The Economic Development of Jamaica

THE ECONOMIC
DEVELOPMENT
OF
JAMAICA

Report by a Mission of the

INTERNATIONAL BANK FOR RECONSTRUCTION
AND DEVELOPMENT

Published for the International Bank for
Reconstruction and Development *by*

THE JOHNS HOPKINS PRESS
Baltimore

The Mission

JOHN C. DE WILDE
Chief of Mission

JOHN HUGH COLLIER   *Economist*

ALBERT WINSEMIUS   *Economic Adviser on Industry*

A. D. SPOTTSWOOD   *Engineering Adviser*

DOUWE GROENVELD   *Agricultural Economist*

W. V. BLEWETT   *Adviser on Agricultural Production*

I. M. LABOVITZ   *Adviser on Social Services*

ANN MARY ROZECK
Secretary and Administrative Assistant

v

INTERNATIONAL BANK FOR
RECONSTRUCTION AND DEVELOPMENT
WASHINGTON 25, D. C.

OFFICE OF THE PRESIDENT

December 19, 1952

His Excellency, Sir Hugh Foot
Governor of Jamaica
Kingston, Jamaica, B.W.I.

My dear Governor:

I take pleasure in transmitting herewith the Report of the Mission to Jamaica, organized by the International Bank for Reconstruction and Development in response to the request contained in your letter of January 2, 1952.

The Bank hopes that the Report will prove a useful guide in working out the development problems of Jamaica. You will understand, of course, that since the Executive Directors and the Management of the Bank have not reviewed the Mission's recommendations in detail, they are transmitted to you as the views of the Mission rather than as positive recommendations of the Bank. We believe, however, that the Mission's Report deserves serious consideration and can be of substantial assistance to the Government in formulating and carrying out a program to provide more employment and higher standards of living.

The Bank will follow with interest the action taken in connection with the Report. The Bank will be prepared, at the request of the Government of Jamaica, to discuss any questions arising from a study of the Report and consider how the Bank can best help in implementing and elaborating the recommendations.

It is my sincere hope that the Report may be of positive and lasting benefit to Jamaica.

Sincerely yours,

Eugene R. Black

INTERNATIONAL BANK FOR
RECONSTRUCTION AND DEVELOPMENT
1818 H STREET, N. W.
WASHINGTON 25, D. C.

December 18, 1952

The Honorable Eugene R. Black, President
International Bank for Reconstruction and Development
Washington, D. C.

Dear Mr. Black:

I am pleased to submit herewith the Report of the Mission to Jamaica, organized by the International Bank at the invitation of the Government of Jamaica. The conclusions and recommendations of the Report are based on studies carried out in Jamaica during the spring of this year.

On behalf of the entire Mission, I would like to express our appreciation for the generous cooperation and warmhearted reception which we enjoyed in Jamaica. The help which we received is no doubt a token of the keen interest which the Government and people of Jamaica are taking in economic development.

In presenting the Report I should like to express my gratitude to all the members of the Mission for their untiring work and co-operative spirit. The Report is indeed a joint product of the entire Mission.

It is our hope that the Report will contribute to the economic progress of Jamaica.

Sincerely yours,

John C deWilde

Chief of Mission.

Preface

On January 2, 1952, H. E. Sir Hugh Foot, Governor of Jamaica, formally invited the International Bank for Reconstruction and Development to send a Mission to make a general economic and financial survey of the Island. This invitation followed an informal exchange of views with the Government of the United Kingdom and the Bank and an exploratory visit by two Bank officials to Jamaica in November 1951.

It was agreed that the Mission should "make an independent and objective study of the development requirements of Jamaica, particularly in consideration of its growing population, and to recommend ways and means of meeting these requirements in the light of the resources which are available or could be mobilized." It was understood that this would involve:

(1) Definition of the goals in terms of the additional employment and national income required;

(2) Consideration of the extent to which further development of agriculture, industry and other economic activities can contribute to these goals, and particularly of the amount of new investment which might be needed to bring about the desired increase in production;

(3) Examination of the financial resources which might be mobilized by the government as its contribution to development in the light of both the total revenue attainable from taxation and borrowing and the indispensable expenditures for other than directly productive purposes;

(4) Study of the measures which the government might take to bring about the desired volume of private investment, especially of the inducements needed to attract foreign capital to Jamaica.

The request for a mission of this character reflected a growing concern in Jamaica with problems of economic development. As an earnest of this interest the Government had already enacted legislation establishing industrial and agricultural development corporations. Steps had also been taken to invite a team of British industrialists to Jamaica and to retain the services of an American consulting firm for the primary purpose of recommending specific industrial projects and promoting foreign investment in Jamaica. All these measures were intended as parts of a concerted, vigorous attack on the principal economic problems of the island.

The Mission consisted of seven experts and a secretarial and administrative assistant. The two agricultural specialists were selected in consultation with the Food and Agricultural Organization which also defrayed a portion of the salary and expenses of one of them. The Government of Jamaica named Mr. W. L. Harrison as liaison officer to the Mission.

The Mission carried out the necessary field work in Jamaica during March and April 1952. All members travelled widely throughout the island and consulted with groups and individuals representing a broad cross section of the community. The Mission enjoyed the wholehearted cooperation of all government officials and departments as well as numerous private individuals and organizations. Some of our proposals were derived from the large number of memoranda we received; still others, particularly those on agriculture, were worked out in close consultation with Jamaican experts. In large measure the Mission acted as the catalyst for the thinking on development problems which was already taking form in Jamaica. We assume, however, sole responsibility for the recommendations set forth in this report.

In framing our proposals the Mission has taken into account the projects already included in the Ten-Year Development Plan drawn up by the Government in accordance with the requirements of the Colonial Development and Welfare Act of 1945. Our recommendations, however, are drawn on a considerably larger and more comprehensive scale. The Mission sought to formulate a broad development program in which all the component parts would be properly balanced and interrelated. At the same time we were deeply conscious that the final planning and execution of development must be the responsibility of Jamaicans. We hope that our report will furnish useful guide lines for the future.

Throughout our work the Mission was keenly aware of the financial implications of development. We have attempted to project the total amount of government expenditures in order to compare them with the probable financial resources. This projection has been built up on the basis of rather detailed estimates many of which are unavoidably subject to a considerable margin of error. The Mission makes no apology for this procedure which was essential, in our opinion, to a proper discharge of our responsibilities. We wish to emphasize, however, that the estimates are only illustrative of the general magnitude of the proposed government outlays in various fields. They reflect no intention to prepare detailed budgets for the future.

The Mission's report consists of two parts. The first contains its findings in the fields of agriculture, mining, manufacturing, tourism, transport, power and social services and its recommendations on the financing of the program. The second part includes a considerable number of annexes which provide either a more detailed factual background on certain questions or a further elaboration and explanation of some of the recommendations.

Table of Contents

TABLES

ANNEXES

Maps

Illustrations

Exchange Rates

One pound sterling (£)	=2.80 U.S. dollars
One shilling (s)	= .14 U.S. cents
One pence (d)	=1.17 U.S. cents

The Economic Development of Jamaica

I.

Introduction

Jamaica with 1.4 million people and an area of 4,400 square miles is the largest of the British West Indian Islands. Its population density of 314 per square mile, while much lower than that of certain industrial countries of Western Europe and some of the densely populated areas of Asia, is undoubtedly high considering the present development of the island. Many would also call it high in relation to the resources available. The island's natural advantages and resources, however, should not be underestimated. While a rugged topography substantially reduces the cultivable area, the available agricultural land, blessed by a mild, warm climate, is potentially very productive. There are ample water supplies for a flourishing agriculture. Annual rainfall varies from over 200 inches to less than 30 inches, and underground water resources are considerable. With a wide range of both rainfall and altitude Jamaica can produce an unusual variety of crops. Although not richly endowed with mineral resources, the island possesses large bauxite deposits now being developed and smaller quantities of other minerals susceptible of commercial exploitation. Its beautiful mountains and coasts, combined with an equable year-round climate, beckon to an increasing number of tourists.

The economy of Jamaica is predominantly agricultural. Almost all its exports consist of raw or processed agricultural products.[1] In 1950 sugar and rum accounted for half of its exports and bananas for another 15%. The production of primary agricultural products amounted to about 27% of the total national output in 1950; and through the supply of raw materials to industry, agriculture probably accounted for 60-70% of the output of secondary industry. In fact, at least 75% of the basic activities in Jamaica are directly related to agriculture. In recent years, however, manufacturing other than the

---

[1] Selected basic statistics relating to Jamaica's economy will be found in Annex 1.

3

processing of local agricultural materials has made considerable progress; and tourism has been making a growing contribution to national income.

Despite a not inconsiderable economic potential and rising production, Jamaica suffers from chronic unemployment and widespread poverty. Wasteful and poor utilization of land, a growing population and lack of sufficient capital have all been responsible for this situation. Preoccupation with the increasing population pressure has in particular tended to produce rather pessimistic evaluations of the island's future. The future does indeed pose serious questions. Jamaica, which does not adequately support its present population, must provide for an additional 18% by the end of the next decade. Although unemployment is already between 15% and 20% of the available labor force, 130,000 more people will be seeking work in the next ten years.[2] There is therefore urgent need for a stocktaking of Jamaica's economic capabilities and for the adoption of a development program which will meet the twin requirements of more jobs and higher living standards.

A rise in production corresponding to the increase in population should not be too difficult to achieve. There is no evidence that national income has not kept pace with population growth in the past. In fact, in more recent years—from 1943 to 1950—we estimate that real output rose at a rate of nearly 4% per year, a figure which yields a significant margin over the increase in population.[3] During this period the production of agricultural commodities, principally sugar, expanded substantially and would probably have risen still further if it had not been for the drastic inroads on banana plan-

---

[2] For data on the population and labor force, see Annex 1.

[3] We estimate net national output in 1950 at £ 85 million or about £ 60 per capita—figures somewhat lower than those hitherto given by the Central Bureau of Statistics. The 1943 output used here as a base should not be regarded as abnormal despite the war. Although much of Jamaica's produce could not be shipped in that year, effective measures were taken to maintain normal production and incomes. War activities compensated for the disappearance of the tourist trade.

JAMAICA

RAILWAYS, PRINCIPAL TOWNS AND HIGHWAYS

JAMAICA

Legend:
- PRINCIPAL ROADS
- RAILWAYS
- PARISH BOUNDARIES
- RIVERS
- CANALS
- SWAMPS

MILES
0 5 10 15 20 25

Parishes:
PORTLAND, ST ANDREW, ST THOMAS, ST MARY, ST CATHERINE, ST ANN, CLARENDON, MANCHESTER, TRELAWNY, ST ELIZABETH, ST JAMES, HANOVER, WESTMORELAND

Towns and places:
MANCHIONEAL, PORT ANTONIO, MORANT BAY, ANNOTTO BAY, PORT MARIA, ORA CABESSA, OCHO RIOS, ST ANN'S BAY, KINGSTON, PORT ROYAL, HARKER'S HALL, BOG WALK, SPANISH TOWN, OLD HARBOUR, OLD HARBOUR BAY, EWARTON, BURNT SAVANNAH, MAY PEN, FRANKFIELD, SHOOTERS HILL, MANDEVILLE, FALMOUTH, Cockpit Country, BLACK RIVER, MONTEGO BAY, LUCEA, SAVANNA LA MAR, NEGRIL

Annotations:
- REYNOLDS METALS CO — HARBOR INSTALLATION, CABLEWAY, BAUXITE PROCESSING PLANT
- JAMAICA BAUXITE CO — HARBOR INSTALLATION, RAILWAY SPUR
- JAMAICA BAUXITE CO — ALUMINA PLANT
- KAISER — BAUXITE PROCESSING PLANT, RAILWAY SPUR, HARBOR INSTALLATION

tations made by the Panama disease. The development of agricultural processing industries and tourism also contributed to rising output. Statistics on consumption of a wide range of articles confirm that the standard of living during this period also rose slightly. Jamaica's capacity for economic growth should therefore not be undervalued in appraising the prospects of the future.

Unfortunately it is much more difficult to increase employment than to raise production. While definitive evidence on past experience is not available, it appears that the substantial rise in output from 1943 to 1950 did not significantly diminish the proportion of unemployed to the "gainfully occupied" population. According to the 1943 census the percentage of unemployed averaged between 18% and 20%.[4] An increase in production often redounds, in the first instance, principally to the benefit of those already employed. In agriculture, where considerable concealed unemployment or underemployment exists, any given increase in production will certainly not bring about an equivalent rise in employment. In industry, too, improvements in efficiency inevitably cause employment to lag behind the expansion in the volume of production.

Another reason why production must increase much more rapidly than population is that the percentage of unemployed must be reduced if Jamaica is to develop a stable economic and political system. If Jamaica could afford to maintain the existing proportion of unemployed to the total labor force (estimated, for want of better data, to be the same as in 1942), then employment opportunities would have to be found in the next decade for only 100,000 to 110,000 people. If, on the other hand, the percentage of unemployed is to be reduced to 5%, jobs would have to be created for perhaps 180,000 to 210,000 people. This would involve a total increase in employment of about 45%.

An appraisal of the economic possibilities of Jamaica has con-

---

[4] In 1943 the "gainfully occupied" population is given as 460,000. In addition there were 54,000 persons under the age of 25 who stated that they were seeking jobs but had never found them. The total labor force would therefore be 514,000.

vinced us, however, that much can be done to meet these future requirements. We have formulated the main outlines of a development program which, if carried out, would in our opinion both raise the standard of living and create enough jobs to diminish the percentage of unemployment substantially. This program, extending over ten years, is undeniably ambitious. It is conceived on a scale which is unprecedented in Jamaica. It envisages public expenditures averaging 27% higher than in 1952-53[5] and total government borrowing amounting to about £ 22 million.

There are compelling reasons for a program of this size. Timid half-measures will not solve the problems of the future. The program must hold the promise of a real advance if it is to capture the imagination of the people and command their continuous support and cooperation. If employment is to be found for a larger population and the potential resources of Jamaica are to be translated into real income, far more must be invested than in the past. Jamaica's problem is to achieve an amount of investment which will provide a more substantial margin over the increase of population. Only in this way can some of the increase in production be devoted to further investment so that economic development will gradually become an automatic process. It is always difficult to get this process started in underdeveloped countries because the low level of production leaves so little for investment. In Jamaica this particular difficulty has been exacerbated by the pressure of unemployment which constantly compels the government to devote the slender resources available for development to relief and make-work projects. The vicious circle must be broken; and this can only be done by an investment program financed to a considerable extent by private capital imports and public borrowing abroad.

We wish to emphasize, however, that all the resources which can be marshalled must, above all, be wisely invested. They must produce an increase in national income which will make it possible to sustain the burden of greater indebtedness and to defray a rising

---

[5] The 1952-53 expenditures, with which the future average expenditures have been compared, are exclusive of expenditures for hurricane relief.

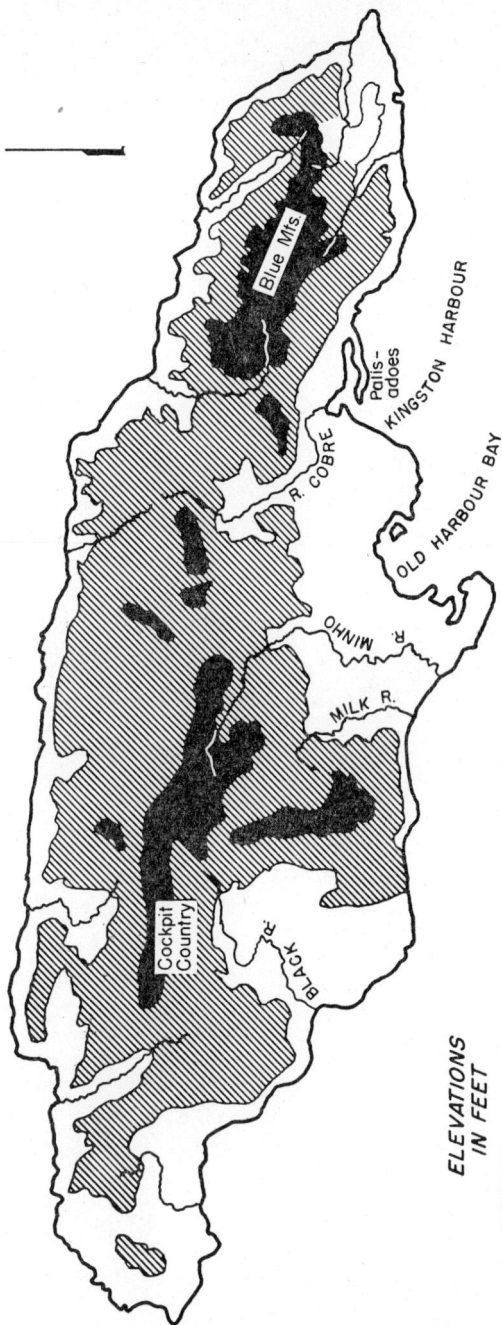

JAMAICA

PHYSICAL FEATURES

ELEVATIONS
IN FEET

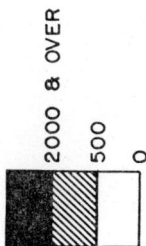

2000 & OVER

500

0

MILES

0   10   20   30

N

Blue Mts.

Cockpit Country

Palis-
adoes

KINGSTON HARBOUR

R. COBRE

OLD HARBOUR BAY

R. MINHO

MILK R.

BLACK

portion of the developmental outlays out of current revenues. For this reason the program we have outlined concentrates primarily on the development of the productive capacity of the country. We have sought to evaluate every type of investment in the light of its cost and its impact on production and income. We have been aware of financial limitations but at the same time cognizant of the fact that these limitations are not absolute but determined in large part by the results achieved with the expenditures.

We do not put this program forward as a definitive blueprint which must be followed in its entirety or at all cost. It extends over a ten-year period because most of the development projects it contemplates cannot be carried out in a shorter time. Definite commitments, however, cannot be made over such a long period, if only because it is impossible to foresee how inevitably changing circumstances will affect the rate of development. The program must therefore be regarded primarily as projecting lines of advance which can be followed more rapidly or more slowly as circumstances dictate, provided always the balance among its components is approximately maintained. There may be unforeseen obstacles—difficulties in obtaining the necessary capital or bottlenecks in organization and administration—which will necessitate adjustment. We hope that every effort will be made to carry out the program along the lines and on the scale set forth in the main body of this report. In the concluding section, however, we have also provided a set of lower targets for the eventuality that the implied pace of accomplishment cannot be achieved. In practice the adjustments will have to depend on the particular difficulties that may arise. This problem is inherent in all economic planning.

We would make one more general observation. Development is not simply a matter of "economics." It can easily be frustrated by purely non-economic obstacles such as adverse political and social attitudes or a lack of the energy and cooperation which it demands from people at all levels in the community. A development program is designed to benefit the people, but at the same time only their work, enterprise and ingenuity can make it succeed.

For a number of reasons we have not given specific consideration to the possibilities of emigration in framing a development program. First of all, this subject has already been rather exhaustively studied. A recent Commission under Sir Geoffrey Evans, for instance, inquired into the possibility of organizing emigration from the populous British West Indian islands to the more sparsely populated territories of British Honduras and British Guiana. Secondly, the prospect of considerable emigration is not very bright. While the Evans Commission recommended schemes in British Honduras and Guiana designed to enable these countries to absorb 25,000 immigrants over ten years, its recommendations have not found general support and it appears unlikely that the proposed immigration target will be achieved. In the recent past emigration has hardly afforded an outlet for the growing population. While there was considerable net emigration in the war years, particularly in 1943 and 1944, the years 1945 to 1950 witnessed an actual net immigration of 4,600 people. Over the entire period 1939 to 1950 there was a net emigration of only 2,300 people. Finally, the creation of possibilities for emigration lies primarily outside the power of the government of Jamaica. It should be the subject for joint action by all the West Indian governments and for individual action by the governments of these territories which are comparatively underpopulated. Whatever success these efforts may have will almost certainly not lessen the need for maximum development of Jamaica's own resources.

The program outlined in succeeding sections of this report places primary emphasis upon agriculture. In part this is a recognition of the dominant place of agriculture in the economy and its role in supplying raw materials to a growing industry. In even greater part, however, it reflects the Mission's conviction that the potentialities in this field are far larger than has generally been assumed in the past. The land is Jamaica's chief asset and, if properly developed and utilized, can be made to yield a much greater output. In projecting the production of primary materials we have also taken into account the expansion of mining. The possibilities in this field, however, are rather limited and we do not envisage that mining will

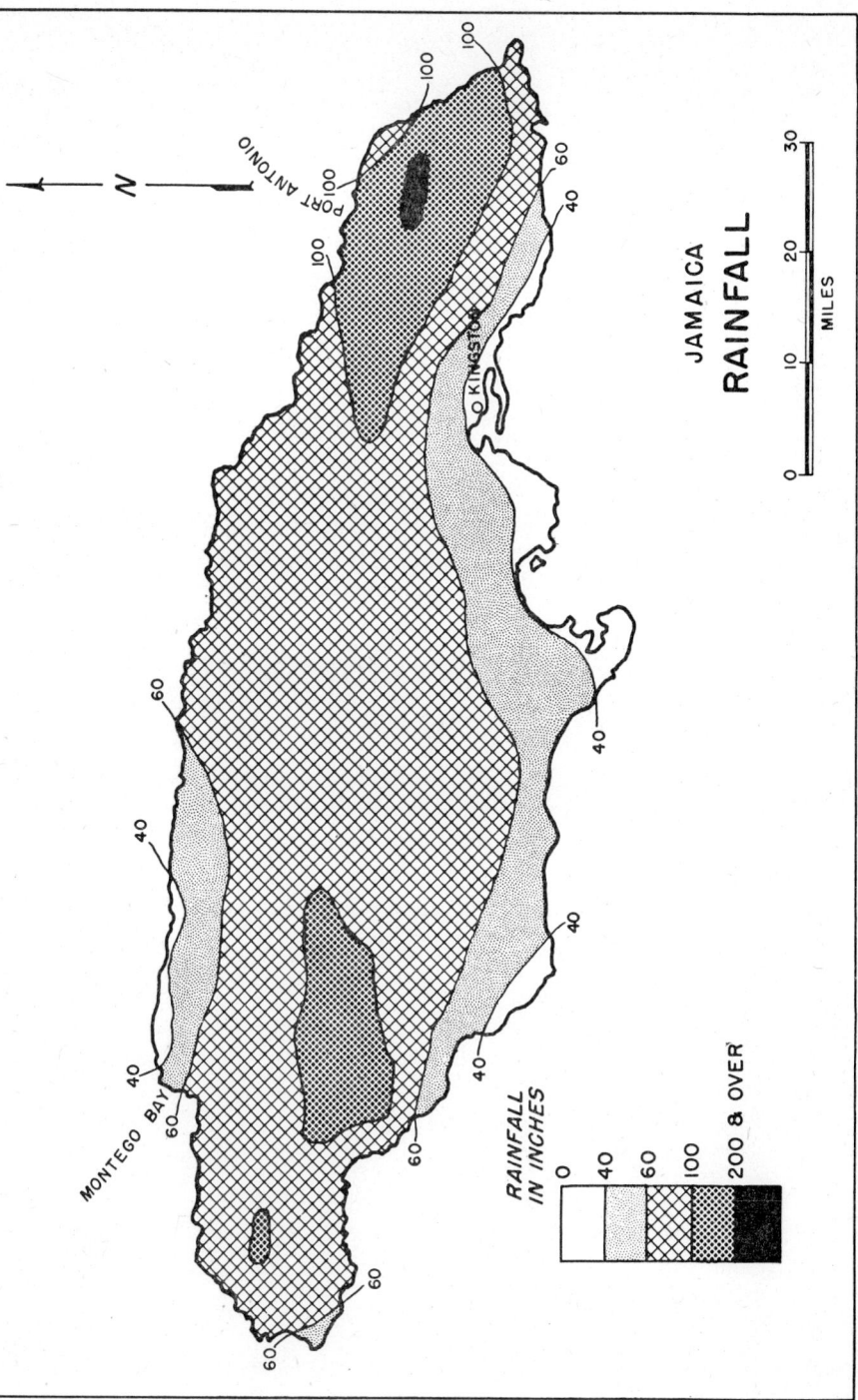

JAMAICA
RAINFALL

RAINFALL
IN INCHES

	0
	40
	60
	100
	200 & OVER

MILES
0   10   20   30

N

PORT ANTONIO

KINGSTON

MONTEGO BAY

100
100
100
100
60
40
60
40
40
40
40
40
60
60
60
60
60
60
40
40
40

ever make a prominent contribution to employment or total production.

We have sought to survey objectively the prospects of the manufacturing industries. Those who look to manufacturing as the principle source of Jamaica's economic salvation may be somewhat disappointed with our conclusions. We expect that manufacturing will provide increasing employment but only as the industrial experience and skills which are still largely lacking are gradually acquired. We have paid particular attention, therefore, to measures to raise the efficiency of production. Jamaica cannot expect to convert its manpower potential quickly into a wide range of manufactures which will find a ready foreign market.

The tourist industry has also been appraised. We believe this is an industry which holds considerable promise and which will develop with a minimum of government assistance.

The recommendations we make on transport and power are largely designed to key the development in these fields to the expansion of capacities in the basic industries.

Finally, we have included the social services, particularly education, public health and housing, in the scope of the development program. Here the primary task was to find an appropriate balance between expenditures in these fields and those more directly related to production. We have recognized that some development of the social services is essential to the improvement of productive efficiency, but at the same time we have been aware of the danger of raising these services to standards which the economy would be unable to support.

II.

Agriculture

CHARACTERISTICS OF JAMAICAN AGRICULTURE

Agriculture is the basic industry of Jamaica. To understand the possibilities of development in this field it is necessary to make a brief diagnosis of the existing agricultural situation and to set forth the facts and features which are relevant to planning a program. Among these the following are of particular importance:

1. *Much of the data needed for framing a definitive development program is lacking.* The facts available on land use are at best fragmentary and not wholly reliable. Not much is known regarding the acreage and yield of crops grown for home consumption. There has been no real soil survey from which the potentialities of agriculture might be more accurately gauged. The agricultural value of the extensive areas not presently under cultivation has never been fully ascertained. Underground water supplies in relation to agricultural needs have not been adequately studied. Little information is extant on income of various types of farmers or on the size and structure of agricultural indebtedness.

2. *Nevertheless, there is no doubt that the available land can be made to yield far more than at present.* Agricultural techniques in many parts of the island can be greatly improved. Very little fertilizer is used outside the sugar estates and some of the banana properties. Wasteful agricultural practices are common. Soil erosion has been allowed to take a frightful toll. The yield of pastures is extremely poor even though natural conditions in many areas are favorable to good pastures. Land under cultivation can be considerably expanded through irrigation, land reclamation and proper soil conservation practices. These conclusions rest upon extensive observation throughout the island. They are also confirmed by such figures as are available. In 1950, for example, it was estimated that:

Approximately one million acres or 36% of the area of

10

Jamaica were devoted to agricultural use. Of this total not more than 423,000 acres were apparently under cultivation. The irrigated area did not exceed 41,400 acres;

Of the 595,000 acres in permanent meadow and pasture only 10% could be characterized as "improved." Part of this land can be cultivated;

1.19 million acres were "unused" or considered "wasteland." Unquestionably the greater part of this area could not be devoted to agriculture because it is either too steep or infertile. Part of the unused land, an estimated 312,000 acres, has been under intermittent cultivation in the past, however, and could be converted to permanent agricultural use if soil conservation measures were applied. Some of the "permanent" wasteland has good soil and could be made productive by irrigation and reclamation of marshes;

500,000 acres were in "woods and forests." A considerable part of this represents scrub forest.[1]

There is little doubt, therefore, that a development program could satisfy the "land hunger" which is said to characterize Jamaica.

3. *Deforestation has had serious effects on agriculture.* Reckless denuding of hillsides has greatly accelerated soil erosion and added to the number and gravity of destructive flash floods. There are continuous inroads on the 500,000 acres of forests,[2] much of which are poor, and frequent demands that part of the 250,000 acres of Crown lands in forest reserves be turned over to cultivation. An afforestation scheme has been in operation over the last ten years, but on a scale insufficient even to keep pace with deforestation. At present Jamaica supplies only about a fourth of its timber requirements.

4. *Hillside agriculture is and will remain a necessity in Jamaica.* Only 20% of the Island's area is flat or slightly rolling. The remainder is hilly and mountainous. In view of the population pressure, it is not feasible to concentrate simply on the development of level or nearly level land. While part of the land now in crops is too steep for cultivation, there can and should be a net extension of hilly land

---

[1] For more detailed statistics on land use, see Annex 2.

[2] For further data, see Annex 3.

under cultivation. At present hillsides are tilled primarily by small farmers under conditions which accelerate soil erosion. One of the principal problems is to make their agricultural practices consistent with soil conservation.

5. *Although Jamaica is known primarily for its export crops, the latter probably account for less than one-third of the value of total agricultural production.* The output of root crops (yams, sweet potatoes, cassava), maize, pulses, rice, coconuts and milk and meat, all of which are produced for the home market, far exceeds that of sugar cane, bananas, citrus and export crops of lesser importance such as ginger, pimento, coffee and cacao.[3] Yet the importance of food crops for local consumption has never been fully recognized and their proper cultivation has not received adequate attention. Yields of food crops and livestock products are generally far below the levels that could be achieved with proper agricultural practices. Both the growth of population anticipated over the next decade and the need for a better balanced diet demand a substantial increase in food production.

6. *The wide variation in rainfall, soil types, altitudes and temperatures makes possible an unusually diversified agriculture.* Tropical, subtropical and even temperate zone crops can be grown in various parts of the island. At different altitudes excellent coffee and cacao can be produced. Sugar and bananas flourish in the plains and valleys and also on hillsides. Dry-area crops such as guavas, limes, cashews and certain fibers can be grown as well as those demanding more rainfall.

7. *Extremely small and very large landholdings and very efficient and inefficient agriculture exist side by side.* According to the 1943 census 74.4% of the number of farms of one acre and over were less than 10 acres in size. They accounted for 11.8% of the total acreage in farms and 30.5% of the area under cultivation. Farms of 100 acres and over constituted only 2.1% of the total but represented 70% of the total acreage, 47.3% of the area under cultivation and

---

[3] For statistics on agricultural production, see Annex 4.

79.3% of the area used exclusively for pasture. Estates of 500 acres and over accounted for 58.5% of the total acreage, 39.6% of the area under cultivation and 68.1% of the area devoted exclusively to pasture.[4] A sample survey made in 1950 disclosed that the number of farms of 100 acres and over had declined by about 6% while the total number of farms had increased by 3%. At the same time there had apparently been an encouraging increase of 15% in the number of medium-size farms (10 to 49) acres. Fundamentally, of course, the 1942 pattern has remained unchanged.

Large landed properties are of two types: estates in the alluvial plains and valleys producing primarily sugar cane, bananas, coconuts and some livestock; and the livestock ranches or "pens" in the uplands. The first of these are generally very efficient. The large sugar estates, for instance, have established a deserved reputation for progressive management. Their yields are at least 60-75% higher than those of the small farmers who deliver their cane to sugar estates for milling.[5] On the other hand, the large livestock properties are for the most part characterized by low yields. In general the small farmers are the most inefficient, partly because they have the least desirable land, partly because their agricultural techniques are the most backward. The small farmers predominate in the hills and produce nearly all the food for local consumption. An increase in their output is a matter of paramount concern.

8. *Certain features of landholding and of the attitude toward land are serious obstacles to agricultural development.* In many cases farmers do not have a properly perfected title to their land and thus cannot put up their land as security for a loan. Through fragmentation by inheritance, land is frequently the object of many and confusing claims which have never been properly adjusted. Land is the most coveted possession. Ever since the days of slavery it has been re-

---

[4] Details on landholdings are given in Annex 2.

[5] This estimate is based on figures supplied by the Sugar Manufacturers Association. The sample survey carried out by the Department of Agriculture in 1950, which also covered the production of cane for "wet" sugar, indicated that estate yields were 120% higher than those of cane farmers.

garded as a guarantee of individual freedom and as a form of insurance against want. The small farmer considers untrammeled, absolute ownership as essential and tends to resist any attempt to restrict his right to use the land as he pleases, however much such restriction may be in the public interest. Unfortunately, absolute ownership in Jamaica has often meant in practice the right of the owner to ruin his land in his own way. The concept of land as a national economic asset has not yet been widely accepted.

The tenancy system also contributes to the reckless use of land. According to the 1943 census, 114,285 acres of farm land were rented. Rented land represented only a little over 6% of the total. but since land is rented primarily for cultivation, its proportion of total land under cultivation—almost 30%—is more significant. Many small farmers in particular rent all or part of their holdings. In 1942 land leased by small farmers (one to nine acres) amounted to 20.6% of all their land and 37.3% of their land under cultivation.[6] Since most land is leased only for one year, there is every incentive to exploit it and avoid making any improvements.

9. *There are a large number of official and unofficial organizations* looking after the interests of the farmers. Among the official organizations are the Department of Agriculture which is charged with agricultural research and experimentation, farm extension and improvement work and operation of the School of Agriculture; the Department of Commerce and Industries which collects, stores, processes and exports a number of agricultural products; the Lands Department which has been charged with settling small farmers on land acquired from large landowners; the Department of Public Works which is responsible for irrigation and drainage works; the Department of Forestry which also looks after fisheries; the Registrar of Cooperative Societies which registers and supervises cooperatives; and the Loan Societies Board which provides funds for agricultural credit to the so-called Peoples Cooperative Banks.

Among the private organizations, the oldest is the Jamaica Agri-

---

[6] See Annex 2.

cultural Society which has always received a government subvention. With its 525 branches throughout the island, it is generally representative of all branches of agriculture although it has tended more recently to look after the interests of the small farmer in particular. It has fostered many commodity associations and has been instrumental in organizing the young farmers' 4-H Club movement. Recently a Farmers Federation has also been established for the primary purpose of championing the producers' interests before the government. It comprises newly organized parish farmers federations and particularly the long-established and powerful commodity associations such as the Sugar Manufacturers Association, the All-Island Banana Growers Association, the Citrus Growers Association and the Cane Farmers Association.

The existence of these numerous organizations is a source of both strength and weakness. On the one hand, they provide many points of contact with the farming community, give the farmers opportunities for self-help and create the framework for close cooperation between the government and farmers. On the other hand, they undoubtedly accentuate the difficulties of framing and carrying out a coordinated agricultural policy. The government departments themselves are often poorly coordinated, and the farmers' organizations frequently work at cross-purposes and engage in internecine strife. The projected organization of a Ministry of Agriculture which will embrace most of the government departments dealing with agriculture is expected to improve coordination within the government, but there is unfortunately little sign as yet that the private agricultural organizations will unite on a common objective and a common program.

NEED FOR AN AERIAL AND GROUND SURVEY

Against the background described above, it becomes apparent that the central problem of Jamaican agriculture is to develop and carry out a pattern of land use which will more fully realize the potentialities of the available land. For this purpose we would strongly recommend that a comprehensive aerial and ground survey be promptly undertaken. More and more countries are finding such

15

a survey essential to development planning. Its use is not confined to agriculture. It is of great value in geologic and mineral exploration, in town planning and in the execution of public works generally. Here, however, we are concerned primarily with its application to agriculture. The objectives of a survey of this type would be (1) to develop proper topographic maps essential for laying out soil conservation and irrigation projects, for planning flood control and for preparing a cadaster; (2) to gather comprehensive data regarding current land use and productivity in relation to soil types, soil conditions and climatic factors on the basis of which actual and potential production can be compared; (3) to delimit individual properties and establish clear titles for the many thousands who cannot qualify for government housing and farm improvement schemes or for farm credit for want of such titles; and (4) to permit a revaluation of land and the gradual introduction of a system of taxation based on unimproved value which would give an additional incentive to development.

The first step would be a complete aerial survey designed to produce topographic maps on the scale of 1:10,000 for the island as a whole, of 1:2,500 for the flat areas and principal townships, and of perhaps 1:1,250 for the larger urban areas. The availability of such maps with 20-foot contour intervals, from which closer intervals could be interpolated on the ground as required, would make it possible to dispense with the many and costly surveys for particular purposes which have had to be undertaken in the past on both private and public account.

The next step would be a ground survey. It could begin as soon as the first topographic maps are available, i.e. about six months after the aerial photography is completed. It would proceed parish by parish under priorities determined in accordance with need. Each ground survey team would consist of a minimum of a soil surveyor with ecological training, an agricultural economist, a topographic and cadastral surveyor, a titles officer and a land valuation expert. Each of these principals would have such assistants as would be required. The soil surveyor would classify the land in each area by its physical characteristics (kind of soil, condition of drainage, degree

of slope, extent of erosion, degree of rock exposure and the like),
and the types of vegetation it supports. Skilled interpretation of aerial
photographs will be of great assistance in revealing existing land use
patterns, particularly the areas devoted to different crops, pastures,
orchards and forest trees. By organizing sample surveys with the
help of local officials of agricultural organizations and the Department
of Agriculture, the agricultural economist on the team will be able
to develop data on yields, prices and costs and other information
pertinent to development, such as population density, size of families
and housing. The topographic and cadastral surveyor would check
the aerial survey maps and, working closely with the titles officer,
delineate property boundaries. The titles officer would determine
ownership in accordance with prescribed procedures and make provision for registration of titles, subject, of course, to appropriate
appeal. Since decisions on titles will be made in conjunction with a
revaluation of land and its incorporation in the tax rolls, it may be
anticipated that spurious claims to land will be discouraged. On the
basis of the information brought to light by the soil surveyor and
the agricultural economist and of such other data regarding land
values as is available in each locality, the valuation expert would then
appraise the value of each holding for different purposes. His valua-
tions when accepted by the owner or altered or confirmed on appeal
would then serve, for instance, as the basis for levying rates (taxes
on real estate) and death duties and as a guide in determining the
loan value of the land and the compensation to be paid in the event
of compulsory land acquisition.[7]

A complete survey of this kind could and should be finished
within six or seven years and would probably cost about £ 650,000.

---

[7] Land will have to be appraised at its (1) improved value, (2) unimproved value, and (3) annual value. The first would be needed in the
assessment of income taxes, the levying of stamp duties, estate duties and
the determination of the loan and acquisition value of land; the second would
be required for levying rates and administration of the Agricultural Holdings
and Land Authorities Laws; and the third would be required for rent restriction purposes and assessment of taxable income.

This sum, however, would be the gross cost. For example, even in the absence of such an over-all survey it would be necessary within the next years to carry out, at a probable cost of £ 125,000, a revaluation of land on the tax rolls. The last valuation was made in 1937 and it is generally recognized that a new valuation is urgently needed to remove the serious anomalies and inequities which have meanwhile developed. Nor does the cost estimate take into account the substantial financial savings which would ultimately be effected. It would make unnecessary special surveys by the Public Works Department, the Central Housing Authority, the Town Planning Department, the Agricultural Department and other agencies. For the Public Works Department alone annual savings of £ 50,000 would be realized. The government could recover the entire cost of the survey within 10 to 15 years;[8] and the availability of cadastral maps would save a portion of the public the cost of private surveys incidental to the transfer and registration of titles to land.

It is, however, the value of the survey to the planning of economic development which is of paramount importance. As far as practicable, it would be desirable to concentrate the survey initially on those areas where regional rehabilitation and development projects are urgently needed. On the basis of the maps drawn from the survey and the data developed by the survey, a comprehensive land-use plan for each area could then be worked out as rapidly as possible. This plan would provide for the proper kind of soil conservation and cropping pattern for each type of slope and soil, for necessary new roads and for minimum housing needs, water supply and other facilities. A program for government assistance to develop holdings in particular areas in accordance with approved plans could then be inaugurated on a large scale, particularly since the survey will also have provided the clear titles to land which holders will need to qualify for government assistance. We do not suggest, however, that economic planning and de-

---

[8] For example, the annual saving to the Public Works Department alone, capitalized at 5% over fifteen years, would be £ 519,000, which, in addition to the £ 125,000 which would probably have to be spent on revaluation in any event, would approximately equal the cost of the survey.

Above: A few years ago this hillside was covered with bananas and was an exceedingly productive area. Now, with any great rainfall this unprotected stream becomes a thick torrent, spreading heavy devastation throughout its lower reaches.

Below: Stone contour barriers on hillsides previously deforested.

velopment is impossible without such a survey or that new projects should be postponed until the survey is completed.

The introduction of a new system of taxation based on the unim-proved value of land is not an indispensable feature of this scheme[9] but it is certainly highly desirable. It will provide a real stimulus to the development of land, whether for urban or for agricultural pur-poses, by reducing the tax burden on improved properties and raising it on undeveloped land. It will provide an additional incentive to take advantage of government assistance for development and will stimulate the transfer of land to owners willing and able to put up their share of capital to improve it. It will help to attract outside capital for investment in landed property.

The use of the unimproved value of land in assessing tax rates is neither novel nor untried. This system of taxation has been success-fully adopted in other countries, including Denmark, New Zealand, South Africa and Australia. It was strongly recommended for Jamaica by the Commission appointed to inquire into land valuation and land taxation under the chairmanship of Mr. Simon Bloomberg. The new tax system will, of course, have to be introduced gradually in order to avoid disruptive effects on the economy.[10]

An Agricultural Development Program

We are convinced that with the proper development of Jamaica's agricultural resources, "land hunger" can be largely satisfied and population pressures to some extent relieved. To this end we have worked out, in consultation with agricultural leaders of Jamaica, a

[9] Taxes on land or real estate are now levied by the central and local governments at specified rates per pound of assessed valuation which is the im-proved value of the property. The total collected in 1949-50 amounted to £ 724,205 or 8.3% of the revenues of the central and parochial governments.

[10] With unimproved value used as the basis of taxation, the actual rate in the pound would have to be higher than at present in order to yield the same revenue. Once this rate is fixed, the tax on improved land could be pro-gressively lowered over a period of five years until it conforms to the new rate on unimproved value; and the tax on unimproved land could be corre-spondingly increased during this period until it also reaches the new rate.

development program which we hope will command general support. It is ambitious, but only an ambitious program will meet the requirements. It must give a decisive impetus to the development of agriculture and must be capable of arresting the flow of population to the cities and lifting the standard of living of the farming classes.

The essential features of such a program are: (1) a soil conservation and rehabilitation campaign designed not simply to save the hillside areas now being tilled but also to bring into cultivation additional areas under conditions which will safeguard and rebuild soil fertility; (2) a rapid acceleration of afforestation as an integral part of soil conservation; (3) a pasture improvement scheme designed to raise livestock yields significantly and to release some pasture land for cultivation; (4) extensive irrigation and land reclamation in order to add to the arable land and increase yields; (5) assistance for rural housing and water supply; and (6) provision of ample agricultural credit to enable farmers to carry out approved land use programs. All of these are interrelated elements of a single program.

1. *Soil Conservation and Rehabilitation*

Soil conservation is the most important and critical feature of the program. It is not exaggerating to say that the fate of the small farmers and of the production of food for home consumption will in the long run depend on the success achieved in rehabilitating Jamaica's hillsides. Even the farmers in the alluvial plains and valleys are dependent on the adoption of proper soil conservation practices in the hills and mountains for protection against destructive floods.

Not long ago the present Governor of Jamaica warned: "If we continue as we are going in our hillside agriculture we are heading for disaster . . . which will come quickly."[11] This warning can hardly

---

[11]Speech at Frome, Nov. 21, 1951. The Governor continued: "Our hill agriculture has been dominated by three terrible tendencies—to scatter, to scramble, to squander. This is no new thing. For a hundred years or more the three tendencies—to scatter, in small uneconomic holdings; to scramble, every man for himself; to squander, like a mad gambler, the fertility of the soil—have been taking their toll."

be made more forceful. For a long time now soil erosion has continued apace. More and more hill and mountain slopes have been burnt over, cleared of trees and put under cultivation without provision for proper terracing, contouring and drainage. As the soil washed away and fertility declined, the land has been abandoned and new areas have been cleared. With this pattern of shifting cultivation much of the top soil has been swept away. In the last few decades the rate of deterioration appears even to have accelerated. The spectacle of abandoned land and eroded hillsides has become only too common.

The time has clearly come to arrest and reverse this process. With its growing population Jamaica certainly cannot afford to live in the future off its "soil capital." The use of the land can no longer be considered as the owner's exclusive concern. Land must be regarded as a public trust to be managed in the nation's interest. Fortunately there has been a growing realization among government officials, agricultural organizations and prominent farmers that this problem must be vigorously tackled. A Farm Improvement Authority began operation in 1949 for the purpose of extending government assistance to small farmers willing to carry out certain improvements in their holdings, including soil conservation works. In 1951 the legislature enacted a Land Authorities Law permitting the establishment of regional land authorities to plan and carry out rehabilitation schemes for designated "improvement areas"; and the Yallahs Valley Authority was set up pursuant to this law. Following the hurricane of August 1951, growers were assisted in replanting about 84,000 acres of bananas, but only on condition that they put into effect certain elementary soil conservation practices such as contour planting and contour drains. Gradually the number of stone and grass barriers has increased throughout the island.

Up to the present, however, the concrete accomplishment has been pitifully small in relation to the magnitude of the problem. There is still no widespread consciousness of the imperative need for soil conservation among the farmers. For instance, very few of the 21,000 smallholders who have been settled on the land under the government land settlement program practice soil conservation, and the government itself did nothing to require the adoption of approved agricultural methods by these settlers. Similarly of the £ 246,-000 of grant assistance committed by the Farm Improvement Authority by April 1, 1952, only £ 52,000 was allocated to soil conservation work.

We strongly urge, therefore, that a soil conservation and rehabilitation program be launched on a really large scale and without delay. This program should aim at the rehabilitation of 300,000 acres within the next decade. It should be large enough to include within its scope almost all of the hillside areas currently cropped and to bring under permanent cultivation part of the land now used for pasture or for intermittent cropping so that about 100,000 acres net would be added to the area under cultivation. Under any such program part of the land now being cultivated would inevitably be reserved for grass or forest either because it is too steep or the soil has deteriorated too far; but such losses would be more than offset by taking suitable pasture and idle land into cultivation.

While the program should extend to the whole island, the effort should focus particularly on the rehabilitation of areas where the need is especially acute and extensive and where accordingly large concentration of resources is necessary. This is the regional approach sanctioned by the Land Authorities Law. We recommend for special attention the Christiana-Upper Clarendon area. Situated in the center of Jamaica and embracing parts of four parishes—Clarendon, Manchester, Trelawny and St. Ann—it comprises some 160,000 acres of agricultural land which for the most part was once very productive. Reckless burning of the hillsides and the cultivation, without soil protection, first of sugar cane and bananas and then of ginger and such food crops as yams and maize, have caused serious erosion and depletion. Our own observations, supported by those of many agriculturists conversant with this region, have convinced us, however, that the damage can be repaired and the land restored to a high level of production.

We realize that a regional program has already been initiated for the Yallahs valley. While we do not suggest that this program be abandoned, the available evidence indicates that expenditures on the Christiana-Upper Clarendon area would yield proportionately far larger returns. The Yallahs valley presents a most difficult soil conservation problem. The slopes are very steep and the soil consists largely of loose conglomerates and shales which, owing to their susceptibility to "slides," are extremely difficult, if not impossible, to contour and terrace. It has already been estimated that of the 50,000 acres scheduled for rehabilitation in this valley less than 6,000 acres can be made available for farming. We would therefore suggest careful testing and experimentation before committing large funds to this project. Even afforestation is likely to be difficult and costly and should proceed on a modest scale in order to test its feasibility in various parts of the valley. In the Christiana-Upper Clarendon area, on the other hand, the type of slopes and soil makes the rehabilitation problem more tractable; and the proportion of the area that can be devoted to agricultural use is much larger— between 100,000 and 150,000 acres. Moreover, the population affected—some 150,000 in 1943—is about ten times greater than that in the Yallahs valley.[12]

A proper soil conservation and rehabilitation program does not, of course, consist simply of laying out contours, drains, terraces, stone or grass barriers and similar works. There must be an appropriate land use pattern established for each project area and a continuous insistance on proper methods of cultivation. An analysis of each area will disclose what parts must be put into permanent forest or grass and what parts can be used for cultivation. Cropping patterns for the cultivable area providing for suitable allocations of land both to annual crops and tree crops will have to be drawn up. In the selection of crops particular attention will need to be paid to crops like sugar cane which will help to retain soil and rebuild its fertility. All crops will have to be planted on contour. Special care will be needed to insure that annual crops such as maize, yams and

---

[12] A recent estimate puts the population of the Yallahs valley at 15,000, although the 1943 census recorded only 7,000.

cassava, which in the past have contributed so much to soil erosion, are planted only on the gentler slopes and then always on ridges rather than on mounds. The importance of mulching to moisture and soil conservation must also be recognized. Khus-khus grass (*Vetiveria zizanoides*), for instance, might be grown both to prevent soil erosion and to supply material for mulching. Lastly, the use of fertilizer will be needed to rebuild fertility once the soil conservation works have been carried out. The program must be not only comprehensive but also continuous in its application.

The appropriate types of soil conservation works and land use patterns must, of course, be worked out for each area, depending on the degree of slope, soil conditions and climatic and economic factors. There may be a tendency toward excessive caution—an insistence in some quarters that protracted experiments with various patterns and methods be undertaken on a modest scale before proceeding vigorously with the over-all program. We urge that this tendency be strongly resisted except in areas where conditions are know to be unusually difficult. The problem is so acute that delay would be dangerous. The projects launched within the first few years of the program will provide practical experience with a variety of methods and patterns. Jamaica can learn by doing. There is no great danger of outright failure because considerable theoretical and practical knowledge on soil conservation is already available in Jamaica, and two experts well versed in soil protection methods used in the United States have been assigned to the island for one year by the FAO. The Mission has no doubt that satisfactory methods of dealing with all types of conditions can be evolved and applied. One technical question—the use of machinery in soil conservation— may call for particular study. In the past work of this sort has been accomplished exclusively by hand with the aid of such simple tools as the hoe and fork. While the hilly and rocky nature of much of the land may preclude the use of machinery in many areas, we believe that the use of bulldozers and plows in contouring and terracing will prove feasible in at least some areas and may effect a considerable saving in time and cost.

A program of the magnitude we have outlined can be carried out only if the participation of farmers is successfully enlisted. Because of their strong individualism and deeply-rooted sense of property rights, primary reliance must undoubtedly be placed on voluntary cooperation. An extensive program of education, coupled with financial incentives, will have to be launched. The educational campaign will require the participation of all groups who have intimate contact with the cultivators—the Jamaica Agricultural Society, the Farmers Federation and commodity associations, the agricultural extension service, the school teachers and religious leaders. All will have to cooperate in a well coordinated effort to persuade small farmers in particular that "saving the soil" is their own and their country's salvation. The major and most difficult task will be to get enough farmers to participate over the next few years in enough projects distributed throughout the island to serve as a practical and effective demonstration of what can be accomplished through proper soil conservation and land use. Once the value of these practices becomes widely known and demonstrated, the whole campaign may be expected to gather momentum rapidly.

Undoubtedly the most rapid progress with the soil rehabilitation program will be made if large landowners can be interested in participating in the program either by developing their properties themselves or by making them available for development on long-term lease. Any properties acquired by the government in this manner can then be made available on long-term lease to selected tenants who are willing to carry out the necessary soil protection works with government assistance and to develop their holdings along approved land use patterns. In this way areas already tenanted under conditions which have led to rapid deterioration of the soil can be rehabilitated, and parts of large properties which landowners have been unwilling to lease because of the destructive practices of tenants may be made available for tenant cultivation under proper safeguards. Such land, however, should be leased for at least 20 to 25 years with a provision that the land-owner at the end of this period make appropriate compensation for the unexhausted improvements which are likely to benefit him. The lease should be sufficiently long so that the tenant feels that he is making improvements for his own benefit and is able to plant long-maturing tree crops.

A number of large property-owners have already offered land to the government provided the land, suitably improved, is returned to them upon expiration of the lease. The government has accordingly announced recently a scheme for improving such land and leasing it to small farmers. The lease, however, is only for five years and it has therefore been necessary to prohibit the erection of a house or the planting of tree crops on such farms. We strongly doubt that this plan affords a sound basis for improvement of the land along the lines we have indicated.

Bringing the thousands of small holdings into the projected soil rehabilitation scheme will be more difficult. By and large the program can be carried out only if an entire slope or drainage area is taken as a unit for development. While it is at times feasible to rehabilitate even a small section of a slope, particularly in the rocky limestone hills, efforts to protect a single holding constituting only a part of a drainage area will generally be jeopardized by the reckless agricultural practices of farmers higher on the hillside or will endanger the holdings below because it is impossible to provide for proper disposal of the run-off water.

In each area singled out for rehabilitation it will be necessary not only to enlist the cooperation of the small-holders in carrying out the necessary soil conservation works, but also to seek their agreement to a land use program for the area as a whole. In many cases this will require a virtual pooling and redistribution of the land. Since part of the land may well have to be taken out of cultivation and put into grass or forest, some reallotment among existing holders may be necessary in the interests of equity. A reduction of land available for cultivation within the project area may necessitate the transfer of some farmers to other land being developed. In all cases there will need to be a reconciliation of existing property rights with the requirement that the area be developed as a unit.

It is difficult to anticipate all the varying conditions which will

Above: Corn planted on stony eroded hillside without any contour barriers.

Below: A close-up of corn planted at Haddo on the contour after stone barriers were laid.

be met and the problems that will have to be solved. In some cases it may be possible to obtain an agreed reallotment accompanied by the necessary change in titles and property rights; in other cases it may be better to leave existing property rights undisturbed and to have the government take over the land on long-term lease with provision for re-leasing it in different allotments to the farmers within the area. Only experience will dictate the best approach. It is essential, however, that the agency charged with the program be given sufficient authority by law to cope with this problem in all its aspects.

In any event, voluntary cooperation will need the stimulation of government incentives. Self-help is, of course, very important, and we urge that all the propaganda for this program stress that the salvation of the farmers depends largely on their own efforts. Agricultural development will require above all a large amount of labor. Of this there is a plentiful supply. Government financial assistance will be necessary to supplement self-help, however, not only because many poorly-educated farmers cannot be readily convinced that certain measures are worthwhile in their own interest, but also because farmers will need help to tide them over an initial period of low production and income and to enable them to purchase some of their requisites such as plant material, fertilizers, implements and livestock. Any program of government financial assistance should be drawn up to make it possible not only to carry out initial improvement works but also to furnish an incentive to maintain the improvement and carry out the land development scheme as initially envisaged.

On the soil conservation works themselves, we suggest that the government be prepared to spend an average of £ 12 per acre. For 300,000 acres this would involve a total outlay of about £ 3,600,000 over ten years. This cost estimate appears to be in line with the experience in Jamaica to date. Following the precedent set in the post-hurricane Farm Recovery Program we recommend that only one quarter of this be considered as a loan repayable over five years. The remainder can fairly be considered as pay to the small farmer for his labor contribution to the rehabilitation project of which his holding is or will be a part; and in the case of the large property owner undertaking to carry out a project it can be regarded as compensation for the labor he must hire to do the necessary work.

Additional funds will also be required to provide production and development credit over a number of years for the purpose of carrying out the agreed cropping scheme. In some cases, too, assistance will be needed for housing and water supply. We shall revert to these requirements later. Here we wish to emphasize the necessity of conditioning all forms of government assistance to farmers on participation in agreed rehabilitation schemes wherever these are considered necessary. Only in this way can any broad farm improvement scheme be carried out and maintained. We regard this not as compulsion, but simply a legitimate and prudent precaution on the part of the government to insure that its funds are "invested" only in farming ventures which are based on sound agricultural practices.

In the last analysis it should be possible to invoke some measure of direct compulsion against the small number of recalcitrants standing in the way of projects desired by the vast majority. This is recognized in the Land Authorities Law which empowers any regional authority set up under the law to carry out works on a farmer's land against his will. In such cases, however, the farmer is not required to pay for any improvements even though he is entitled to claim compensation for any damage, no matter how temporary, inflicted on his land. In essence, therefore, the law encourages rather than penalizes non-cooperation, for the farmer can get all the benefits of improvement schemes without any effort on his part. We strongly urge that this stipulation of the law be amended. The government might consider whether under certain circumstances, particularly when the overwhelming majority of farmers wish to participate in an improvement program for a given area, it might not be feasible to acquire the land of the few who are unwilling to cooperate at a value determined primarily by the annual yield of the land in the years immediately preceding its acquisition. Such acquisition might be in the form of a long-term lease, with the provision that the owner could resume possession on payment of his share of the improvement cost. In a country where land is scarce in relation to the population and its intensive and efficient use is a matter of paramount public interest a way may have to be devised to control in some measure the individual's right to use the land in any way he sees fit.

Compulsion will probably need to be invoked but rarely. In most cases the minority opposing the proposed rehabilitation scheme will tend to yield in face of the declared wishes of the overwhelming majority of potential participants. At the same time the mere possibility of using the powers of compulsory acquisition will help to persuade the minority of the futility of holding out.

2. *Afforestation*

Afforestation as an essential part of the soil protection program has already been stressed. Afforestation combined with other soil conservation measures can in the long run provide the only insurance against the destructive floods which now plague Jamaica. Even in the few places where the construction of flood control dams may prove possible, there is under present conditions a serious danger that the storage basins will silt up rapidly.

Up to the present afforestation has been on a wholly inadequate scale. Under a scheme approved in 1941 and to be financed out of Colonial Development and Welfare grants, 23,000 acres of Crown lands were to be afforested by 1956. By 1950, however, only 4,288 acres had actually been planted, and at the present rate only 7,000 acres will be completed by 1956. Present planting is at the rate of only 500-600 acres per year, and private persons are assisted in planting another 500 acres per year.

We strongly urge the adoption of a more ambitious program with a target of about 100,000 acres over a ten-year period. On the basis of such cost estimates as were obtainable in Jamaica, we believe that this would involve a government expenditure of about £ 1,000,000. Part of it would be devoted to accelerating the afforesta-

29

tion of Crown Lands, and part would be spent in subsidies for afforestation on private lands. The first step in such a program should be a rapid expansion of government nurseries. At present private property owners wishing to plant trees are unable to obtain planting material.

Wherever land rehabilitation projects of the type outlined above are carried out, it will generally be desirable to afforest the ridges and steeper slopes. In such areas and other areas accessible to the surrounding population it would be well to experiment with the planting of mixed forests including food trees such as mangoes, avocados, naseberry, ackee, breadfruit, cashew and the like. These would then provide not only needed soil cover, but ultimately a welcome addition to the diet of the people as well. On the Crown lands and less accessible areas plantings would be of timber trees, including such hardwoods as mahogany, teak and mahoe, and quicker-growing softwoods such as wattle, cedar and pine. Both the selection of areas and the type of trees for afforestation would be greatly facilitated by the soil and ecological survey which would be carried out as part of the aerial and ground survey we have already recommended.

Particular study will have to be devoted to the best methods of establishing forests on the degraded soils of the steeper slopes. In such cases special care will be needed to avoid excessive disturbance of the soil. Where some scrub forest already exists, it may be advisable to remove it gradually as the more permanent tree cover is established.[13]

Equally important with afforestation is more adequate protection of existing and future forest areas. The attitude of law enforcement authorities toward encroachment on forest reserves, trespassing and indiscriminate burning of hillsides has been far too lenient. Strict enforcement of the Forest Law and the Country Fires Law is necessary. Every effort must be made to develop real community responsi-

---

[13] The larger trees, for example, could be stumped or lopped instead of burned or dug out; and the smaller trees might be ringed or poisoned once the young trees are established. These practices would be particularly important in the establishment of "food forests."

bility for the protection of forests, and the schools must do their part in educating children to a realization of the importance of forests to the economy.

3. *Pasture Improvement*

Another important objective of the agricultural development program should be to intensify the livestock industry. The output of livestock products must be substantially increased to meet the needs of the growing population and provide a better diet;[14] and gradually part of the pasture now "extensively" utilized for the production of beef cattle will have to be released for cultivation. Productivity in the livestock industry is now deplorably low. In general three acres of pasture are required to carry one beast, and one acre produces about 60 pounds of beef (liveweight) per year which at present prices is equivalent to a yield of only about £ 2 ($5.60) per acre. Dairy cattle produce on the average only three quarts of milk per day.

The improvement of feed supplies through better pasture management can do more than any other measure to raise the output of livestock products. In the breeding of cattle Jamaica has made substantial progress; and the island has even been exporting pedigreed cattle to the Caribbean area and South America. By the introduction of Zebu (Indian) blood into European milk and beef breeds the island has produced excellent heat tolerant types.[15] No doubt more can be done to upgrade indigenous herds, but the primary need now is to improve feeding.

The potentialities are great. Natural conditions in Jamaica are more favorable to good pastures than in most tropical and subtropical countries. On the government farm at Hope near Kingston it has already been demonstrated that one animal can be carried to the acre even though the rainfall there is much lower than in most of the island. In Natal in South Africa two beasts have been car-

---

[14] For the same reason an increase in the production of fish by means of the establishment of fish ponds would be desirable. A note on fisheries appears in Annex 5.

[15] See Annex 6.

ried per acre of properly managed and fertilized pastures even though the rainfall is only 30 to 40 inches per year. The principal problem is how to realize the potentialities for higher production in Jamaica through practices which will be effective in raising output and at the same time give the livestock farmer a return substantially greater than his additional outlay.

Yields will be significantly increased only if grass is grown, fertilized and generally treated as any other crop. It is particularly important to improve feed supplies during the dry season when the growth of most cattle receives a serious setback. Sometime before the advent of the dry season row grasses such as Napier and Elephant grass should be fertilized and mulched with cut grass.[16] At the same time sod-forming grasses should be disked or harrowed and fertilized. Wherever possible grass should be cut in the flush season (preferably shortly after the application of nitrogenous fertilizers), stored in inexpensive pits or trenches and converted into silage with the use of molasses and water.

Ways and means of increasing the necessary protein intake of cattle should be fully utilized. Legumes might be used in combination with grasses (tropical Kudzu with Elephant grass; indigofera with Wynne grass) in such a way as to raise the protein content and simultaneously reduce the requirements for nitrogen fertilizer.[17] Striking increases in the protein content of grasses can often be obtained through the use of fertilizer. More extensive planting of

---

[16] The Mission observed that in a number of places grass accidentally mulched had remained green and vigorous in growth while adjoining non-mulched grass had become brown and unproductive in the dry season.

[17] It is said that Kudzu will crowd out other grasses, but this may be controlled if vigorous grasses are used in combination with Kudzu and their growth is stimulated by nitrogenous fertilizer. An experiment in Puerto Rico has shown that the dry yield of fertilized cultivated pastures in which Kudzu was included was three and a half times that of natural pastures similarly fertilized. The protein yield of such cultivated pastures was almost double that of the natural pastures. See Jose Vincente, "Los Pastos Mejorados Conservan y Mejoran la Tierra y Producen Mas Leche y Carne," *Revista de Agricultura de Puerto Rico*, Vol. XLII, Nos. 1-2, 1951.

fodder trees such as "Quick-Stick" (*Gliricidia*), whose leaves are rich in protein, should be encouraged. It will also pay to make fuller use of locally available protein concentrates such as rice bran and dried cassava leaves. It has already been demonstrated that the leaves of cassava, which is extensively grown in Jamaica, have a high protein and carotin value when quickly dried at high temperatures.

More intensive pasture management is also needed. Pastures might be subdivided into small paddocks which are grazed intensively for a few days. This will not only permit fuller utilization of the grass but also the subsequent scattering of the concentrated cattle droppings by improvised (if necessary) wooden harrows, thus saving on fertilizer. This will require, of course, more labor, more fencing (which can be of the portable or the electric type) and better water supplies.

Experience and experiments outside Jamaica have demonstrated the great response of grass to fertilizer, particularly nitrogen. In Florida and Southern Georgia, for instance, the dry matter yield of plots fertilized with a standard dressing of 400 lbs. nitrogen (equivalent to 2,000 lbs. ammonium sulphate) has been five to six times that of unfertilized plots. In southern Georgia the carrying capacity of fertilized pastures with a new strain of Bermuda grass has been increased to two and a half beasts per acre. In Florida one pound of nitrogen produced, on the average, an increase in dry grass yield of 25 to 30 lbs., containing about 4 lbs. protein, or enough to produce 2.5 to 3.5 lbs. of beef (liveweight). We are aware that experiments in Jamaica have not shown such startling results even though soils, temperatures and rainfalls are more favorable than in Florida or southern Georgia. For instance, in experiments conducted in three parishes over a sixteen month period (1946-48) applications of four cwt. ammonium sulphate, together with potash and phosphates, generally produced an increase in dry matter yields of only 50% to 100% and little increase in protein content. They were carried out in an unusually dry period, however, and for various reasons cannot be regarded as conclusive. We are convinced that far better results can be achieved with further experiments varying, among other things, the timing of grass planting and fertilization and the quantity and proportions of fertilizers applied and using a combination of mulching and fertilization.[18]

Intensification of the livestock industry along the lines indicated above will, of course, require much more labor, equipment and supplies. It will be argued that the cash investment involved will not be economic in view of the returns which may be anticipated, and that in any event the livestock farmer does not have the necessary capital. We fully agree that the investment is not attractive on the basis of beef prices existing in Jamaica. If it is assumed, for instance, that one pound of nitrogen costing perhaps a shilling or a little more (14 or 15¢) will produce an extra pound of beef yielding 1s.2d. (17¢), the livestock man will not risk the additional outlay, particularly since he will probably also have some extra expenditures for other fertilizers and labor.

In the interest of the consumer beef prices have been kept at a level which is among the lowest in the world. In 1951 the price obtained by the livestock farmer in Jamaica (102s.6d. per 100 lbs. warm dressed weight) was less than a quarter of the price in the United States, half of that in the United Kingdom and 15% less than that in Argentina. Since then the price has been raised by 30% (to 135s. per 100 lbs.), but it still effectively discourages investment in the raising of livestock. Since it applies to all grades of beef indiscriminately, it also fails to provide an adequate incentive for the production of better grade beef. Thus at present the demand for "fancy" or high grade beef is largely met either by black-marketing of the better livestock or by high-priced imports from the United States.

The price of milk, although somewhat more satisfactory, also appears unremunerative. The expansion of milk production has

---

[18] For a description and analysis of pasture fertilization experiments, see Annex 7.

Above and below: Results of the Aenion Town Coffee demonstration plot. This land, derelict five years ago, now produces coffee, bananas, breadfruit, citrus, and cocoa. With the breadfruit and citrus developing well, in a few years the temporary shade can be removed and the final plan of orderly rows of coffee and shade attained.

tended to level off in recent years, and the price at best offers no incentive for a further increase in production.[19]

An increase in the price of beef, and perhaps of milk, is indispensable, in our opinion, to a needed intensification of the livestock industry. Jamaica cannot afford to maintain a price which promotes uneconomic use of the land. If the consumer must be subsidized, it is better to do so directly from public funds than to keep the price at an artificial level which discourages production.

Once the price is raised to make intensive livestock practices worthwhile, the government should provide the funds necessary to get an intensification program started. We suggest that such a program aim at the improvement of about 100,000 acres of pastures over a ten-year period and that approximately £ 1.6 million be allocated for this purpose. Since most farmers may doubt that these intensive practices pay, the government must be prepared to pay the greater part of the extra cost in labor, equipment and supplies over a period sufficient to produce results—say two years. We suggest that as an incentive three quarters of the assistance be made available as a grant.

In each case it will be desirable to work out with the individual farmer the type of practices which are most likely to yield good results on his land. Experiments may also demonstrate the profitability of fertilizer applications. On the poorer land where only extensive grazing and beef production are likely to prove possible, controlled grazing and improvement of water supplies will be of paramount importance. On the better lands, where intensive beef or dairy production is feasible, the use of fertilizer or manure, the conservation of fodder grasses and legumes for the dry season, as well as rotational grazing, will need to be fostered. Increases in yields up to 50% can probably be achieved in these ways. In dairy farming better pasture management will have to be complemented by the cultivation, in rotation with cash crops, of legumes and grain fodders for green feeding in stalls or for conservation.

---

[19] The price of milk—6s.1/2d. per quart—has increased by 160% since 1940, while the price of beef has risen by only 135%.

Since the type of practices we recommend will require a great deal of labor, it is especially important to bring into the program[20] the small livestock farmers who can invest their own labor. The large penkeepers, however, should be persuaded to apply the improvement scheme to at least a portion of their better pastures. The big bauxite producing companies who have ample capital and large tracts of pasture land may well be induced to lead the way and should not require a government subvention.

While undertaking this program, the government should at the same time greatly expand its pasture research and experimentation program to acquire more data on the responses of different grasses to fertilizers under various conditions and on various problems of pasture management. For Jamaica a pasture research center is as necessary as a sugar cane research organization.

4. *Irrigation and Land Reclamation*

Irrigation and reclamation provide another possibility of greatly expanding agricultural output. Parts of the island, primarily on the south coast but to some extent also on the north coast, have insufficient rainfall. In other parts the rainfall distribution is such that prolonged and damaging droughts frequently occur. Along the southern coast there is much good land now producing little or nothing which could be made highly productive with water. On other lands crop production is hazardous because of uncertain rainfall. Moreover, in many parts of the coastal areas there are swamps which can be reclaimed for agricultural use. Portions of these swamp areas bordering on sugar estates have already been reclaimed by private initiative. The Mission found a widespread conviction that a well-considered program of irrigation and reclamation could bring about a substantial increase in the production of sugar, bananas, rice, vegetables and other crops. The lack of capital and the absence of data on the economic justification of particular projects have hitherto been the major deterrents to such a program.

---

[20] Farmers with less than 10 acres had almost one-quarter of the cattle on the island in 1950; and those with less than 25 acres had well over a third.

Irrigation

At present there is some irrigation in all of the parishes except Manchester.[21] With the exception of a few experimental plots of overhead irrigation, all of the 47,200 acres now irrigated are supplied with water by gravity systems.

The largest irrigation project is the Rio Cobre System which irrigates 22,000 acres in the parish of St. Catherine where the average annual rainfall is approximately 30 inches. It was constructed by the government in 1872-76 and is still operated by the government. Water is sold at rates sufficient to pay all operating costs and return a small surplus to the government. A project to augment the Rio Cobre System by water from three wells which discharge into the existing canals was put into operation in the summer of 1952. It cost about £ 28,000 and provides enough water to cultivate about 2,000 additional acres or to permit more intensive cultivation of some of the irrigated lands now growing grass.

Another large project is the Cockpit System, completed in 1917, which irrigates about 4,000 acres in Clarendon parish. Privately constructed, it was financed by loans guaranteed by the government. It has been successfully operated by a commission since its completion.

The most recent irrigation development is the Mid-Clarendon Scheme. This project, which was about 85% completed in May 1952, is being constructed by the Mid-Clarendon Irrigation Authority established under the Irrigation Law of 1949 by Order of the Governor in Executive Council in February, 1950. About 10,000 acres can be economically irrigated under the scheme, but initially only 5,000 acres will be provided with water. The funds for the construction were raised by the government through public loans and relent to the Authority. The area will be irrigated by water diverted from the Milk River and its two tributaries, the St. Toolies and St. Jago Springs, into two separate mainline canals. Since the Milk River and the St. Toolies Spring fail in periods of drought, the water supply

---

[21] See Annex 8 for the area under irrigation in each parish.

from the river and springs will be supplemented by seven deep wells which will discharge either directly into the canals or through short subsidiary canals. Water will be sold to both large and small land-owners by the Authority. A large part of the scheme is expected to be in operation by the end of 1952.

A considerable number of relatively small irrigation projects have been undertaken in various parts of the island by individual landowners and large companies. In recent years the government has authorized the Department of Agriculture to spend up to £ 100,000 for assisting in the development of minor irrigation schemes (50 to 500 acres), mostly using water from deep wells. Money is loaned for such schemes if they are approved by the appropriate Parish Farm Improvement Committee, the central Farm Improvement Authority and the Public Works Department. The government takes the loss on any wells which prove to be dry. Since 1950, 48 such schemes have been in-vestigated but to date only a few have actually been carried out.

There is no doubt that both land and water are available for a substantial extension of irrigation.[22] Studies of the underground water resources are far from complete and a hydrological survey is urgently needed. However, sufficient knowledge has been gained to permit greater utilization of underground supplies. Since 1929 wells have been sunk for irrigation on a considerable scale. The advent of the deep well, coupled with successive reductions in power rates for pumping and the relatively low cost of diesel pumping, has revolution-ized the expansion of irrigation in recent decades.

There are probably about 83,000 acres of reasonably good land

---

[22] While the number of rivers that can be tapped are limited, there are large underground supplies of water. Broadly speaking, water can be ob-tained from two formations: alluvial and white limestone. In the alluvial formations the water is much closer to the surface, but in the limestone yields are much higher. The limestone formations act as huge underground reser-voirs storing a high percentage of the rainfall which occurs in the wetter portions of the Island. Water from these reservoirs flows through the porous limestone to the sea in underground streams which occasionally appear on the surface and feed existing rivers. Sometimes rivers disappear underground into the side of a hill and reappear on the other side as springs.

which might eventually prove worth irrigating. A preliminary survey of possible projects made in consultation with Jamaican agriculturists and experts from the Public Works Department has persuaded us that during the next decade an additional 46,000 acres, in addition to the 10,000 acre Mid-Clarendon Scheme, might profitably be brought under irrigation. Of this total, 12,000 acres would be in St. Catherine; 3,000 in Clarendon; 5,000 in St. Elizabeth; 2,000 in Trelawny; 4,000 in St. Thomas; and 20,000 in minor irrigation schemes scattered throughout the island.[23] The total cost of these projects might be roughly estimated at £ 2 million to £ 2.25 million. We would emphasize, however, the tentative nature of this recommendation. While we have reason to believe that these projects are worthwhile, thorough surveys and investigations should be undertaken to determine the advisability of each project in the light of costs and probable returns. Funds for these investigations should be made available as soon as possible so that a definitive and comprehensive irrigation program can be drawn up and begun. Undoubtedly this will require a considerable expansion of the Hydraulics Branch and possibly of the Surveys Branch of the Public Works Department. A list of the proposed schemes, together with the priority rating and estimated cost of investigating each of them, is included in Annex 9.

One of the schemes—a multiple purpose project—merits special mention. It is the proposed Harker's Hall dam on the Rio Pedro, the principal tributary of the Rio Cobre. This project contemplates the construction of a dam 150 feet high with a crest length of 600 to 800 feet to provide storage for flood control, irrigation and power. The proposed dam site and the reservoir area above it appear to be free of the porous limestone formation which would make it impossible to construct a storage reservoir. A preliminary study indicates that a reservoir with a capacity of 47,800 acre-feet might be created by the dam. This capacity could probably store the runoff from most major storms and considerably reduce flood damage to crops, roads, bridges and an existing hydroelectric plant on the

---

[23] For a list of these projects, see Annex 9.

Rio Cobre. Over the last 15 years this damage has averaged £ 10,000 to £ 15,000 annually.[24] In addition, the project could provide for irrigation of about 8,000 acres in the parish of St. Catherine, might develop as much as 1,000 kw of power at the dam and increase the firm power available at the existing hydro plant on the Rio Cobre. While a rough, preliminary survey points to the soundness of this project, it is necessary to make a thorough study, including topographic surveys, subsurface investigations of the dam foundation, a geological investigation of the entire reservoir area, and hydrological studies of storm and normal runoffs. This might cost as much as £ 30,000.

Since all of the projects on the list, except the Harker's Hall project, would require pumping, one of the governing factors in the further development of irrigation in the Island is an ample supply of electricity at low rates. The Jamaica Public Service Company, a privately owned concern, has not been inclined in the past to extend its lines into any area unless it could be assured of an adequate income at the outset from a line. This has been an obstacle to the development of new irrigation schemes requiring pumping in areas not now served by power lines. This handicap might be overcome if the government advanced the necessary funds for transmission line construction with provision for repayment over a long period similar to that applied to the Mid-Clarendon Scheme—namely by surcharges on the bills due the Public Service Company, with the Company taking title to the lines at the end of the repayment period.

Pumping costs are critical not only because much of the water for irrigation will have to come from wells, but also because overhead irrigation will probably become increasingly prevalent. Not only will overhead irrigation be necessary in areas where the rolling nature of the land precludes irrigation by gravity flow, but it may be preferable even in areas where canal irrigation is feasible. Overhead irriga-

---

[24] Capitalized at 5% over 30 years, this would amount in round figures to between £ 153,000 and £ 230,000. While floods are not an annual occurrence, their frequency and destructiveness have apparently been increasing. The last four floods occurred in 1939, 1944, 1950 and 1951.

tion requires only about half as much water, and experiments conducted by some sugar estates in Jamaica have indicated that on heavy clay soils its use produces much higher yields. While the capital investment for overhead irrigation is higher, considerable progress has been made in producing lower cost equipment, particularly of the portable and semiportable type. It is likely to prove worthwhile for crops with a high cash return per acre such as sugar and bananas. Before making large investments in overhead irrigation, however, it would be prudent to undertake a number of experiments to determine the best combination of equipment for various types of crops and land, the cost of installation and operation, and, most important of all, the effect on yields and returns per acre for different crops.

Reclamation

While we are confident that a considerable expansion of irrigation will prove worthwhile, recommendations on reclamation projects can be made with much less certainty. A few sugar estates have undertaken reclamation projects but under conditions which make it difficult to determine whether they would normally be profitable. The only government land reclamation scheme in operation is one that resulted from studies undertaken in 1926. The investigations revealed the possibility of reclaiming the Upper Morass of the Black River and indicated that by deepening the existing channels and keeping them clean, conditions in the area could be considerably improved. Since then, the government has established a Drainage Board which supervises the cleaning of the channels. Some of the lands bordering the Morass have been drained and are used for feeding cattle and more recently for the cultivation of rice.

No adequate investigation of the cost of reclaiming various swamp areas has ever been undertaken and little information is available on the soils of such areas. After marshalling such fragmentary data as are available, we have come to the very tentative conclusion that possibly 20,000 acres of swamp land might be reclaimed over the next decade at a total cost of perhaps £ 570,000. Before undertaking such a program, detailed surveys of each project should obviously be undertaken. The first step should be a soil survey since further investigation would be useless if the soils should prove unsuitable for the cultivation of high-yielding crops. The next step would be to investigate the technical problems and estimate the cost. The cost of the surveys is estimated at about £ 25,000. The projects which may qualify for inclusion in the program are listed in Annex 10 in the order of priority in which investigations should be undertaken. It is quite probable that about a quarter of the area tentatively selected for reclamation will prove to be unsuitable.

The reclamation program, if carried out in whole or in part, would require a substantial increase in the staff of the Hydraulics Branch for supervision of the projects. Additional earth-moving equipment would also be required. As most of the land included in the projects is privately owned, measures would be required to distribute the cost of improvements equitably among the owners and to draw up a coordinated program for the development of the reclaimed area. One solution of this problem would be the creation of drainage districts under a general statute which would authorize the formation of such districts and outline the general terms under which they would be developed. These districts would have the advantage of permitting all owners interested in reclamation to join the district voluntarily. In case some recalcitrant owner refused to cooperate, the law should provide for acquisition of the land at a cost generally determined by its current value. Annual payments made by the owners to retire the cost of improvements over a period of years might, for tax purposes, be regarded as operating costs, thus providing a distinct incentive to participation in land reclamation.

We are, of course, aware of the fact that irrigation and reclamation projects should be undertaken only if the beneficiaries can be expected to pay the full charges, including interest and amortization on the capital investment and the cost of operation and maintenance. Unless the required capital investment proves much greater than indicated above or the soils are not fertile, there is little doubt that these charges can be met. Sugar and bananas are grown profitably under irrigation on private estates. An examination of cost figures

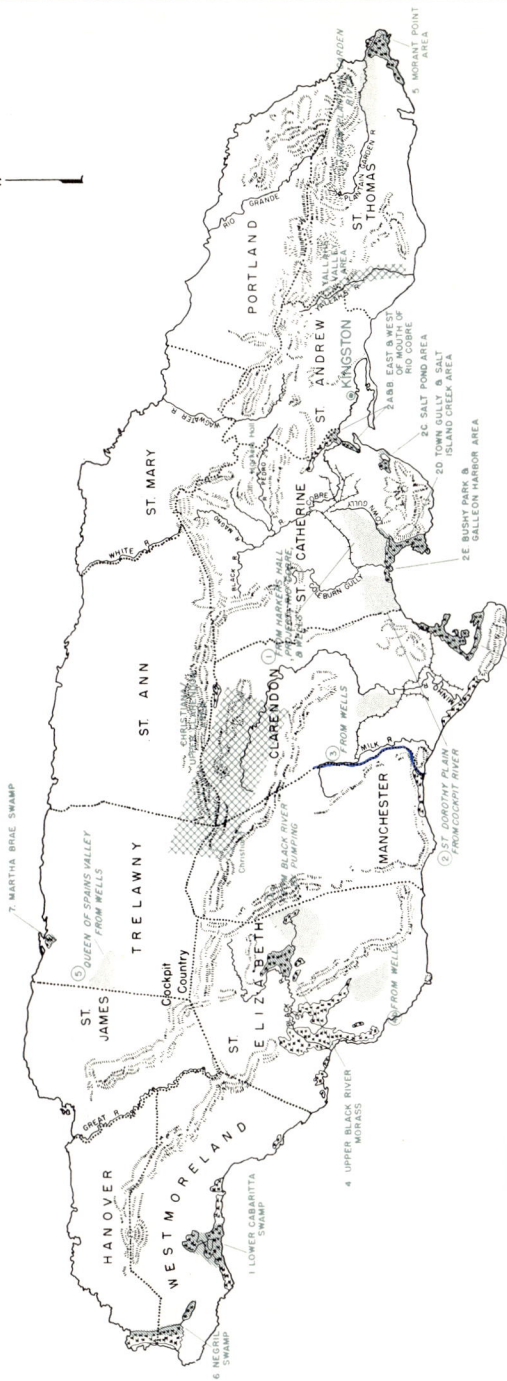

JAMAICA

AGRICULTURAL PROJECTS

MILES
0   5   10   15   20   25

IRRIGATION PROJECTS

LAND RECLAMATION PROJECTS

REGIONAL SOIL
CONSERVATION PROJECTS

RIVERS

CANALS

SWAMPS

PARISH BOUNDARIES

N

HANOVER

WESTMORELAND

ST. JAMES

TRELAWNY

ST. ANN

ST. MARY

PORTLAND

ST. ELIZABETH

MANCHESTER

CLARENDON

ST. CATHERINE

ST. ANDREW

ST. THOMAS

KINGSTON

Cockpit Country

2A&B EAST & WEST
OF MOUTH OF
RIO COBRE

2C SALT POND AREA

2D TOWN GULLY & SALT
ISLAND CREEK AREA

2E BUSHY PARK &
GALLEON HARBOR AREA

3 CLARENDON GULLEY
WEST HARBOR AREA

5 MORANT POINT
AREA

1 LOWER CABARITTA
SWAMP

6 NEGRIL SWAMP

4 UPPER BLACK RIVER
MORASS

7. MARTHA BRAE SWAMP

① FROM MARKET MILL

② ST. DOROTHY PLAIN
FROM COCKPIT RIVER

③ FROM WELLS

5 QUEEN OF SPAINS VALLEY
FROM WELLS

FROM WELLS

BLACK RIVER
PUMPING

RIO GRANDE

WAGWATER R.

YALLAHS VALLEY
AREA

RIO COBRE

RIO MINHO

BLACK R.

WHITE R.

GREAT R.

for the government Twickenham Park farm discloses that both sugar and bananas on irrigated land yield a good net profit which is particularly high for bananas.[25] Included in these costs are £ 5 per acre for water and from about £ 3 to £ 6 for applying water and maintaining canals. It seems unlikely that the charges for water which will have to be made under most of the proposed irrigation projects will significantly exceed £ 5 per acre. Even in cases where bananas or sugar cane can be grown without irrigation, the increased yield made possible by irrigation will in many cases pay for the cost.[26] Considering the probable capital cost of reclamation, it may be expected that the reclamation of reasonably good land will also pay. Both irrigation and reclamation, however, are likely to be profitable only if crops with a rather high cash value per acre can be grown. These include, besides sugar cane and bananas, such crops as tomatoes and other truck-garden vegetables. Rice could probably also be grown profitably on irrigated or reclaimed land, for although the gross yield is only about £ 30 per acre, it requires less labor than sugar, bananas and truck-garden crops and can be grown in combination with another crop within a period of a year.

5. *Rural Housing and Water Supply*

In the agricultural development program outlined above we believe it will be essential to make some provision for rural housing and water supply. We do not propose any scheme for general improvement of the admittedly very low housing standards in the rural areas. However desirable, this can be undertaken only after production and income have been significantly expanded and the country

---

[25] For 1951 the indicated net profit on sugar after all costs was £4 14s. per acre; on bananas it was as high as £ 36 6s. 1d.

[26] Thus on the basis of costs at Twickenham Park it may be estimated that an increase of nine tons of sugar cane per acre or of 23 count bunches of bananas per acre will be sufficient to pay the cost of irrigation. An acre of cane under cultivation can be expected to yield about 35 tons, and an acre of bananas at least 200 count bunches. See Annex 11.

can afford it. We would suggest an attack only on certain outstanding deficiencies.

At present many farmers must trudge miles before they reach the plot or plots which they till. If they lived on their holdings they would be able not only to work them more effectively but also to protect their crops against serious losses from praedial larceny which is one of the banes of Jamaican agriculture. Moreover, the proposed development program will result in a very considerable extension of the area under cultivation—by perhaps as much as 150,000 acres. This will mean the creation of many new farms and a corresponding need for houses. The available financial resources will obviously permit assistance only on a modest scale. We suggest it take the form of help in moving existing houses to the farm site and of supplying materials for reconstruction and repair and, where necessary, for new houses. Great reliance will have to be placed on self-help, with the owner supplying the labor required for building and repair. The assistance should be given as a loan repayable over 10 years and the maximum loan should be £ 100 for a new house. On these conditions we would suggest that £ 2 million be allocated for this purpose over the ten-year period.

Access to some water supply is essential both for farmers and their livestock. Sources of water are often remote and then frequently polluted. Only a beginning can be made with the solution of this problem over the next decade since the provision of water is inevitably costly. According to the Lands Department a water catchment with a tank of 50,000 gallons costs £ 2,500 and a well £ 2,000. Each of these will, of course, have to supply a considerable number of families, and there can be no question of piping water into houses. For the purpose of supplying water and other facilities it would obviously be desirable to have farmers settled in communities. A practicable compromise between this need and the requirement for living close to or on the land tilled by farmers will have to be worked out in each settlement. We would recommend that about £ 1.5 million be spent on water supply over ten years. Three quarters of this will probably need to be a grant.

6. *Agricultural Credit*

The program of assistance for soil conservation, pasture improvement, rural housing and water supply all envisage an extension of credit to cover part of the cost. Far more credit will be needed, however, to enable farmers to pursue improved agricultural practices on new and rehabilitated land and to establish crops and purchase livestock in accordance with approved land use patterns. Requirements for this type of credit will rise as additional land is brought into use. Basically the need will be for (1) short-term crop or production loans, and (2) longer-term development loans.

The first of these would be intended to meet part of the farmer's living expenses as well as part of his operating expenses, including fertilizer and planting material, until the crop can be harvested. Such credits would represent in essence a short-term crop advance and would be repaid in a period ranging from six months for most food crops to eighteen months for sugar cane. The second would be to finance the establishment of long-maturing crops such as citrus, coffee and cacao, the acquisition of cattle or the purchase of equipment. Repayment would usually be spread over five years with amortization deferred, in the case of loans on orchard crops, until the crop starts bearing.

We have attempted to estimate the total amount of production and development credits that will be needed in line with the expansion of agricultural output we envisage. We anticipate that the peak need for short-term production credit will be £ 3.3 million. For development credit a peak demand of close to £ 900,000 may be anticipated. A total revolving credit of about £ 4.2 million will therefore be required.[27]

We recommend that these credits, as well as the loan portion of the government assistance programs mentioned above, be admin-

---

[27] For detailed estimates, see Annex 33. The calculation assumes that crop or production loans will be granted in an amount equal to half of the expected cash yield, and development loans at half of the total cost of establishing tree crops.

istered by the existing agricultural credit banks—namely, the Peoples Cooperative Banks.[28] There are some 120 of these banks which are organized on a cooperative basis and have about 75,000 members. Administration by these banks would not only be the most economical way of providing credit, but would also permit maintenance of an adequate check on the total indebtedness assumed by each farmer for various purposes. The government funds might best be supplied through the Agricultural Loan Societies Board as hitherto, with the proviso that the criteria for extending loans be established by the agency or agencies charged with responsibility for the over-all agricultural development program. This Board, which should ultimately be converted into a central bank for cooperatives, will need to keep a careful check on the repayment record of each of the Peoples Cooperative Banks.

It may be objected that the program will add excessively to existing farm indebtedness and that a substantial part of the loans will not be repaid. Undoubtedly, the total increase will be very large, for to the estimated £ 4.2 million for production and development credit must be added about £ 2.9 million for soil conservation, pasture rehabilitation, rural housing and water supply. Unfortunately no figures are available on the total of existing indebtedness which must also be taken into account. The census of 1943 indicated a total mortgage indebtedness of £ 1.7 million. It is quite probable that this has risen to at least £ 2.5 million. If one excludes short-term credits which may be considered as crop advances and allows for some repayment of loans now outstanding, it may be expected that the volume of longer-term indebtedness will ultimately rise to about £ 6.3 million under the contemplated program.

This increase in indebtedness must be related, however, to the rise in production that can be expected from the development program as a whole. In the past the creditworthiness of Jamaican agriculture has not been high because lending could not be geared to a definite, comprehensive and coordinated program for raising output.

---

[28] For a description of the existing agricultural credit machinery, see Annex 12.

If in the future loans are granted only for the purposes specified in the program outlined above, the increase in debt should not prove too burdensome. As will be indicated elsewhere, we believe that the proposed development program will raise the gross value of agricultural production from about £ 25 million to £ 36 million. The volume of indebtedness could therefore be kept within the limit of 20% of the value of output which has proved feasible in a number of countries. We have also analyzed the prospective economic position of individual farmers participating in the improvement program and have come to the conclusion that they should be able to carry the contemplated debt charges.[29]

This presupposes, however, the will as well as the ability to repay. Often there has been an inclination to regard government credit as a grant rather than a loan and to criticize sharply attempts to proceed against those who default on their payments. If there is to be a sound system of agricultural credit, there must be strict insistence on repayment. It is important to develop among the members of each Peoples Cooperative Bank a feeling of joint responsibility for repayment of credits granted by the bank. If the Loan Societies Board withholds further credit from a bank with a bad repayment record, there must be a firm resolve to uphold the action of the Board in the interest of credit to farmers as a whole. If there is a default on loans secured by a mortgage, political pressures against the foreclosure of the mortgage should be firmly resisted. In assessing the cost of the agricultural development program we have not considered it possible to make a specific allowance for "bad debts." Failure to collect debts will, of course, make it necessary either to curtail the credit program or to cover the losses out of additional government funds. We believe it will be possible to avoid serious losses by avoiding general purpose loans and by taking advantage of all opportunities to secure loans by crop liens which can be automatically discharged through the controlled marketing of agricultural commodities. Organized marketing has already made commendable progress in Jamaica and covers such products as sugar cane, bananas, citrus, tomatoes, coffee and

---

[29] See Annex 13.

cacao. We urge that it be extended as far as possible, particularly to cover crops grown for local consumption. We therefore strongly support the proposal of the Registrar of Cooperatives to establish in each parish a few marketing and credit cooperatives to experiment with joint financing and marketing of food and other crops for which organized facilities do not yet exist.

IMPACT OF THE PROGRAM

We believe that the proposed ten-year agricultural development program will ultimately raise production by about £ 11 million.[30] Part of this increase will result from higher yields. We expect, for example, that the soil conservation and rehabilitation program will gradually increase the productivity of the land already under cultivation. Similarly we anticipate that the present low output of those pastures included in the pasture improvement program will at the least be doubled. Higher yields will also be achieved through the extension of irrigation. The greater part of the increase will, however, be realized through an expansion of the area under cultivation by approximately 150,000 acres. Of this total some 100,000 acres will be on the hillsides and uplands, about half representing pastures not hitherto used for cultivation and the rest hillside land which is either idle or intermittently cultivated. The remainder of the increase will be in the more or less flat areas and will result from reclamation and the extension of irrigation to dry lands which now produce little or nothing. The rise in output attributable to these new lands will be especially large if appropriate emphasis is given to the cultivation of crops with a high cash value per acre, including not only bananas and sugar cane, but also longer maturing tree crops such as coffee, cacao and citrus. On the whole we have been conservative in estimating the total increase in output which might be achieved by the development program. We have not allowed for

---

[30] Estimated at the prices prevailing in 1950.

any fall in prices which may prove to be optimistic, but on the other hand we have tended to underestimate quantitative yields. We have not take into account any general advance in productivity other than that which might be ascribed to particular factors directly influenced by the development program.

The expansion of acreage under cultivation will make possible a new land settlement program but on a basis quite different from that which has prevailed in the past. Under the old land settlement program carried out under the auspices of the Lands Department, some 115,000 acres were acquired and turned into 144 settlement projects with 24,000 allotments at a total cost exceeding £ 1.5 million. While this program has undoubtedly resulted in some increase in food production, it is now generally acknowledged to have been a failure.[31] Part of the land acquired for settlement proved unsuitable; the selection of settlers left much to be desired; a considerable portion of the cultivable land has never been tilled; half of the settlers have fallen behind in their payments; and, most important of all, the land has rapidly deteriorated because there was no insistence on soil conservation and other proper agricultural practices. Nearly all of the land on these settlements requires urgent rehabilitation. In the new settlement program the defects of past land settlement policies and practices must be avoided. We have proposed that any land opened to cultivation should first be rehabilitated with the help of prospective settlers selected on the basis of their farming experience. A land use scheme will have to be adopted for each holding and adherence to it enforced by a combination of incentives and penalties. Meanwhile, the land in existing settlements should be included in the general rehabilitation program. We do not suggest, however, that it be given special priority over other farms equally needing attention.

Occasionally doubts are raised concerning Jamaica's ability to

---

[31] For an analysis of this land settlement program, see Annex 14.

make use of the additional land that could be brought under cultivation. Such doubts may seem strange in a country long said to have suffered from "land hunger," but the anxiety stems principally from a fear that Jamaica will experience serious difficulties in marketing the output of such land. We have accordingly paid special attention to the crops which might be grown in the light of both agricultural and marketing considerations. Our recommendations for the expansion of specific crops are given below, but we emphasize that any final determination of a cropping pattern must await an appropriate land use survey.

1. *Sugar*

We recommend that the area under cane be increased by about 26,000 acres of which 16,000 might be on rehabilitated hillsides and 10,000 on newly reclaimed and irrigated land in the plains and valleys. As already indicated, cane would be an excellent soil conserving crop on the hillsides. The marketing of the additional amount of sugar thus produced should not prove a serious problem. In terms of sugar the output would probably rise from 268,000 tons in 1951 to approximately 380,000 tons in 1962, primarily as a result of the increased acreage but also to some extent in response to improved agricultural practices. After allowing for a domestic consumption of 60,000 tons, the exportable surplus would be 320,000. Under the Commonwealth Sugar Agreement which is valid at least until 1960, Jamaica has an export quota of 270,000 tons to which "local exports" of about 5,000 tons may be added. It is not unreasonable to expect, however, that Jamaica will be able to obtain an increase in the quota because of a continued shortfall in exports by other Commonwealth countries, particularly South Africa and Australia and because of a rise in United Kingdom consumption. The United Kingdom is obliged to buy the greater part of the quota (188,348 tons) at a remunerative "negotiated price," and the balance is for sale in Canada, where the preferential market gives Commonwealth sugar a substantial differential over the price fetched by sugar from other sources.[32]

The existing mills can handle most of the increased cane production, partly by extending the grinding season and, even more, by "balancing" their capacity through the elimination of particular bottlenecks. We anticipate, however, that an additional mill or mills with a production of up to 30,000 tons of sugar will have to be erected to grind some of the additional farmers' cane grown on the hillsides. All or the bulk of this additional capacity will be needed in the Christiana area where we envisage a considerable expansion of cane production in the interest of soil conservation. This will involve an investment of £ 2 million to £ 3 million. Since private capital is unlikely to consider such an investment remunerative on the basis of present prices of farmers' cane, we suggest that the government put up £ 2 million of the necessary capital and that the remainder be financed out of Jamaica's share of the United Kingdom's profit on the resale of Commonwealth sugar to Canada, and, possibly, out of some increase in the present cess or levy on sugar exports.

2. *Bananas*

We believe Jamaica should aim to raise production to about 22 million stems or not far from the peak of 27 million stems reached in 1937. This would involve an expansion of about 50,000 acres in the existing area which amounts to approximately 95,000 acres and which will produce between 12 million and 15 million stems for export in

---

[32] Until this year, when the price of Cuban sugar fell sharply, the price at which the United Kingdom bought Commonwealth sugar was actually below the so-called world market price. The amount paid by the United Kingdom is calculated according to a base price in which annual adjustments are made to take into account certain changes in costs of production. The Canadian preference assures Commonwealth producers an additional return of $17.35 per long ton over the world price. There is, however, some agitation in Canada against the continuation of a substantial preference on Commonwealth sugar owing to the discrimination against dollar imports by the Commonwealth countries. Jamaica may find it necessary to obtain the United Kingdom's consent to some relaxation of restrictions on dollar imports.

1952-53. Some increase in yields can be expected to result from soil conservation, the use of fertilizers and irrigation. The rapid expansion of the acreage to present levels following the ravages of the Panama disease and the 1951 hurricane has been achieved by the adoption of the disease-resistant Lacatan banana and the energetic rehabilitation campaign carried out by the All-Island Banana Growers' Association with the cooperation of the government. Prospects for the development of new banana strains resistant also to leaf-spot disease are good and should, if realized, significantly reduce the cost of production.

Marketing prospects in the United Kingdom and the European continent are good. Supplies to the United Kingdom, where bananas have always been a popular food, have been only a little over half of the prewar annual imports of over 22 million stems; and the demand in a number of continental European countries is also far from satisfied.[33] The only real competition which Jamaica has to face is that from the Cameroons which may be expected to produce up to 8-10 million stems and which before the last war marketed its output in Germany. The rise in population in Europe since the prewar period has increased the potential market.

The recent announcement that the United Kingdom would not renew the bulk-purchase contract in 1953 has aroused considerable protest in Jamaica. It should not be too difficult, however, to make alternative marketing arrangements, particularly since established private companies have in fact handled the bananas for the Ministry of Food. The contract has, of course, offered a firm price, but effec-

---

[33] Imports into continental European countries which draw their supplies from their own possessions or have little or no foreign exchange restrictions (France, Spain, Sweden, Switzerland and Belgium) increased from an average of 11,167,000 "count bunches" in 1935-39 to 17,041,000 in 1951 or by almost 53%. In the remaining countries, however, imports fell from 8,741,000 to 5,938,000 "count bunches" or by 32%. If these countries had free access to bananas from "soft-currency" sources, their consumption might be as high in relation to prewar years as that of the others. In that event they might take 7 million to 8 million more "count bunches." See U.S. Department of Agriculture, *Foreign Crops and Markets*, Vol. 65, No. 1.

tive cooperation among producers in dealing with private marketers, together with the favorable supply-demand situation should make it possible to maintain remunerative prices.

3. *Citrus*

We recommend that the present area in citrus be expanded from about 34,000 acres to 44,000 acres. With some improvement in cultural practices and in the care of trees it should be possible to raise the present very low yields to nearly two boxes per tree, so that total output may increase from almost one million boxes to 2.6 million boxes. This proposal is in line with the recommendations of the Citrus Growers Association and should focus principally on an expansion of the production of oranges. Of the increased output, 500,-000 boxes would probably be consumed at home and 1,100,000 boxes would be used to make concentrated juice for the Ministry of Food which has undertaken to buy 2,750 tons of this juice annually for a ten-year period commencing in 1950.

The expansion program is likely to prove profitable only if (1) the present arrangement under which the price for juice will be reduced progressively from 30 shillings per gallon to 22 shillings can be modified to maintain the price at the present level, and (2) an export market can be found for about one million boxes of fresh fruit. Realization of the first condition depends on negotiations with the Ministry of Food. The second condition should, in our opinion, not be too difficult to meet. We fully realize that since the termination of the bulk-purchase agreement by the Ministry of Food in 1950, exports of fresh fruit have languished. Owing to a few unfortunate marketing experiences, the Jamaica citrus growers have virtually abandoned attempts to sell fresh citrus in the United Kingdom. The latter imports only about 60% as much fresh citrus as it bought before the war. While supplies are particularly short during the summer season when Jamaican oranges are not available, there should be room on the winter market for the comparatively small additional supplies from Jamaica.[34] The principal competition would be from Israel where production has been declining and from Spain. Jamaica is said to be greatly handicapped by its high freight rate of 10 shillings per box as compared with about 7 shillings on Israel oranges and 3 to 5 shillings on Spanish oranges. The latter, however, have to pay an import duty of about 3 shillings per box. On the basis of current prices, Jamaica should be able to sell oranges in the United Kingdom at 35-40 shillings per box. After allowing for handling, selling and transport charges of about 23 shillings, the grower should realize about 12 to 17 shillings or more than he obtains for oranges processed into juice. A rationalization of the packing houses of which there are at present far too many, may increase his return by an additional 2 shillings. Present prices in the United Kingdom also point to the possibility of selling grapefruit.

We suggest, therefore, that a vigorous attempt be made to establish a market for fresh fruit as well as for citrus juice. This means, however, that growers and packers will have to improve the quality of their fruit which now often suffers from avoidable skin blemishes and poor color.

4. Coffee

Since natural conditions in Jamaica are favorable for production of coffee and world market prospects are promising, we recommend that present efforts to raise production be intensified so as to increase the area by about 20,000 acres and output from about 4.4 million pounds in 1950 to 30 million pounds. Jamaica still enjoys a reputation for high-quality coffee and once, before soil erosion took its toll, produced far more than at present. A considerable portion of the area to be covered by the soil conservation program could profitably be planted to coffee. The expansion of coffee production will require, of course, a substantial increase in nurseries, the establishment of additional pulperies and strict quality control over exports.

---

[34] We understand, however, that Jamaica could extend its marketing season into the summer by growing a range of known varieties.

5. *Cacao*

The area in cacao might well be expanded from about 12,000 to 22,000 acres. Conditions for this crop are excellent, and the island is free of the diseases which have impaired output in Africa and South America. Long-term marketing prospects are good. With the high-yielding clones now available it should be possible to increase production from 4.8 million pounds to 16.5 million pounds. To achieve this goal nurseries will have to be rapidly expanded, central fermentation plants established and the quality of exports adequately controlled.

6. *Coconuts*

Successive hurricanes have reduced coconut production so that it is no longer sufficient to meet the island's need for water coconuts and edible and inedible oils. We suggest an increase of 30% in the number of trees, involving perhaps 15,000 additional acres. With better selection of seed nuts and improved cultural practices, output may be raised 50% over that of 1950 when about 100 million nuts were produced.

7. *Tomatoes and Vegetables*

There should be a growing market for fresh and processed vegetables and tomatoes, both at home and abroad. An increase of 20-30% in the present area of about 11,000 acres might be envisaged. We realize that the cultivation of tomatoes has undergone many vicissitudes, but with the provision of water for irrigation and proper spraying it should be possible to put production on a more secure footing. The wholesale price of about one shilling per pound obtainable during the winter season in the United Kingdom should prove an incentive to the marketing of fresh tomatoes in that country. The Canary Islands, however, have a great advantage in "know-how" over Jamaica. Jamaica needs expert assistance in improving the packing of tomatoes and in determining exactly the right stage at which the fruit is to be packed.

8. *Pineapples*

The high prices obtainable for fresh and processed pineapples in the United Kingdom, together with the favorable climatic and soil conditions in Jamaica, should make commercial production of pineapples attractive. If high-yielding suckers can be obtained from abroad, a target of 3,000 acres may prove feasible in a few years.

9. *Fibers*

Jamaica can grow a wide range of fibers for both bagging and cordage although at present only a small amount of sisal is grown. Kenaf, ramie, furcroea (Mauritius hemp) and sanseveria (Bowstring hemp) all grow well in Jamaica. The attractiveness of growing jute substitutes such as kenaf will, of course, depend on the price of jute which has recently declined sharply. The planting of sanseveria, however, will be an aid in the prevention of soil erosion; and the cultivation of furcroea in some of the drier areas may prove useful. The cultivation of these fibers is unlikely to absorb more than 3,000 acres.

10. *Rice*

The area grown to rice, which is an important staple in the local diet increased from only 500 acres in 1942 to an estimated 5,400 in 1950. Although production in the latter year amounted to 2,670 tons, 9,000 tons still had to be imported. Organized efforts are now being made to expand the cultivation of rice. We think it might be feasible to increase the area by about 8,000 acres, particularly on reclaimed land. We would advise, however, against promoting self-sufficiency by offering prices above the cost of importing rice. The production of rice should not be artificially fostered at the expense of a possible expansion of competing crops with a high-cash value per acre such as sugar cane and bananas. In connection with the rice program, the installation of facilities for parboiling rice to preserve its full nutritive value might well be considered.

11. *Root crops*

Root crops, including yams, sweet potatoes and cassava, make the most important contribution to the local food supply. The area devoted to their cultivation can only be very roughly approximated and is probably in the neighborhood of 50,000 acres. By and large we envisage no extension of the area. With the rehabilitation of the hillsides on which these crops are grown and an attendant improvement in agricultural practices output should be able to keep pace with the growing population. Some expansion in the area planted to cassava might, however, be desirable, since, as already indicated, the protein-rich cassava leaves make a fine cattle feed and a process for dehydrating these leaves appears to be ready for commercial application.

12. *Other Food Crops*

Among other food crops, maize or corn and pulses are of importance. We would advise against an expansion of the area grown to maize which is at present some 58,000 acres. In fact, some conversion of the maize acreage to other food crops appears desirable. It is not an ideal crop for Jamaica and in the past has greatly contributed to soil erosion. On the other hand, the production of various types of pulses which are a cheap source of protein might well be encouraged. In order to provide an incentive for an increase in acreage, the government might consider the advisability of re-establishing a minimum prices for pulses.[35]

It may be objected that these tentative suggestions for the utilization of the additional acreage which will be released lay too much emphasis on the production of export crops. We have no intention, however, of underestimating the importance of food production for domestic consumption. We believe the necessary increase in local food output can be achieved without a significant expansion of acreage. The major effort must be to raise existing low yields of pastures and local food crops by such measures as fertilization, crop rotation,

---

[35] Observations on a few additional crops are given in Annex 15.

soil protection, development and cultivation of better varieties and other improved agricultural practices. Elsewhere we shall have occasion to emphasize the need to devote more attention to research and experimentation on local food crops.

Effect on Employment

The probable effect of the program on production is easier to estimate than the impact on employment. Much of the anticipated rise in output will be achieved by the fuller employment of those already engaged in agriculture who probably number between 225,000 and 235,000. At present there is considerable underemployment or concealed unemployment. Nevertheless, a substantial increase in employment can be expected. About 150,000 acres will be added to the area under cultivation. The program envisages a particularly large expansion in the production of crops such as sugar and bananas which require considerable labor. Intensification of the livestock industry should also create an additional demand for labor. Altogether we estimate that agriculture may in the end furnish employment opportunities for between 30,000 and 40,000 more people. This represents an increase of 13% to 18% as compared with the increase of 44% which we hope will be achieved in production.

ADMINISTRATION OF THE PROGRAM

A development program of the scope we propose is unquestionably a formidable undertaking. Its success depends not only on the enthusiastic endorsement and cooperation by all farmers' organizations, but above all on effective planning and organization by government. It is difficult to determine what agency or agencies should be given responsibility for carrying out the program. A suitable answer to this question cannot be devised simply on the basis of general principles of administration, but must also take into account local conditions. No group of outside experts can pretend to evaluate correctly all the factors which must influence the decision. We have, however, given much thought to this question and believe that over-all direction and coordination of the program must be entrusted to a single agency. The agricultural development program we have pro-.posed has many interrelated aspects. It seeks to accomplish revolutionary changes in land use through soil conservation, afforestation, pasture improvement, irrigation and land reclamation and envisages a comprehensive system of government grants and loans, extending also to rural housing and water supply, as a means of enlisting the participation of the rural population in this entire program. It touches the activities of many government departments or agencies including the Department of Agriculture, the Forestry Department, the Department of Public Works, the housing authorities, the Loan Societies Board and the Peoples Cooperative Banks; and it impinges also on the work of the many private agricultural organizations. In our opinion, therefore, a single agency is necessary to provide the requisite leadership and direction and to insure that all aspects of government assistance in the agricultural field are administered in such a way as to achieve the targets of the program. Such an agency would not displace existing government departments but would coordinate and supplement their developmental work.

In line with this thinking, the Agricultural Development Corporation might well be entrusted with the over-all direction of the program. It is a government corporation created by law in 1951 with a comprehensive mandate "to stimulate, facilitate and undertake the development of agriculture." Its establishment recognized that development is an extraordinary task which requires an agency staffed by persons of outstanding ability and permitted to operate under flexible and expeditious procedures. The Corporation already has a capable board and a vigorous chairman who has been prominent in developing large agricultural enterprises both in and outside of Jamaica. The stature of its chairman and the members of its board makes it less susceptible to political pressures which would impede the execution of the program. Since it is not subject to the same restrictions with respect to salaries and methods of operation as the regular government service, it should be in a favorable position to recruit the people of managerial ability and technical qualifications who are needed to help carry out the program but who would otherwise be unobtainable.

We do not suggest, of course, that the formulation of agricultural policies and programs should be delegated to the Corporation. The Governor in Executive Council, advised by the regular government departments, and the legislature cannot abdicate this responsibility. The law setting up the Corporation specifically provides that it is subject to policy direction by the Governor in Executive Council. The latter will have to approve the principal features of the program, and the legislature will have to authorize the necessary funds. Within the broad framework of the approved program, however, the Corporation should be given considerable latitude in working out the program and allocating funds to specific projects.

If this recommendation is accepted, the Agricultural Development Corporation would assume responsibility for the activities of both the Yallahs Valley Authority which has been established under the Land Authorities Law, and the Farm Improvement Authority which has been administered by the Department of Agriculture with the director of the department serving as chairman of the Authority. We found considerable sentiment in Jamaica in favor of confining the Corporation's responsibility to regional areas requiring special attention such as the Yallahs valley and the Christiana-Upper Clarendon region, and of entrusting the task of carrying out the development program in the rest of the island to a strengthened and expanded Farm Improvement Authority. We question, however, the advisability of such a division of responsibility. We have already indicated our belief that a single agency will be more effective in insuring the coordinated execution of the development program so as to achieve the maximum results for the economy as a whole. If the Farm Improvement Authority were to take on a large part of the over-all program, it would have to be expanded and given more independence and a full-time director in place of the Director of Agriculture who is so overburdened by other tasks that he cannot pay adequate attention to the Authority. In that event, the coordination of the various agencies concerned with development would become extremely difficult.

It is important to emphasize once more that the Corporation should confine itself principally to central direction and coordination. The actual administration of various parts of the program can and should be delegated as far as possible to existing government departments and agencies.

The government will have to give special attention to ways and means of bringing about the continued cooperation of all those concerned with the program. This could perhaps be assured through an interdepartmental committee which would serve in an advisory capacity to the Corporation.

The Corporation's own staff might well consist principally of managerial personnel and technical experts who could not be recruited by the regular government departments. The rest of the personnel required could best be obtained by strengthening and expanding the government departments who will share the task of carrying out the program. The Department of Agriculture will have to play a particularly important role. It might well be given primary responsibility for the necessary field work with the farmers. A large field staff of senior agricultural officers, supplemented by a large corps of junior officers and assistants, will be required. In a development program of such large dimension much of the field work can undoubtedly be broken down into rather specialized tasks for which it will be possible to train people in a relatively short time. Many of the graduates of the School of Agriculture and of the Practical Training Centers who are not now in government service might be mobilized for this work.[36] In this connection we strongly recommend that the capacity of the School of Agriculture at Hope, which provides a three-year course in agriculture, be expanded so that the yearly number of graduates will be raised from about 20 to 40. Similarly, we suggest that the number of Practical Training Centers which provide at a lower level a good

---

[36] Of the 480 men who left the Practical Training Centers from 1948 to 1951, only 70 are at present working for the government. Of the balance, 242 are engaged in other agricultural pursuits.

combination of theoretical and practical training in agriculture and associated crafts be increased from three to six. These measures will not solve the immediate staffing problem, but they will help to ease the shortage in the future.

In recruiting staff for the development program care will have to be taken to insure that the Department of Agriculture also has sufficient personnel to discharge its normal functions. The department will continue to be solely responsible for advising the government on over-all agricultural policy, maintaining farmers' advisory or extension service, conducting research and experimentation and providing technical guidance of the nurseries which supply the farmers with planting material. The department will therefore have a large assignment, particularly since we are convinced that some of these normal activities also need to be expanded. The nursery program, which might well be entrusted to the commodity associations under the supervision of the department, will have to be greatly enlarged if targets for the increased production of certain crops such as coffee and cacao are to be achieved. We strongly recommend that a considerably larger research program be undertaken. Extensive work should be done on the response of various crops to fertilizers. The Sugar Manufacturers Association has shown how much can be achieved through applied research and experimentation in this field, but comparatively little has yet been done to determine the proper applications of fertilizers for other crops.[37] We have already alluded to the need for more experimentation on pastures. Work on local food crops which are of such importance to the island has been largely neglected in the department's research program. To carry out this extended research program we believe that the department's staff should be strengthened by the addition of at least ten experts.[38]

The Corporation will undoubtedly find it necessary to bring the

---

[37] A note on fertilizers appears as Annex 16.

[38] This would provide for one expert in each of the following fields: fertilizers, particularly in relation to food crops; pastures; selection, breeding and cultivation of root crops; citrus; food trees; cacao; vegetables; tomatoes; pineapples; storing, drying and processing of crops; and soil conservation.

farmers' organizations into the program. Without their active support it will be impossible to enlist the participation of the farmers. Only the farmers' own organizations can convince them of their vital stake in the program and of the need to make their own contribution to its success. The field staffs of these organizations should prove a valuable adjunct to the Corporation's own staff and that of the Department of Agriculture. In some cases they may also be able to assume responsibility for carrying out certain parts of the program, especially those involving the expansion of particular crops.

The importance of obtaining the participation of the three companies mining bauxite on the island should also be underlined. These companies own large tracts of land, only a small part of which will actually be mined. By the terms of their concessions they are required to maintain their lands in good agricultural condition; and their spokesmen have frequently expressed their willingness to contribute to the advancement of agriculture. They should be encouraged to carry out an extensive soil conservation and pasture improvement program. Presumably they will not require financial help, for they have ample capital resources and they can the more readily assume the investment risk in view of their ability to offset possible losses against their income tax liability.

III

Mining

Compared to agriculture, mining is likely to make only a small contribution to primary production. Nevertheless, the output of minerals can confidently be expected to increase substantially in the years immediately ahead. Deposits of bauxite, cave phosphates and gypsum are already being exploited, and there is reason to believe that it will also prove commercially feasible to mine a number of other minerals on a modest scale.

Bauxite

The recent development of Jamaica's large bauxite reserves has already considerably stimulated economic activity in some parts of the island. Three companies—Reynolds Jamaica Mines Ltd., Jamaica Bauxites Ltd. (a subsidiary of Aluminum Ltd. of Canada) and Kaiser Bauxite Company—are engaged in developing these deposits; and a fourth company is reported interested in entering the field. Reynolds has built a six-mile aerial tramway to transport its pelletized bauxite to the northcoast port of Ocho Rios where storage facilities and a new loading pier have been constructed. It began shipment in May 1952 and by the fall expects to be producing at an annual rate of 750,000 tons which may ultimately be increased to one million tons. Kaiser has built a twelve and a half mile railway to the southcoast port of Pedro where a new dock has also been constructed. It will commence export in the fall of 1952 and will be mining about 650,000 tons of bauxite per year. Jamaica Bauxites will also be converting bauxite into alumina in Jamaica. The first part of its plant, with an alumina capacity of 66,000 tons per year, is scheduled to begin operations in the fall of 1952; and the second part, with an additional capacity of 98,000 tons, is scheduled for completion toward the end of 1953. A further extension to 245,000 tons may be undertaken. Bauxite production will be at an annual rate of about 200,000 tons at the end of 1952 and 500,000 tons by the end of the following year. The alumina is to be shipped by the regular Jamaica railways and a new connecting spur of two and a half miles to Old Harbour on the south coast where a port has been constructed. Altogether the amount of bauxite mined by the three companies is expected to increase to between two and two and a half million tons per year. Total bauxite reserves are currently estimated at 200 to 300 million tons.

Despite this expanding output, the peak employment anticipated in the bauxite industry—about 1,200 people[1]—will actually be smaller than the number of workers engaged in the past on the construction of necessary installations. At the height of construction activity in the winter 1951-52 about 4,500 workers were employed.

The government, however, may derive a substantial amount of revenue from the industry. Royalties at the rate of one shilling per ton will bring in £ 100,000 to £ 125,000 per year, and income taxes paid by the companies are expected to yield considerably more than this sum. The transport of alumina and supplies for Jamaica Bauxites will also help to improve the financial position of the government railway.

OTHER MINERALS

Of the other minerals, gypsum and phosphates have already been mentioned. Large reserves of gypsum estimated at 84 million tons have been discovered in eastern St. Andrew and more will undoubtedly be found through further prospecting. Some gypsum is now being exported. Perhaps as much as 100,000 tons of so-called "bat phosphates" are available in the limestone caves. These phosphates, which take the form of calcium diphosphate are being mined on a very modest scale. They deserve much wider use in Jamaican agriculture, particularly because they will in many cases produce much better results than imported superphosphates.

While Jamaica is evidently not rich in other minerals, a number may well prove worth exploiting. Recent surveys have revealed the

---

[1] This is exclusive of the workers employed in the companies' agricultural operations.

presence of considerable bodies of magnetic iron ore in addition to already known deposits of hematite and limonite. We suggest that a magnetometric survey be undertaken to ascertain the extent of these high-grade ore bodies which are known from a surface survey in localities in the parishes of St. Andrew and Portland.

Prospecting licenses have been given for petroleum, lead, zinc, manganese, copper and ilmenite. Slight indications of petroleum have been found and a survey now in process by a private company should determine whether exploratory drilling will be worthwhile. Detailed prospecting of copper occurrences should be carried out in (1) Upper Clarendon, where the old mines of Charing Cross, Stamford Hill and Gold Mine used to operate, (2) Portland (southwest of Port Antonio), and (3) southern St. Mary and northern St. Andrew (Job's Hill and adjoining areas). Lead, zinc and manganese occur in small but workable quantities. Prospecting is in progress at Marshall's Hall, Portland; and at the old Hope Mine in St. Andrew the mining and concentration of modest quantities of lead and zinc ores with a zinc content of 4.9% and a lead content of 1.7% will begin in the fall of 1952. At this mine, however, reserves are sufficient for only five years' operations.

Since new technical developments have made the development of low grade ores commercially feasible, we suggest that the exploration of mineral resources be vigorously pushed. To this end the Geological Survey Department should be strengthened. The addition of one or two field geologists would considerably expedite the work; and the appointment of an experienced petrologist-chemist would help in overcoming the present long delay in obtaining analyses of rocks and minerals from the Government Chemist or the Mineral Resources Division of the Colonial Geological Surveys in London. Establishment of a small geophysical branch in charge of one geophysicist would also be advisable. These appointments would need to be accompanied by corresponding additions to the equipment and subordinate staff.

IV.

Manufacturing Industry

In recent years increasing attention has been given to the development of manufacturing industries. Significant tax benefits have been held out to attract "pioneer industries" and special concessions have been granted to promote the establishment of particular plants. A revised tariff schedule, which lowered duties on raw materials and provided moderate protection for manufactures, was adopted in 1951. Recently responsibility for stimulating industry was concentrated in an Industrial Development Corporation. At the same time steps were taken to enlist the help of an American consulting firm and a team of British industrial experts for the primary purpose of determining what specific industrial projects might be undertaken.

Our task in this field was not to work out particular projects, but to examine the general prospects of industry in the light of the various factors which might be expected to hinder or foster it. The possibility of industrial development has been the subject of very wide differences of opinion. At one end of the scale is the school of thought which sees little hope for the expansion of agriculture and views rapid and forced industrialization as the only salvation for Jamaica and other heavily populated islands of the Caribbean. It would convert the plentiful supply of manpower into an industrial asset and looks to the industrialization program of Puerto Rico as an example to be followed. At the other end of the scale is the view that Jamaica does not have the natural resources or the industrial talent to warrant the hope that manufacturing will ever make a substantial contribution to its economic development.

It will already be apparent that we do not subscribe to a pessimistic evaluation of Jamaica's agricultural prospects. The question therefore is not whether industrialization must come about, but whether it can develop on a sound economic basis. It must be determined whether the factors affecting industrial development are sufficiently favorable to enable Jamaica to produce manufactures in competition with established manufacturing countries.

CHARACTER OF EXISTING INDUSTRY

The 1943 census recorded 60,000 people as engaged in "manufacturing." Of these, however, only 14,373 were employed in "factories"; the remainder might be described as "manufacturing craftsmen" such as dressmakers, shoemakers and the like. As the accompanying table indicates, factory employment rose sharply to 23,098 by 1951 and the number of establishments increased from 365 to 627. The manufacturing accounting for this employment can be roughly divided into four categories. The first is the processing of locally produced agricultural products, which employed at least 63% of all factory workers. The sugar industry alone accounted for 27% of factory employment.[1] The processing of local agricultural materials altogether contributed 60% of the gross value of secondary production in 1943. In the processing of these generally bulky and perishable materials Jamaica can be said to have a definite advantage. The second category, employing almost 17% of the total in 1951, comprises the manufacture of such products as beverages and bakery goods which, because of their high cost of transport or their perishability, are normally manufactured in the market where they are consumed. The third category, accounting for 11% of the employment, includes printing and publishing, automobile and railway repair and similar service industries, all of which are intimately tied to the home market. The last category, with less than 10% of factory employment, consists primarily of the manufacture of goods from materials partly or wholly imported. These goods include garments, boots and shoes and, to some extent, furniture and other woodworking products.

---

[1] These figures are calculated from the more detailed breakdown of factory employment given in Annex 17.

TABLE 1

FACTORIES AND FACTORY EMPLOYMENT

	No. of Plants	1943 Total Number of Employees	Average Employment per plant	No. of Plants	1951 Total Number of Employees	Average Employment per plant	Index of Employment 1943-1951
ALL MANU-FACTURING	365	14,373	39.4	627	23,098	36.8	160.7
Vegetable products	230	10,144	44.1	384	15,937	41.5	157.1
of which: sugar	29	4,465	153.9	23	6,809	296.0	152.5
other	201	5,679	28.2	361	9,138	25.3	160.9
Animal products	10	92	9.2	9	138	15.3	150.0
Leather products	12	211	17.6	21	428	20.4	202.8
Textile products	14	592	42.3	23	1,406	61.1	237.5
Wood and paper products	55	1,125	20.4	122	2,209	18.1	196.4
Iron products and repair	19	1,233	64.9	31	1,445	46.6	117.2
Chemical products	13	822	63.2	9	1,018	113.1	123.8
Misc. products	12	155	12.9	28	517	18.5	333.6

In all these branches of manufacturing except the last, Jamaica might be said to have a natural advantage. In most of them production and employment will rise either as the volume of available agricultural raw materials expand or as population and income increase; and it is therefore possible to forecast their development with some degree of accuracy. Evaluation of the prospects of that small portion of industry now manufacturing goods from largely imported materials is much more difficult. Unquestionably this branch of manufacturing faces serious handicaps by comparison with the established industries of the more experienced industrial countries.

OBSTACLES TO DEVELOPMENT

First of all Jamaica, unlike Puerto Rico, cannot expect to have free access to a large and expanding market. Exchange restrictions and Commonwealth tariff preferences give it a certain degree of protection, but only against competition from countries outside the sterling area. There is the prospect of a customs union among British Caribbean territories, but even if realized it will create a market of only 3.3 million customers with rather low incomes. Principal reliance will have to be placed on the local Jamaica market which is shielded by a moderate degree of protection against outside competition. The initiation of manufacturing on a scale sufficient to be economic is difficult in such a limited market, the more so because many consumer goods must be manufactured in a wide range of styles.

Secondly, Jamaica suffers from high transport costs on both its imports and exports. Highly industrialized countries with large populations inevitably enjoy more adequate and cheaper transport services than islands such as Jamaica with small populations and a relatively low volume of production.

Thirdly, capital costs are higher than those in more industrialized countries. The investor expects a greater return in less developed countries and will not risk his funds without such an assurance. Working capital requirements are generally greater, for larger inventories of materials and spare parts must be kept. The maintenance costs on equipment are also likely to be higher.

Finally, the necessary industrial skills, managerial talent and marketing experience are largely lacking. In this respect the more established industrial countries have a tremendous headstart which will be difficult to overcome.

Wage Rates and Labor Costs

These handicaps do not necessarily represent insuperable obstacles to the development of general manufacturing industries largely dependent on imported materials. A few of them may gradually be overcome. The real question, however, is whether Jamaica has one or more advantages which more than compensate for these difficulties. The one great advantage which Jamaica, like other populous, underdeveloped countries, may claim to possess is a plentiful, cheap labor supply. For this reason the expectation is frequently harbored that Jamaica will be able to develop on a considerable scale so-called "labor-intensive" industries, i.e. types of manufacturing in which labor costs ordinarily represent a very large share of the total costs of production. We have accordingly paid special attention to the analysis of this alleged advantage.

Wages are undoubtedly low compared to those in industrialized countries. A comparison with wages in the United Kingdom appears most relevant because competition with Jamaican manufactures will come primarily from that source. We have made this comparison both by using published statistical data and by gathering information from manufacturers in Jamaica with knowledge of wages in both countries. The latter information was perhaps most valuable because it pertained to identical or almost identical activities. The comparison, details of which appear elsewhere,[2] reveals that the wage differential, while still great, has significantly decreased since 1946. Data compiled by the International Labor Office on wages in a number of occupations indicate that the wages for skilled and nonskilled labor were in that year respectively 25-50% and 50-65% lower in Jamaica than in the United Kingdom. The information collected from manufacturers, on the other hand, showed a differential of only 20-25% for skilled labor and about 50% for unskilled labor at the beginning of 1952. This reduction in the disparity is confirmed by official data which indicate that from 1946 to 1951 earnings in manufacturing in the United Kingdom increased approximately 33% while earnings in Jamaica rose by 55%.[3]

The relative level of wages is not, of course, alone decisive. The question is whether at existing wage rates labor productivity is such that labor costs per unit of product in Jamaica are markedly lower than in competing countries. This implies the need for a comparison

---

[2] See Annex 18.

[3] Information on earnings in the United Kingdom is from "Earnings in Manufacturing" published by the Statistical Office of the United Nations; that on Jamaican earnings was supplied by the government of Jamaica.

of labor productivity. Unfortunately such comparisons are notoriously difficult to make even where data are fairly plentiful, which is certainly not the case in Jamaica. Opinions on labor productivity expressed by plant managers are apt to be subjective and prejudiced. Keeping in mind these pitfalls, the Mission did make a special attempt to gather enough information to permit the formulation of a rough conclusion. In this task it was obviously important to take into account factors other than the quality of labor which affect productivity. These include the quality of management, the available capital equipment and the scale and variety of production. Fortunately, it was possible to make a comparison in a number of cases where differences in the latter factors were relatively small and the difference in costs could be attributed primarily to the labor factor. A study of these cases indicates that labor productivity is on the average 20-25% lower than in the United Kingdom. If wage rates are also taken into account, it may be said that in general manufacturers in Jamaica have virtually no advantage over the United Kingdom with respect to skilled labor costs and an advantage of approximately 25% with respect to the cost of unskilled labor.[4] In actual practice, average labor productivity is lower and labor costs are higher than the above comparison would indicate. This additional differential is attributable to deficiencies in capital equipment, poorer management and supervision, less efficient work flow and similar factors unrelated to the quality of labor.

Since, as has already been pointed out, costs other than labor are also higher, the conclusion seems warranted that in the years immediately ahead there is little prospect of building up a manufacturing industry processing imported materials for a highly competitive export market. In the first instance efforts must be devoted to increasing the efficiency of existing industry and accumulating the necessary industrial experience. Production will have to be almost entirely for the home market where moderate tariff protection plus proximity to the market give industry some advantage. In this con-

---

[4] See Annex 18 for a more detailed discussion of labor productivity.

nection it is to be hoped that the proposal for a customs union among British Caribbean territories can be realized before long. This would at least enable Jamaica as well as a few of the other larger British territories in the Caribbean to develop production for a somewhat larger market and thereby to acquire the industrial skills which may ultimately make possible expansion into wider markets.

This conclusion should not be regarded as too discouraging provided that the problem of labor productivity is vigorously tackled. A few enterprises have already shown what can be accomplished with good management and training. Extensive discussions with management have given us the impression that the Jamaican is basically well adapted to work in the manufacturing industry. This impression is borne out by the findings of an investigation conducted by the United States Bureau of Labor Statistics of the experience with Jamaican laborers in American factories during the last war. Two-thirds of the companies surveyed reported that the Jamaican's output compared favorably with that of other employees, although it was acknowledged that the Jamaican required more intensive training than was normally given. The general observation was that Jamaicans did best in light work and worked more slowly, but at the same time more steadily, than American laborers. The report concluded that "It was apparent that greater success in obtaining satisfactory production from Jamaicans was achieved when more effort had been devoted to fitting them into their new working environment by means of special attention to orientation, training and supervision."[5]

Need for Higher Productivity

The important task of the future is to increase productivity. The steps that might be taken to this end are outlined below. They will require contributions from labor, management and the government.

---

[5] "Wartime Utilization of Jamaicans in U.S. Industrial Establishment," *Monthly Labor Review*, November, 1945.

1. *Labor Training*

In this field we strongly recommend prompt enactment of an apprenticeship law and an expansion of vocational and prevocational education. Apprentices are employed in industry today, but systematic training is only rarely provided and no certificates of proficiency in a trade or craft are granted. Often apprenticeship tends to become a mere device for hiring labor at sub-standard wages. As early as 1943 an Apprenticeship Committee set up by the government to study this question recommended that (1) a regulation be drafted to govern the character and duration of training and the working conditions of apprentices, (2) only "approved" employees be permitted to employ apprentices and (3) an Apprenticeship Board be established to frame the standards and license the employment of apprentices. A law embodying these proposals has since been drafted, but no action has been taken despite almost universal recognition that a proper apprenticeship system is necessary.[6]

Apparently the inaction stems largely from a fear on the part of employers that the training of apprentices under the proposed law would be too burdensome, particularly in view of the lack of instructors and equipment. This fear would probably be at least partly overcome if the government were to undertake simultaneously to improve and expand technical vocational education. In-plant training and technical school education should in any event go hand in hand. We shall have occasion elsewhere to stress the need for introducing more of a vocational bias into the regular school system in order to develop basic manual skills and a general familiarity with tools. Here, however, we want to deal with technical education proper.

The only technical institution in the country is the Kingston Technical School which has an enrolment of about 500 daytime and 900 evening students. It is generally recognized that the buildings of the school are woefully inadequate and that the equipment is insufficient and largely obsolete. Aside from departments teaching domestic science and commercial subjects, the school has a "technical" and a

---

[6] See Annex 19 on Apprenticeship.

"trade" department. The latter trains craftsmen and artisans; the former, "technicians" equipped with more theoretical and academic background. Inadequate accommodations and equipment make it necessary to reject many applications. In September 1951, for instance, only 56 out of 599 applicants could be accepted for training in these departments. The bottleneck is most acute in the "trade" department which primarily stresses training with tools, so that many students have to go instead into the "technical" department. The latter turned out 28, 30 and 23 pupils in the years 1949, 1950 and 1951 respectively; and the "trade" department trained 26, 13 and 19 apprentices in those years.

The Technical Education Exploratory Committee appointed in 1948 recommended (1) erection of a new building to accommodate the trade and technical departments of the Kingston Technical School, doubling of the capacity of the trade department and an almost complete renewal of equipment, and (2) establishment of additional trade schools at May Pen, Mandeville, Montego Bay and St. Ann's Bay. We fully endorse these proposals. Expansion and rehabilitation of the Kingston School would probably involve a capital outlay of £ 240,000 and an additional annual recurring expenditure of £ 18,000. The new trade schools would cost about £ 200,000 and £ 70,000 in annual operating expenditures. In connection with at least one of these schools we would suggest that facilities be also provided for the training of hotel staff.

The same Committee proposed also the ultimate establishment of a Technological Institute to train qualified engineers. We do not believe, however, that the need for engineers would warrant such a rather costly investment at present. Instead, we suggest that five scholarships at £ 600 per year be provided for training engineers abroad. Allowing for a four-year training course, a total annual expenditure of £ 12,000 would be required. Technicians at the lower level would, of course, continue to be trained in the technical department of the Kingston school.[7]

---

[7] For further details on technical schools, see Annex 20.

The technical schools could also contribute to the training of foremen and supervisors through part-time courses. The government might also make grants to enable qualified men to obtain practical experience abroad.

2. *Recruitment and Screening of Labor*

One of the functions of the Labor Department should be to assist employers in recruiting labor. The Department already performs this function with respect to workers recruited for seasonal agricultural labor in the United States. Through simple aptitude tests employers could be assisted in the selection of labor suitable for industrial work. The Department's staff, however, needs to be strengthened and regional offices must be established if it is to undertake this task and at the same time cope with its growing responsibility in the adjustment of labor-management relations.

3. *Attitude of Labor*

It is important that labor be aware of the stake it has in improving its own efficiency. It should not only support all efforts to bring about better training, but also to develop a feeling of greater responsibility for the quality of work. Too often workmen are careless and indifferent in the performance of their tasks. There is little pride in workmanship. Labor union leaders tend to believe that productivity is the exclusive responsibility of the entrepreneurs. They show little appreciation of the fact that real wages can in the long run increase only if labor productivity improves. Nor do they fully understand that in a country where capital is scarce, investments in new enterprises are unlikely to be made unless there is an assurance of a greater return than is normally earned where capital is more abundant. The creation of additional employment opportunities for the working classes will largely depend on the investment of private capital which will venture only if labor efficiency is high enough to warrant an expectation of reasonably low labor costs.

4. *Capital Equipment*

The availability of adequate capital is a critical determinant of productivity. Many small enterprises are struggling along with inadequate equipment and insufficient working capital. Despite these handicaps, a number of them have a creditable record in pioneering industry, often with little or no government help. They need financial assistance which they cannot obtain through regular banking channels. The newly established Industrial Development Corporation is authorized to make loans and do equity financing. We suggest that its first concern should be to supplement the financial resources of existing enterprises which have a good record of accomplishment but need additional capital to insure greater productivity. The existence of efficient and profitable local industries will of itself act as a magnet to attract additional foreign capital. The corporation will, of course, also have to be prepared to assist in the financing of new undertakings.

5. *Technical Assistance*

In our survey of existing manufacturing establishments we were impressed by the fact that a considerable increase in efficiency could probably be effected by a better layout of plant and machinery, improved organization of work and installation of cost accounting. This is particularly true of the large number of small enterprises whose management often does not possess enough experience to get the best out of the available plant. We therefore recommend that the Industrial Development Corporation equip itself to furnish advice and assistance on such matters as plant arrangement and work flow, cost accounting, marketing, proper wage systems and the like.

ROLE OF INDUSTRIAL DEVELOPMENT CORPORATION

As already indicated above, part of the task outlined above will devolve on the Industrial Development Corporation. It might be appropriate, therefore, to indicate here our conception of the principal functions and organization of this Corporation. In general these functions might be grouped as follows:

1. *Industrial Promotion*

This would involve enlisting the interest of both domestic and foreign capital in particular industrial ventures and continuous study of the various factors, including government policies, affecting Jamaica's ability to attract private capital into industry. The promotion effort should center not on any general campaign to advertise industrial opportunities, but rather on attempts to solicit capital for specific projects which have been sufficiently investigated to warrant the assumption that they would be feasible.

2. *Technical Services*

This would require the organization of a small staff to provide technical and economic advice to existing industries and work up industrial projects for promotion. Consultants for particular projects could, where necessary, be obtained abroad.

3. *Financing*

The resources and accounting for this activity should clearly be separated from the other activities of the Corporation. While the Corporation must be prepared to take more than ordinary risks in financing industry, this operation should as far as possible be self-supporting.

LABOR-MANAGEMENT RELATIONS

Another important factor in the development of industry is the relationship between labor and management. This subject merits special mention because the history of labor relations in Jamaica has been rather troubled. No doubt part of these troubles represent a transitory phenomenon. Labor-management relations still suffer from "growing pains." Although labor unions have existed on the island for some decades, they did not really strike root until the last decade. Ever since 1939 trade-unionism has grown rapidly until in 1950 21% of the wage-earning labor force was organized. The first period of this growth featured demands for recognition and better working conditions which were resisted, almost inevitably, by employers. There was a wave of strikes in the mid-forties. Gradually, as the unions became more firmly established and employers became reconciled to collective bargaining, the number and severity of conflicts rapidly diminished.

TABLE 2

INDUSTRIAL DISPUTES 1945-50

Year	Number of Disputes	Number of Strikes Begun	Man Days Lost
1945	154	97	91,655
1946	110	76	238,540
1947	27	25	258,700
1948	23	19	10,347
1949	7	—	2,656
1950	161	60	75,212

In 1950 there was another recrudescence of strikes incidental to the elections of that year. It brought to the fore a distinctive feature of the unions—their virtually indissoluble link with political parties. The union connected with the minority party began a campaign to attract members and in several cases demanded recognition from employers hitherto recognizing the other union. Both unions attempted to increase their support by outbidding each other in promises to the work men, and the strike weapon was frequently used to settle the issue. This outcropping of jurisdictional strikes prompted the government to set up a special Board of Enquiry to make recommendations for the settlement of such disputes. The board subsequently proposed the enactment of legislation empowering the government Labor Adviser to determine bargaining agents through secret polls of the workers and establishing machinery to resolve disputes arising out of the application of this procedure. [8] While the government felt it unwise to pass legislation in this period of dynamic development of labor-management relations, the Labor Adviser in practice adopted the board's proposals and developed reasonably effective techniques for dealing with jurisdictional disputes.

---

[8] See Annex 21 on Labor-Management Relations.

After a period of relative quiet, a new complication arose in 1952. In the spring of that year the second largest political party ejected from its ranks a minority of leaders suspected of Communist leanings. This group took with it the labor union connected with the party, thus leading the majority to form its own union. Meanwhile, still another union had been founded. Thus four unions were vying for the allegiance of the workers. A sharp increase in strikes, primarily jurisdictional in character, took place. Employers have been bewildered by rapid shifts in the allegiance of their labor force. They have frequently been troubled by outbreaks of strikes long before collective bargaining contracts were due to expire. The Labor Adviser has required extraordinary ingenuity and patience to resolve the complicated problems which have thus arisen.

All these difficulties should not be allowed, however, to obscure the fact that real progress has been made in the long run in developing more stable and responsible relations between workers and employers. Collective bargaining has become an established practice and disputes are, for the most part, settled amicably around the table. Strikes are generally rather brief and often attended by an amount of publicity out of proportion to their importance. There are some indications that the present confusion stemming from the existence of four rival unions will not be permanent. Ultimately two major unions may again emerge. Moreover, there are some encouraging signs of collaboration between unions. The last contracts in the sugar industry were jointly negotiated by two unions. In the port at Kingston a joint industrial council representing two unions as well as employers and the government has recently been established to stabilize labor relations.

Nevertheless, there is still ample justification for the adoption of measures to effect further improvement. For one thing, we think the time has come to strengthen the hands of the Labor Adviser whose office has assumed growing importance. His overworked staff should be increased and his department provided with funds to establish a number of regional offices. If the Labor Adviser is to assist in settling disputes before they erupt into strikes, he must have more listening posts throughout the island. It has now also become desirable to give legislative sanction to the powers and procedures for settlement which he has gradually developed. Any such legislation should stipulate the general circumstances and procedures under which polls to determine the bargaining agent among workers may be taken. It will need to provide that new polls can be conducted only toward the termination of the labor contract unless the Labor Adviser is convinced that there has been a substantial alteration in circumstances affecting the relationship of the workers to their existing bargaining agent. In any event any such change in allegiance revealed by a poll should not generally affect the validity of an existing labor contract.

We would further suggest that the Labor Adviser encourage industry-wide bargaining wherever this is likely to be conducive to stable labor relations and efficiency. This type of bargaining now takes place only in a few cases, notably in the sugar industry. While the abolition of all wage differentials within each industry may be impracticable, it seems desirable to work toward a more uniform wage standard which will discriminate as little as possible between efficient and inefficient producers. At present the unions tend not unnaturally to extract the largest concessions from the more efficient employers in each branch of industry and to treat the inefficient producers much more leniently for fear of putting them out of business. In the long run, however, this may be short-sighted, for it prevents the most efficient producers from taking full advantage of their lower costs to expand their markets and production and thus create in the end more employment opportunities in the industry as a whole.

Legislation is obviously not the only or even the primary remedy for a troubled labor situation. A constructive and responsible attitude by labor and management is far more important. A greater understanding of each other's views and, above all, of the implications of their developing relations for the economy of Jamaica, must be cultivated. It is encouraging that the University College of the West Indies, near Kingston, has taken the initiative bringing labor and management together in a seminar for discussion of their problems.

For the labor unions the development of good leadership, particularly at the local and regional level, is all-important. Lack of experience and poor education make many trade union officials poorly qualified for their jobs. In part this is a financial problem. The unions have been unable to pay salaries adequate to attract good officials or to pay for their training. Their resources have been limited because the Jamaican laborer generally pays his dues only during the limited time when the union carries an active agitation for higher wages and better working conditions or has just achieved notable concessions. More recently a growing number of employers have agreed to a voluntary check-off of union dues which should help to improve union finances. In their own interest and that of the Jamaican people the unions should now begin to pay much more attention to the education of their officials and members.

The development of sound and stable relations between management and labor is essential if a steady increase in the production of goods and services is to be achieved. The national product must be divided in such a manner as to enable labor to share the benefits of growing productivity and at the same time assure capital sufficient profit to provide an incentive for the additional investment without which no development program can succeed. Management and labor will have to work hand in hand to improve the efficiency of production so that a proper basis for new enterprise and expanding employment opportunities will be created. Progress toward higher levels of production must be arrested as little as possible by prolonged interruption through strikes. The private foreign capital which is so indispensable to development will be attracted only if Jamaica can establish a reputation for orderly settlement of labor disputes.

The Attraction of Capital

We turn now to a consideration of the special measures which the government has taken or might take to attract more private capital to industry. Such measures must obviously be used with caution. It is unwise to foster artificially industries which in the long run cannot stand on their own feet. It may be justifiable to give special assistance and protection to an industry during the period of critical growth while it is acquiring industrial experience and developing a market, but only in cases where the industry in question has a reasonable prospect of becoming competitive after the initial period. The need to increase employment opportunities should not lead Jamaica to promote industries which cause significant losses in import revenues and at the same time produce higher-priced or poorer-quality goods than can be imported.

One type of measure adopted to foster industry offers the investor the prospect of higher profits, rather than protection against competition.[9] Of this type the most important enactment adopted in Jamaica is the Pioneer Industry (Encouragement) Law of 1949, which is due to expire at the end of 1952. Under this law any entrepreneur in an industry declared to be a pioneer industry may import equipment and building materials for his plant free of import duty and tonnage tax and may reduce his income tax liability by writing off 20% of his permitted capital investment in each of any five years of the first eight years of operation. In addition, sums so set off may be distributed within the following two years to shareholders or debenture holders as capital monies on which the recipients are exempt from income tax and surtax. More recently any enterprise making new investments was given the right to write-off 20% of this investment in the first year of the life of the plant and equipment in addition to the normal depreciation allowance.

We believe that this type of income tax concession has been and will be of some value in attracting capital and stimulating initiative and we accordingly recommend that the Pioneer Industry Law be renewed at the end of 1952.[10] We suggest, in addition, the advisability of permitting enterprises to carry forward losses for a maximum

---

[9] For a fuller description of the measures taken to foster industry, see Annex 22.

period of six years instead of three years as at present. We would oppose, however, sweeping measures such as the tax "holiday" which has been granted to new enterprises in Puerto Rico. A tax holiday might attract too many industries interested in continuing operation only as long as complete tax exemption lasts. It would also involve too large a sacrifice of potential revenues and discriminate sharply against existing industries.

Unfortunately, these income tax concessions are of more value to domestic than to foreign capital. A United Kingdom company operating in Jamaica, for instance, must in any event pay the full income tax levied in its own country. Any reduction in the income tax collected by Jamaica correspondingly decreases the amount which the company can offset against its income tax liability in the United Kingdom. Even if the company is registered in Jamaica and controlled by a local board of directors, any income transmitted to a parent company in the United Kingdom must pay the full rate assessed by the tax laws of that country. The government of the United Kingdom has resisted all efforts to change the law in this respect, primarily because such a change would violate the principle of equity requiring that all incomes irrespective of source be taxed at the same rate, and possibly also because it would unduly stimulate the export of capital. The tax laws of the United States also operate to nullify foreign tax concessions on income earned abroad, although only to the extent that such income is actually transmitted to the United States. The Pioneer Industry Law, however, gives the American investor an important assurance that, if the income from his investment is sufficient, he will be permitted to repatriate, within a period of eight years, the equivalent of the entire value of his capital investment as "income."

---

[10] The provision permitting the distribution of sums set off against income tax as capital monies within two years of the year of assessment may be conducive to an unduly generous dividend policy at a time when it might be more important to encourage reinvestment of profits in the business. The government might therefore consider whether or not this danger could be avoided if the period were extended beyond the two years now allowed.

The tax concessions of the Pioneer Industry Law give no help to existing industries. We have already stressed the importance of assisting these industries to increase their capital investment and thus improve productivity. In view of the scarcity of capital they must depend in part on reinvestment of profits for the extension and modernization of their plant and equipment. [11] We strongly recommend that the reinvestment of profits be encouraged by levying a substantially lower tax rate on profits retained for capital improvement. If this recommendation is adopted, the government might consider whether this concession should be confined to companies registered and controlled in Jamaica since, as has been indicated, United Kingdom companies would derive no benefit from it in any event. The objection will no doubt be urged that the proposal involves a loss of revenue which Jamaica can ill afford. The loss, however, will not be permanent and will ultimately be more than offset by increased taxes on the distributed profits derived from the enlarged investment. The sugar industry already enjoys in effect a concession of this kind, for it has been enabled through a cess on the export of sugar to set up a tax-free capital rehabilitation fund.

Another advantage which the government is prepared to offer industry is the benefit of a planned industrial site. The government has set aside about 300 acres adjoining Kingston harbor as a site for new plants. The area will be supplied with water and electric power and is conveniently located with respect to both maritime and inland transport. It will be primarily useful for industries working largely with foreign raw materials. The suggestion has also been made that the government should build factories for rental and ultimate sale to entrepreneurs willing to start a new manufacturing business in Jamaica. A program of this sort might provide a real incentive, but, once begun, it would be difficult to abandon, and its

---

[11] Information on 25 enterprises made available to the Mission showed that the capital investment of these concerns rose from 1948 to 1950 by £ 455,584 or 19%. Of this increase, 61% was supplied by new share capital, 26% by long-term loans and short-term credits and 23% from reserves and undistributed profits. See Annex 23 on the capital structure of Jamaican industry.

benefits might have to be extended to all potential investors irrespective of whether they really needed such assistance. The large amount of capital required, [12] while ultimately recoverable, would severely tax Jamaica's slender financial resources. It might also attract a disproportionate amount of highly speculative enterprise which because of its rather small capital stake in Jamaica might have less incentive to stay and work out any serious difficulties that it might encounter. We doubt, therefore, that the government should undertake an obligation of this kind, the more so because it may well prove possible to attract sufficient capital without such an incentive.

INDUSTRIAL PROTECTION AND ITS DANGERS

Another set of measures adopted by the government to promote industry is specifically designed to protect production against foreign competition. The general revision of the tariff in 1951 which we have already mentioned was a measure of this kind, but moderate in character. In our opinion it struck approximately the right compromise between excessive protection and free trade. Far more important, however, has been the special protection granted in connection with the establishment of specific industries. By means of licensing, high import duties and other import controls the domestic market has on a number of occasions been exclusively reserved for selected new enterprises, thus in effect ensuring them a virtually monopolistic position. This is true, for instance, of the plants producing matches, condensed milk and cornmeal which were established under the Safeguarding of Local Industries Law. Special protection was also given to the vegetable oil industry. Although the availability of raw materials and the high freight costs on imported cement seemed to make the manufacture of this product in Jamaica economically advantageous, a considerable number of special concessions were granted to the company which established the cement

---

[12] In Puerto Rico, where the government has undertaken such a program, an outlay of about $2,000 per worker employed has been necessary. The cost in Jamaica might be 15% lower, but it would still be extremely burdensome.

plant. It obtained not only an exclusive license and complete protection against imports but also a very favorable price arrangement and provisions for the write-off of capital which are even more far reaching than those under the Pioneer Industries Law.

While recognizing that special protection may occasionally have to be granted, we believe that Jamaica's experience clearly demonstrates the danger of fostering monopolies. Monopolistic concerns not only tend to encourage inefficiency at the expense of the consumer, but they also whet the appetite of other potential entrepreneurs for similar concessions. The government has tried to guard against this danger in a number of cases by conditioning a monopolistic license on efficient production. It is difficult in practice, however, to determine a proper standard of efficiency and the highest efficiency is generally attained only under the pressure of competition. The milk condensery and vegetable oil factories, for example, work on a guaranteed manufacturing margin which does not provide the best possible incentive to improve efficiency. The match factory, which operates under government fixed prices and a guaranteed dividend, is particularly inefficient. Because of the conditions surrounding its operation, it has been unable to install labor-saving machinery which would have reduced costs of production substantially.[13] Jamaica has nothing to gain and much to lose from encouraging inefficient industries of this type.

THE FUTURE OF MANUFACTURING EMPLOYMENT

By and large we conclude that further opportunities for the development of a sound manufacturing industry exist, especially if more attention is paid to increasing productivity. Just how rapidly factory production and employment can be expected to increase over the next ten years is difficult to prophesy. As already indicated, factory employment was 8,725 higher in 1951 than in 1943. This

---

[13] In 1946 the output per man-year in Jamaica was 3.92 million matches as compared with 23.5 million in a factory of comparable size in Australia. As early as 1935 production in the United Kingdom reached 23.3 million per worker, and in the United States it was 77.2 million in 1939.

represents a rise of almost 61% or about 6% per year. If this rate of growth were maintained, factory employment would reach 44,000 in 1962 or about 20,000 more than in 1951. We believe, however, that this is clearly the outside limit of what can be achieved. Actual accomplishment will probably fall short of this total. The processing of local agricultural materials, for example, is unlikely to increase more rapidly than gross agricultural production for which we envisage a total rise of 44% by 1962. In fact the increase may well be less. Some of the expansion in agricultural output will be in commodities which require no processing (bananas) or little processing (coffee and cacao); and the amount of materials processed in a number of industries, particularly sugar, can be raised without a fully equivalent increase in employment. Altogether employment in this branch of industry, which amounted to 14,550 in 1951, probably cannot be expected to expand by more than 30% or by about 4,400 workers. In the remaining branches of industry, however, it would not be unreasonable to expect a continued rate of growth of at least 6% annually, which would result in an increase in employment of 7,700. The output of the products and services of these industries can be expected to rise more rapidly than the population and the general level of income particularly because many of them will produce goods hitherto imported. There are many opportunities for expansion. Not only will the output in already established industries rise, but new industries will presumably be started. The range of goods which can be manufactured for the domestic market can be increased to include such things as various types of building materials, small tools and other hardware items, household articles, ceramics, packaging materials and the like. A limited export market in the Caribbean area may be gradually developed as the efficiency of production improves. The growing tourist industry will expand the market for distinctive Jamaican products made from locally available materials.

The total increase in manufacturing employment which may be expected by 1962 is therefore likely to fall within the range of 12,000 to 20,000 with the total probably nearer the lower than the upper limit.

It is difficult to know how much capital will need to be invested to obtain this employment. One may assume, perhaps, an investment need of about £ 1,200 per person employed, and if it is further assumed that the rise in employment will be about 15,000, the total industrial capital requirement can be estimated at £ 18 million. It is unlikely that private foreign and domestic capital will be able to supply this entire sum. A considerable part, perhaps half, may be obtained from abroad. The sugar, building materials and textile industries, for instance, have been able to attract a considerable volume of foreign capital in the past. Of the rest, it is possible that somewhat more than half may be found by building up the reserves of existing concerns, by selling shares in Jamaica and by obtaining working capital from the commercial banks. It is not improbable therefore that the Industrial Development Corporation may have to put up between £ 3 million and £ 4 million. The total, however, cannot be forecast with any accuracy.

V

The Tourist Industry

Next to agriculture and manufacturing, the tourist industry is likely to furnish the largest increase in future employment. Prospects for its further development are excellent. In no industry does Jamaica possess so decisive a natural advantage. With its rugged mountains, its striking coastline and its abundant tropical and sub-tropical vegetation, Jamaica is perhaps the most beautiful of all the Caribbean islands and can offer an almost unequalled range of natural attractions. It has an ideal climate in the winter, and the prevailing winds narrow the seasonal range of temperature, particularly on the north shore, to such an extent as to make the island attractive to tourists even in summer. In the United States it has nearby a large and growing market for its "product." Moreover, pricewise it is well able to compete with most American resorts offering equal facilities.

In certain other respects the tourist industry possesses notable advantages for Jamaica. Its development has required, and will probably continue to require, proportionately much less government assistance than is needed by agriculture and other industries. It has enabled Jamaica to diversify its market. Whereas nearly all of Jamaica's agricultural exports go to United Kingdom, about 93% of the tourist traffic comes from the United States and Canada. Finally, less investment is required per person employed in the tourist industry than in manufacturing. The hotel industry requires at the most an investment of £ 1,000 per "tourist bed" which in turn gives direct employment to at least one person. This investment, of course, also stimulates employment in transport, entertainment, commerce and agriculture which supply goods and services to the hotels and directly to the tourists.

The tourist trade has expanded rapidly. The number of visitors to Jamaica rose from 62,690 in 1938 to 93,626 in 1951 or by about 50%. In the last two years alone an increase of almost 37% was registered. Of perhaps greater significance is the fact that the proportion of visitors remaining for longer stays has considerably risen. Thus from 1948 to 1951 the number of "long-stay" visitors increased by about 93%, while that of "short-stay" visitors rose by only 41%. The summer traffic has also assumed much greater importance than in prewar years. In 1948 and 1951, 42% and 39% of the tourist traffic fell in the months of May-September, inclusive, as compared with only 23% in 1938. It has been estimated that tourists spend between £ 3 and £ 4 million annually in Jamaica, which makes tourism the island's second largest "exporter," ranking only after the sugar industry.

TABLE 3

NUMBER OF TOURISTS VISITING JAMAICA

Year	Short-stay	Long-stay	Total
1929	n.a.	n.a.	18,631
1938	n.a.	n.a.	62,690
1947	42,817	10,653	53,470
1948	48,971	12,860	61,831
1949	54,908	13,720	68,628
1950	56,909	17,983	74,892
1951	68,827	24,799	93,626

How much employment is given today by the tourist industry is difficult to estimate. The tourist hotels probably employed about 2,200 people in 1951. Perhaps another thousand were engaged in catering to tourists in transport, entertainment and allied fields. To this direct employment, however, must be added a considerable amount of indirect employment, arising out of the purchase of local food and other supplies by hotels and the purchase of both locally produced and imported articles by the tourists themselves. Altogether an analysis of tourist expenditures led us to the conclusion that directly and indirectly employment is created for the equivalent of perhaps 12,000 people. This does not mean, of course, that this many people derive their entire livelihood from the tourist industry. A much larger number of people are affected by tourist expenditures, but most of them derive only a small part of their income from it.

As the attractions of Jamaica become more greatly publicized, the tourist industry can be expected to develop rapidly, the more so since rising incomes in the United States and cheaper air fares have brought foreign travel within the reach of larger numbers of Americans. Most of the development can be left to private enterprise, but the government can help in a number of respects to stimulate it.

PUBLICITY

Wider and more effective publicity is certainly needed. Since 1922 Jamaica has had a Tourist Trade Development Board of ten members appointed by the Governor. It has been financed in part from the receipts of passenger duties, in part from annual government grants. Its resources, while gradually increasing, have been far from adequate. In 1951-52 they amounted to £ 68,109, of which approximately £ 50,000 was spent on advertising and publicity. In the current fiscal year the board has apparently been assured a government subvention of £ 100,000 as compared with £ 56,109 last year. We recommend that the resources available to the board be increased gradually to at least £ 200,000. Part of this might be financed by raising the passenger duty. [14] Most of the increase might be spent on the promotion of summer traffic. A more balanced year-round trade would help greatly to reduce costs and improve the profitability of hotel investments.

In addition, we strongly urge a reorganization of the board to make it truly representative of the tourist industry. At present most of the people actively engaged in the industry regard the board as ineffective and they accordingly take little interest in its activity. We suggest that the various groups interested in the tourist trade— the hotel owners, the Chamber of Commerce, the airlines and shipping

[14] The duty payable by short-stay visitors might be raised from 4 to 10 shillings, that payable by long-stay visitors from 10 to 30 shillings.

companies—each be allowed to nominate a number of members. The board itself should then be allowed to appoint a managing director. Only a board directly representative of the industry can be expected to promote tourism with maximum vigor and effectiveness. Moreover, a board which has the confidence of the industry will have more success in supplementing its resources with voluntary contributions from those in the tourist trade.

HOTEL CONSTRUCTION

As more tourists are attracted, accommodations will have to be increased. Since the war considerable sums of money have been invested in modernizing and equipping existing hotels and in building new ones. American capital has become interested in the hotel industry. In 1951 hotels catering to foreign tourists had about 1,100 rooms with accommodations for 1,800 guests. We suggest that the target should be to raise the total number of rooms to about 6,000, with accommodations for 10,000, by 1962. This may require an investment of perhaps £ 10 million.

In the past the government has encouraged such investment through the Hotel Aids Law of 1944, which permits accelerated depreciation allowances and imports of building materials and equipment free of duty and tonnage tax, similar to those granted under the Pioneer Industries Law. We strongly recommend that this law be continued and suggest that its benefits also be extended to the renovation of existing hotels. In view of the large investment desirable in the future, we would also urge the government to consider a limited guarantee of mortgages on new hotels. Although adequate profits are apparently being made in the hotel industry as a whole, investment in the industry is still regarded as rather speculative, so that it is difficult to attract mortgage capital either at home or abroad. Only in areas where a considerable nucleus of hotels already exists is additional investment considered relatively safe; but it is obvious that if the tourist industry is to expand, development will have to be pushed in new areas. The opening of such new areas to the tourist trade, however, is likely to involve abnormal risk. It may take considerable time before a sufficient number of tourists are attracted to make the investment profitable. In such cases the government might guarantee at its discretion, payments of interest and principal on mortgages in order to give a needed stimulus to development. Certain conditions would, of course, have to be made. It would be necessary, for example, to stipulate that equity investment provide a sufficient proportion—say 30%—of the total cost. It might also be advisable to limit the duration of the guarantee to a period at the end of which the investment should reasonably be expected to become profitable. In this way unsound ventures would be discouraged. The government should make a small charge for such guarantees.

A limited guarantee of this type might be particularly appropriate in connection with the development of the mineral baths on the south coast. The desirability of developing these baths which are said to have definite therapeutic value, might first be investigated by a recognized expert on mineral spas. Even if his report is favorable, however, private investment in the baths would inevitably entail considerable risk which could be mitigated by a partial government guarantee.

COMMUNICATIONS

The establishment of the airport at Montego Bay has greatly stimulated the tourist trade; and the extension and improvement of the Palisadoes airport at Kingston, which has now been decided upon, should have the same effect. We strongly doubt, however, the economic feasibility of the oft-advanced proposal to establish additional airports. It will be more important and more economical to give high priority to the improvement of the road along the north shore and of the road connecting Kingston with the north coast via Bog Walk.

Development of the tourist trade is undoubtedly handicapped by the virtual lack of a regular steamship passenger service linking Jamaica with the United States. Many tourists will still travel only by sea.

The Tourist Board has made several attempts to interest shipping companies in such a service, but it is unlikely to succeed unless the government is prepared to guarantee the line some minimum income. We suggest that the board continue to seek an arrangement of this kind on a basis which would not involve the government in financial risks out of proportion to the benefits that would be obtained.

VI.

Transport

The expansion of agriculture, industry and tourism will inevitably impose a greater burden on the island's transport facilities. It is accordingly necessary to review the adequacy of the railway, roads and ports and determine what must be done to enable them to play an effective role in the development of Jamaica's resources.

THE RAILWAY

In recent years the government-owned and operated railway has carried between 300,000 and 375,000 tons of freight and between 600,000 and 800,000 passengers annually. It is a standard-gauge railway with 207 route miles and serves about 60% of the total population. Its principal lines connect Kingston with Montego Bay in the northwest and Port Antonio in the northeast. While the railway showed an operating profit in the prewar years, it has never earned enough to cover its debt charges. The railway's balance sheet indicates a cumulative loss, after taking into account debt and depreciation charges, of £ 7,432,900 since 1896 when the government took it over from an American syndicate. In the last few years the annual operating deficit which has had to be met from the government budget has exceeded £ 300,000.[1]

Because of these losses and the development of road transport, demands have been made from time to time that the railway be abandoned. The last expert survey made by Mr. C. E. Rooke in 1945 urged in essence progressive abandonment of the railway. At first glance there seems ample justification for halting the operation of the railway. The recent volume of traffic appears hardly sufficient to warrant operation, and the cost of moving freight, estimated by the

---

[1] Statistical data on the operations and freight rates of the railways are given in Annex 24.

railway administration at 9d. per ton-mile, is among the highest in the world. Neither of these, however, need be permanent. As the result of the development program a growing volume of freight, particularly of bulky commodities ideally suited to rail movement, will require transport; and costs can be substantially reduced by more efficient operation. Under these circumstances we are convinced that abandonment of the railway would be unwise; and this conviction is supported by the views of responsible leaders whom we consulted. Without the railway it would be necessary to invest a large amount of capital in roads and vehicles which the island can ill afford at its present stage of development. The railway is well adapted to handle agricultural commodities and alumina. It has demonstrated, for instance, its ability to meet the requirement for rapid and safe movement of the important banana crop to loading ports. It also exercises a moderating influence on road trucking charges. For these reasons we recommend that a firm decision be made to retain the railway for a period of at least fifteen years. At the end of this time the situation might once more be reviewed in the light of conditions then prevailing.

It is, however, essential that prompt steps be taken to put the railway on a sounder financial footing and to remedy some of the serious deficiencies in equipment which otherwise might make it unable to cope with the increasing traffic.

Freight Rates

While there was still a small operating profit in prewar years, the postwar period has witnessed a progressively larger operating deficit. Operating expenses in 1950-51 were 95% and in 1951-52 78% more than gross revenues. The heavy postwar deficits are primarily attributable to the serious decline in the profitable banana traffic, the maintenance of low rates, increases in staff and rising costs of supplies, materials and labor.

A substantial reduction in the deficit is needed to stop the drain on the budget and thus release more funds for development. This can only be accomplished by curtailing operating costs, increasing traffic and raising freight rates. A rise in freight rates is particularly important because at present rates an expansion of traffic might even increase rather than lower the deficit.

Freight rates are too low. They bring the railway an average return of about 4d. per ton-mile, and yield only 2d. per ton-mile on sugar. In 1950-51 freight rates on most commodities were but 10-60% above prewar even though operating costs were 130% higher than the average in 1935-39. On sugar cane and raw sugar, which accounted for 60% of the total tonnage and 22% of the ton-miles in 1950-51, the rates were actually still below prewar levels. Average revenues per ton-mile were almost 10% less than in 1938-39. In February 1952 modest increases were put into effect. Rates on general merchandise were raised 25% and rates on other commodities, except bananas, 10-15%. Even so, only one commodity, bananas, is carried at a rate which covers the reported operating costs.

Passenger rates are also low. They were raised one third during the war but were brought back to the prewar level in 1948. In February 1952, fares were increased 12½% and a small extra fare instituted on first class tickets on the new diesel trains running to Montego Bay. These fares, however, are of less importance than the freight charges since passenger revenues amounted to only 20% of total revenues in 1951-52.

We strongly urge that freight rates be substantially increased. While the users of the railway should not be asked to carry the burden of unjustifiably high operating costs, they should be expected to pay adequately for the transport services received, thus in effect making it possible for the government to save substantial sums for economic development. We are unable to make firm recommendations on specific rates. It may be possible, however, to increase the rates on sugar by 100% and to raise rates on all other commodities, except bananas, by 10% to 60%, with the larger increases applicable to the more valuable commodities. The railway management will have to recommend precisely what increases should be effected. This decision will need to take into account, of course, the possibility of road competition. It is difficult to determine what truck haulage rates are since, in the absence of common carrier trucks, rates are fixed on a contract basis. We believe, however, that they are high enough to leave some margin for an increase in railway rates, particularly on bulk commodities. In any event, the fear of a possible diversion to road traffic will not justify maintaining rates at a level which does not even pay the out-of-pocket cost of transporting the goods.

Reduction in Operating Costs

Part of the relatively high cost of operating the railway can be attributed to the rugged, mountainous terrain of the country. The high proportion of steep grades and sharp curves on the railway[2] greatly increases operating costs by limiting the number of cars per train and accelerating wear and tear on equipment. Nevertheless, costs can be significantly reduced by more efficient utilization of existing equipment and staff and by better maintenance. The railway has long been overstaffed, and is even more so now than before the war. The staff increased from 1,480 in 1938-39 to an average of 2,056 in 1950-51. Even after allowing for the 20% reduction in working hours which has meanwhile been effected, this increase is out of proportion to the traffic which remained about the same.

The railway management can effect the necessary economies and improvement in operating efficiency only if it is as free as possible from political interference and pressures. This condition can never be assured as long as the railway is operated as a government department. We recommend, accordingly, that it be given autonomous status under an independent Board of Directors. The board should consist of no more than five members appointed by the Governor in Executive Council. The majority should be reputable businessmen or other

---

[2] For example, the 112-mile line to Montego Bay leaves the plains 42 miles from Kingston, rises about 1500 feet in 19 miles (to an elevation 1703 feet above sea level) on a practically continuous 3% grade, falls to an elevation of 378 feet, rises again to an elevation of 1084 feet and then slopes to the sea at Montego Bay. The percentage of curvature on the total route mileage is 41%.

qualified private citizens. Members ought to be given sufficient compensation for attending meetings of the board to insure that they will devote adequate attention to railway affairs. The board should be empowered to appoint the Managing Director who would be an ex officio member of the board, to fix railway rates, approve the budget, determine policy, including personnel policy, and supervise all railway operations. It is important that the board also control all expenditures except for capital expenditures in excess of £ 50,000. Government control should be exercised only through the appointment of the directors, appropriation of any funds necessary to cover any deficit and capital outlays, and review of the board's annual report. We suggest that one of the first acts of such a board might be to engage a firm of management consultants to assist in reorganizing the railway administration along efficient lines and maintain a periodic check on its operations.

Investment Requirements

Some capital outlays are needed to permit more efficient operations and the handling of a larger volume of traffic. Needed replacements and improvements have been too long deferred owing to the railway's precarious financial position and the uncertainty of its future. Most of the freight cars and passenger coaches are old. Of the 650 freight cars, only 41 or about 6% are reported to be in good condition; 387 are in fair condition and 222 are so poor that the majority ought to be scrapped. We believe that about £ 670,000 will be required in the period up to 1962 for necessary capital improvements and replacement. Of this sum about £ 437,000 should be spent on the acquisition of rolling stock including 166 new freight cars, and the balance on civil works, particularly the extension of the railway workshops and the strengthening of bridges. In this connection it might be noted that one of the Mission's recommendations on the Kingston port should result in a considerable saving in the use of freight cars.

Anticipated Reduction in the Railway Deficit

With a rise in freight rates and a reduction in operating costs, the railway will be in the position to profit greatly from the increase in traffic flowing from the development program. Thus, the very considerable expansion in the production of such commodities as bananas and sugar and the general quickening of economic activity would greatly enhance the revenues of the railway. The haulage of alumina and supplies for Jamaica Bauxites should also add substantially to these revenues.[3] Altogether we estimate that it will be possible to decrease the deficit progressively from about £ 370,000 in 1952-53 to less than £ 60,000 in 1961-62. The total saving effected over this period should approximate £ 2.3 million. Even after deducting the sum required for capital investment, a substantial amount of the saving should remain available to assist in financing the whole development program.

ROADS

Jamaica appears on the whole to be served by a better network of roads than most comparable countries. In 1951 there were 2,566 miles of main roads suitable for motor traffic and 2,200 miles of parochial roads capable of carrying light motor traffic. For every square mile there were 1.08 miles of motor roads. The existing network should in general be adequate as long as the railway remains in operation. The urgent need today is not for building new roads, but for better maintenance and improvement of the existing road system.

The work on roads falls into two categories: (1) improvement and construction, and (2) maintenance. Each is characterized by serious deficiencies.

Construction and Improvement

Road construction has always been far more influenced by political considerations than by the requirements of the economy. The Public

---

[3] It has been estimated that revenue from this source will increase from something over £ 50,000 in 1952-53 to more than £ 100,000 in 1954-55.

Works Department has little voice in programming this work. Under such conditions, a real road program has been impossible. Each year funds are earmarked for an incredible number of projects. In 1951-52, for example, provision was made for no less than 168 projects involving an average expenditure of £ 2,241. This has inevitably resulted in a tremendous waste of funds and little accomplishment. The annual allocation to each project is generally sufficient for only a short time after which work is suspended. Great waste is involved in stopping and resuming work and in repairing the damage to the uncompleted work which traffic and heavy rains frequently cause in the meantime. Thus the cost of building new roads and bridges in the five-year period ending March 31, 1951 was apparently over £ 50,000 per mile including overhead.[4] Progress is unbelievably slow, as is evident from examples of road construction projects picked at random from the 1950-51 report of the Public Works Department:

(1) Scotland Gate to Danvers Pen, St. Thomas. Distance six and a half miles; started in 1947; one and a half miles completed.

(2) Annotto Bay to Port Maria, St. Mary. Distance twelve miles; started in 1948; one and a half miles completed.

(3) Content Gap to Pleasant Hill. Distance four and a half miles; started in 1943; still uncompleted.

We strongly recommend that a definite long-range program of road building and reconstruction be drawn up and implemented without interference. Such a program ought to be formulated by technically trained people. It must focus on a rapid completion of some of the more worthy projects which have been under construction in the past and on a strictly limited number of new projects which can be clearly justified on economic grounds. The roads which in the Mission's opinion should have the highest priority are listed in

---

[4] Annual reports of the Public Works Department disclose that during this period the roads under its supervision increased by 24 miles or less than five miles per year. Although the exact amount spent on new roads cannot be determined from the Department's reports, it was evidently in the neighborhood of £ 1.2 million in this period.

an Annex[5] to the report. Above all, it is imperative that the appropriations for this program be voted as a lump sum and not earmarked for specific projects. The Director of Public Works must be able to spend the funds in accordance with sound engineering and economic considerations. We suggest also that the road improvement program be carried out with the use of modern machinery and techniques and by a special section of the Public Works Department not concerned with maintenance. If these recommendations are adopted, it would be possible to accomplish a great deal more than is achieved at present.

Maintenance

By far the most important problem is maintenance. Inadequate maintenance has resulted in a very serious deterioration of roads. The amount spent for this purpose in postwar years has fallen far behind the rise in cost of labor and materials and the increase in road mileage. In 1951-52 the allocation for maintenance—£ 315,000—was only 8% higher than the average in 1938-39 and 1939-40. Since road mileage meanwhile increased 6%, wages 160% and materials 200%, an allocation of at least £ 516,500 should have been made in 1951-52 to make expenditures comparable to those in prewar years. We therefore urge that in the future £ 525,000 be set aside annually for maintenance.

In addition it would be highly desirable to allocate about £ 70,000 annually for the repair of flood damage. This type of damage is particularly severe in a country which often suffers from torrential rains and floods. Annual allocations for flood damage repair are very small, so that work often cannot be started until special funds are made available. Adequate funds are seldom voted to complete work which has been begun. Partial repair of flood damage has thus been an important contributory factor in the gradual deterioration of the road system. The annual appropriation of adequate funds which can be carried forward from one year to the next would greatly help the Public Works Department in coping with this situation.

---

[5] See Annex 25.

While the Director of Public Works does control the programming of maintenance and repair work as distinct from road construction, considerable improvement could be made in carrying out this work. First of all, far too much is done by hand labor alone. The same labor provided with adequate tools could accomplish several times as much work with only a slightly larger total expenditure of funds. Secondly, the productivity of road workers is low because there are not sufficient trained foremen and junior engineers to provide adequate supervision. These faults can be corrected in time by the acquisition of more equipment, better organization of work and training of more personnel. They will require, however, the personal attention of the senior engineers in the department who are unfortunately preoccupied far too much with details and unnecessary paper work.

Machinery

An improved road program along the lines indicated above will require additional road machinery and better workshops and stores. We would recommend an investment of about £ 375,000 for road equipment over the next three or four years and an annual allocation of funds for replacement of equipment equal to approximately 12½% of that in use. Requirements for replacement funds would be in the neighborhood of £ 60,000 a year. For new shops and stores about £ 110,000 should be made available.

If this entire program is to be carried out efficiently there must be a thorough reorganization and streamlining of the functions of the Public Works Department. More detailed proposals on this subject are given in an Annex to this report.[6]

Finally, we have also included in an Annex certain suggestions for amendment of the regulations governing road traffic.[7]

PORT FACILITIES

Jamaica is served by one major port, Kingston, and 15 outports. Only Kingston is equipped to handle general cargo in large quanti-

---

[6] See Annex 26.
[7] See Annex 27.

ties. At 12 of the outports only bananas and sugar are handled. At 10 of these the bananas and sugar are loaded on vessels from lighters; at the other two there are wharves, but no facilities for handling commodities other than bananas and sugar. The three remaining outports have piers built recently by the three bauxite mining companies. They are equipped to handle bauxite ore or alumina outbound and oil and other supplies inbound, and are available only for the use of their owners.

At Kingston there are eleven general cargo piers capable of accommodating ocean-going vessels, one for loading gypsum in bulk, three for handling oil from tankers or for bunkering fuel oil and one for bunkering coal. Only three of the general cargo piers have railway connections. These are government-owned. The remainder are privately owned.

Although the future will bring a great increase in shipments of bauxite, alumina, bananas, sugar and other agricultural commodities, we foresee no need for a general expansion of port facilities. Special ports have been built to handle bauxite and alumina, and the greater part of the bulky agricultural commodities, such as sugar and bananas, will continue to be shipped through the outports. The heavy expenditure entailed by the oft-proposed port development at Montego Bay, for instance, could hardly be justified by the traffic likely to develop. In Kingston the need for more facilities will arise only when the volume of cargo increases about 25% above the present tonnage, which is unlikely to take place for some time.[8]

The principal problem which requires solution at Kingston is the serious congestion of the waterfront area. This congestion results from (1) the inability of streets and alleys leading to the waterfront to handle the traffic when ships are loading and discharging, (2) the lack of through streets paralleling the waterfront, and (3) the use for long-term storage of facilities which should be used only for transit or short-term storage.

In 1949 a committee of government officials and a representative

---

[8] Data on the number of ships calling at Kingston and the volume of cargo handled can be found in Annex 28.

of the Shipping Association formulated a plan to relieve traffic congestion, prevent pilferage and provide better fire protection in the waterfront area. The committee recommended that the plan be carried out in stages by waterfront owners at no cost to the government or to the city except for additional fire protection and road construction. The plan provided for a waterfront or pier road, the opening up of through streets parallel to the pier road, and the closing of the lanes or alleys which lead to a dead end at the waterfront, together with the establishment of a controlled or protected waterfront with only a few guarded entries and exits. Such a plan would permit the free flow of traffic throughout the waterfront area and would give all piers access to the railroad by the use of trucks and trailers along the pier road.

The report was not approved even in principle by the government because of objections raised by some of the waterfront owners. In our opinion the recommendations made in the report were reasonable and some formula should be found to eliminate the objections to the plan or at least put it partially into operation. The government should immediately adopt the committee's recommendations in principle. If necessary, it should condemn and pay for the property required to carry out these proposals. More adequate fire protection should be provided as soon as possible.

This plan can be carried out only if steps are taken to replace the outmoded Wharfage Law. Enacted in 1895 this statute still governs the rates which can be charged for handling and storage of goods moving over the wharves and piers in Kingston and other ports. It requires the wharf owner to give three months free storage on outward cargo and fourteen days on inward cargo. The charges it fixed have been increased only 50% since 1895 and are so low that it pays exporters and importers to store their goods at the waterfront rather than elsewhere. As a consequence long-term storage warehouses are practically nonexistent in Kingston and vicinity and the waterfront transit sheds, in which goods should remain only for short periods, are used for long-term storage. Merchants withdraw their goods from storage as they need them and add to the congestion of trucks and drays attempting to handle goods directly to or from ships through the narrow streets leading to the waterfront.

We recommend, therefore, the enactment of a new wharfage law with the following provisions:

(a) Limitation of free storage to six days, exclusive of Sundays and holidays; and the application of penalty rates thereafter in order to give shippers and consignees a real incentive to clear sheds promptly (enforcement of this should be deferred until adequate warehouses can be built outside the waterfront area);

(b) Determination of proper remunerative charges by a non-political Board appointed by the Governor in Executive Council; enforcement of these new charges or subsequent revisions therein within 60 days after their publication, with provision for hearings, followed by a final decision of the Board, in case objections are filed;

(c) Application of the charges to weight or measurement tons (except in the case of liquids normally shipped by the gallon) instead of, as at present, to such indeterminate measures as bags, boxes, puncheons, etc.;

(d) Continuation of the "side wharfage" or berthage now charged against ships on a net registered ton basis, with the charges applied as in (c).

Such a law would have many beneficial results. It would greatly relieve congestion and make it profitable for wharf owners to provide better facilities. It would give an incentive for the construction of warehouses away from the waterfront area. Finally, it would be of great assistance to the railway by enabling it to earn some money on the three wharves it now owns and by freeing for other employment at least 100 freight cars which, because of lack of warehouse space, are now regularly used during the crop season for sugar storage.

Conditions in the waterfront area would also improve if the Harbor Master's operations were moved to a less congested point in the harbor and if the waterfront property now occupied by the Public Works Department and the Ordnance Department were vacated. These properties could be more effectively used for waterfront development.

Airports

Jamaica has two major airports, the older Palisadoes airport at Kingston and the newer one on the north coast at Montego Bay. The runway at Montego Bay has recently been lengthened to accommodate stratocruisers and jet airliners, and, except for changes in the terminal building, the airport should prove adequate to handle the increase in traffic anticipated in the next few years. The Kingston airport, however, must be extended if it is also to handle the stratocruisers or the commercial jets which are expected to begin service to Jamaica in October 1952. Without adequate air service tourist traffic cannot be expected to develop.

The Palisadoes airport is located on the long narrow peninsula or sand spit which forms the southern boundary of Kingston Harbor, about one and a half miles airline distance south of Kingston across the Bay. Since lengthening either of the two runways along their present alignments would require a considerable amount of fill in the Bay, consideration was given to the construction of a new airport at Cumberland Pen near Kingston. It has now been found feasible, however, to construct a new runway, 7,000 feet long, along an entirely new alignment close to the shore in relatively shallow water. This definitely makes it more economical and expeditious to extend the existing airport than to build an entirely new one.

VII.

Electric Power

If the electric power system is to serve the needs of an expanding economy within the framework of the development program we have projected, it will be necessary to expand capacity somewhat more rapidly than is now planned and to convert the frequency at which power is now generated from 40 to 50 cycles.

CAPACITY AND GENERATION

In May, 1952, the generating capacity installed in all power stations in Jamaica totaled approximately 40,000 kw. Of this total, 27,129 kw were operated by the privately owned Jamaica Public Service Company, 8,925 kw by the three aluminum companies and the new cement plant, and the remainder by sugar mills and three small communities. With a generation of 86 million kwh, the Jamaica Public Service Company accounted for probably about 90% of total production in 1951, and supplied approximately 99% of the electric energy sold in Jamaica. As of May 1952 the Jamaica Public Service Company, a Canadian controlled concern, operated under exclusive licenses[1] in eleven of the fourteen parishes of the island and served about 27,500 consumers. Of the 27,129 kw operated by the company, 9,500 kw were in one steam station, 13,450 kw were in four hydro plants and 4,269 kw were in five diesel plants. All of the plants, except four diesel plants having a total capacity of 1,936 kw, generated at 40 cycles per second and were interconnected. The four diesel plants generated at 60 cycles. For the transmission of energy generated by the inter-connected 40 cycle system, the company operated 331 miles of high tension lines varying in capacity from 6,600 volts to 66,000 volts.[2] In 1951 the peak load on the system reached 16,150 kw

---

[1] Provisions of licenses governing the generation of electric power are given in Annex 29.

[2] For details of installations, see Annex 30.

(compared with an effective capacity of about 17,750 kw) and is expected to reach 21,000 in 1952. The addition of the 3,200 kw hydro station on the Lower White River in March, 1952, and the use of pondage in peak periods will enable the company to meet the 1952 peak demand.

The amount of power generated has been comparatively small. Per capita production in 1951, for example, was only 23% of that in Puerto Rico. The rather small output is in part a reflection of the low standard of living, in part perhaps a result of a rather conservative policy of expansion. It should be noted, however, that the company has expanded its facilities considerably since 1938 despite postwar difficulties in obtaining equipment. In 1938 its installed capacity was 7,200 kw, consisting of a steam plant in Kingston of 6,300 kw capacity and a hydro station at Bog Walk of 900 kw capacity at maximum river flow. Since then it has added three hydro plants with a combined installed capacity of 12,400 kw and a 3,500 kw steam unit, expanded the Bog Walk plant to bring its capacity up to 1,050 kw, and rented a 2,283 kw diesel unit which was installed at a United States Army Airfield during the war and thereafter transferred to the Jamaican government. At present the company is constructing a 10,-000 kw steam plant at Hunts Bay, near Kingston, which is expected to be in operation in mid-1953.

TABLE 4

TOTAL POWER GENERATION BY JAMAICA PUBLIC SERVICE COMPANY
(thousands of kilowatt hours)

Type of Station	1938	1945	1951	1952
				(est.)
Steam	12,120	18,705	29,452	20,454
Hydro	3,631	16,036	51,957	68,686
Diesel	1,140	1,334	4,636	6,989
Total	16,891	36,075	86,045	96,129

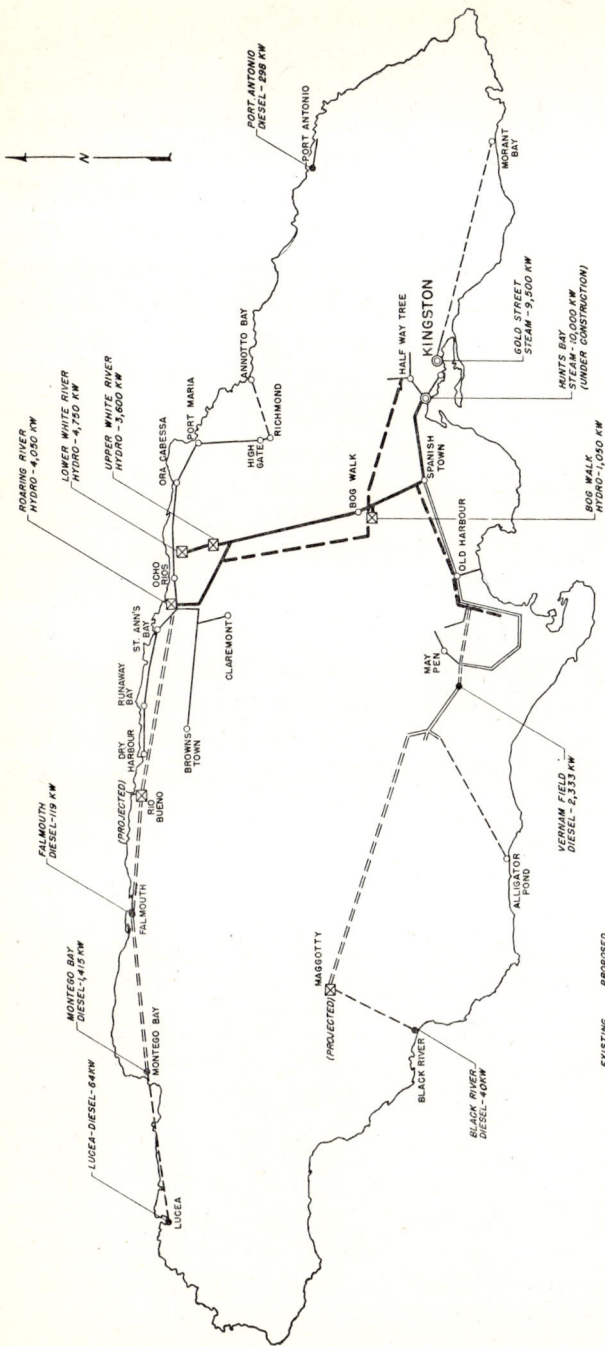

JAMAICA

ELECTRIC POWER SYSTEM

PORT ANTONIO
DIESEL – 298 KW

ROARING RIVER
HYDRO – 4,050 KW

LOWER WHITE RIVER
HYDRO – 4,750 KW

UPPER WHITE RIVER
HYDRO – 3,600 KW

FALMOUTH
DIESEL – 119 KW

MONTEGO BAY
DIESEL – 1,415 KW

LUCEA – DIESEL – 64 KW

(PROJECTED)

BLACK RIVER
DIESEL – 40 KW

(PROJECTED) MAGGOTTY

VERNAM FIELD
DIESEL – 2,333 KW

BOG WALK
HYDRO – 1,050 KW

HUNTS BAY
STEAM – 10,000 KW
(UNDER CONSTRUCTION)

GOLD STREET
STEAM – 9,500 KW

PORT ANTONIO

MORANT BAY

KINGSTON

HALF WAY TREE

SPANISH TOWN

OLD HARBOUR

BOG WALK

ANNOTTO BAY

RICHMOND

HIGH GATE

PORT MARIA

ORA CABESSA

OCHO RIOS

ST. ANN'S BAY

RUNAWAY BAY

DRY HARBOUR

RIO BUENO

BROWNS TOWN

CLAREMONT

MAY PEN

ALLIGATOR POND

BLACK RIVER

FALMOUTH

MONTEGO BAY

LUCEA

N

MILES
0   5   10   15   20   25

STEAM GENERATING STATIONS
HYDRO GENERATING STATIONS
DIESEL GENERATING STATIONS

EXISTING   PROPOSED
◎
⊗
●

69 KV TRANSMISSION LINES
33 KV TRANSMISSION LINES
12 KV TRANSMISSION LINES

69 KV LINES PROBABLY REQUIRED FOR FREQUENCY CONVERSION – 1953-'54.
33 KV LINES FOR ADDITIONAL HYDRO INTERCONNECTIONS.

ELECTRIC POWER

The company now has sufficient firm capacity to meet all demands by virtue of the addition of the lower White River hydro station to its system in March, 1952; and the new 10,000 kw Hunts Bay steam station coming on the line in 1953 will assure adequate capacity for a few more years (probably until 1956 or 1957).

For planning purposes, the company estimates that the peak load on its interconnected system will grow at an annual rate of at least 10% until 1962, reaching 42,000 kw in that year. It also anticipates that its total kilowatt hour sales will increase in proportion to the peak load and will reach 245 million kwh in 1962. These assumptions appear to be rather conservative. It is more likely that the peak load will reach 50,000 to 60,000 kw[3] and that the generation will be 290-300 million kwh in 1962, particularly if agricultural and industrial development of the island go forward as anticipated. We accordingly suggest that the company review the potential requirements in consultation with the government.

In line with its projection of demand, the company has tentative plans to add a 12,500 kw steam unit to the Hunts Bay Station now under construction. It is also investigating, and has already made application for permission to develop, two additional hydro projects (Rio Bueno and Maggotty Falls), which will add a total of about 5,000 kw to its capacity. The latter two projects are likely to leave only about 8,000-10,000 kw of hydro-power potential available for development. The company contemplates extending its transmission lines to include in its network the two projected hydro plants and some of the localities now inadequately served by independent stations.

CHANGE IN FREQUENCY

We believe it essential to the development of Jamaica that prompt steps be taken to convert the power frequency to 50 cycles. About the turn of the century when the original power franchise was granted,

---

[3] For instance, the peak loads on the company's interconnected 40 cycle system in the period 1945-51 actually increased at a rate of 13.4% annually and kilowatt hours generated increased 15.4% annually in the same period.

111

40 cycles was regarded as the ideal frequency. Since then, however, 50 and 60 cycles have become standard in almost the entire world. Since manufacturers no longer produce 40-cycle equipment except on special order, retention of the present frequency significantly increases the cost of new electric motors and other items of electrical equipment. The Jamaican purchaser must often content himself with 50-cycle motors which can only operate at 80% efficiency on 40-cycle current and therefore increase the cost of power. Now that Jamaica is on the threshold of a period of considerable development, delay in shifting to a standard frequency, which will in any event be necessary some time, will only raise the ultimate cost.

Since 1946 local businessmen, led by the Jamaica Chamber of Commerce, have been agitating for a change in frequency. In 1946 and 1947 the Company opposed the change primarily because it was experiencing extreme difficulty in obtaining even the necessary equipment for ordinary operations and normal expansion. It did agree, however, to make all future extensions and additions to generating and distribution facilities with the frequency change in view. Accordingly the company installed in the new hydro station on the Lower White River, and will install in the new Hunts Bay Steam Plant, 50-cycle equipment which, with minor modifications, will generate at 40 cycles until such time as the whole system is converted to 50 cycles.

The conversion should now be undertaken as soon as the necessary arrangements can be made. It might be conveniently begun in 1954 when some surplus generating capacity will be available following completion of the new steam plant and delivery schedules for the required equipment may also be easier. The conversion should be to 50 cycles rather than 60 cycles for the following reasons:

(a) The new Lower White River station and the new steam station at Hunts Bay are designed to be changed to 50-cycle with relatively small alterations;

(b) A considerable number of motors sold as 40-cycle are really 50-cycle;

(c) Most of the standard equipment in the United Kingdom is 50-cycle and most of the United States manufacturers can readily supply 50-cycle equipment;

(d) Sixty cycle current has no particular operating advantage over 50-cycle.

As the first step in the conversion program, the amount of equipment which would be affected should be surveyed and the cost accurately estimated. The Jamaica Public Service Company is willing to undertake this survey which would probably require six months or more to complete. In 1947 the cost was estimated at £ 250,000 by a consultant retained by the Chamber of Commerce. The cost at present may be in the order of £ 325,000 to £ 350,000 because the number of power consumers and the amount of installed electrical equipment has meanwhile increased and the cost of new equipment, materials and labor has also gone up.

While the Jamaica Public Service Company can be expected to carry out the conversion operation, it would be unreasonable to ask it to defray the cost. The company will not directly profit by the change and will in fact suffer some loss through interruption of service and the extra cost of operating temporarily at two frequencies during the period of conversion which may last two to three years. We recommend therefore that the company be allowed to recover the cost by levying a surcharge of 5% on all existing rates except residential rates. In this way the total cost could probably be paid off in about eight or nine years. The government should help to reduce the cost as far as possible by admitting free of duty all equipment required for the conversion.

Power Rates

Power rates are fixed by the Jamaica Public Service Company although the licenses under which it operates provide that "the Governor in Privy Council may from time to time make, alter and amend rules which shall be binding on the undertakers as to the maximum prices to be charged from time to time by the undertakers and the reduction of the same." We consider the rates generally reasonable. Through reductions in 1935, 1936, 1938, 1941, 1942, and 1945, the company brought rates down to a point where they encouraged larger use of electricity for many purposes and made private installations for pumping irrigation water uneconomical where pumps could be served from the Company's lines. In February, 1952, the company raised its basic charges for electricity by about 7%. This was the first increase since 1923, except for changes made in line with the rising cost of fuel. In spite of this recent increase, the industrial and commercial rates of the Jamaica Public Service Company are lower than those of Puerto Rico, Cuba, or Trinidad and compare favorably with those in Miami, Florida. Compared with Puerto Rico, the Jamaican charges to industrial consumers are about 20% lower and the commercial rates are about 23% lower.[4] Only residential rates are somewhat higher.

---

[4] Rural consumers in Jamaica purchased 32% of the power in 1951 (chiefly for pumping and irrigation); industrial consumers, 26%; commercial consumers, 17%; and residential consumers, 17%. The remainder was purchased by municipalities and miscellaneous consumers.

VIII.

The Social Services:
Education, Health, and Housing

In the program for developing more fully the economic potentialities of Jamaica, better education, better health, and better housing
play a double role. They are among the tools that will boost the
productivity of the people, and they are at the same time part of
the dividend resulting from that improvement. In the present state
of economic development, an appreciable dividend of this kind is not
readily achieved. Indeed the immediate need is, as the government
has said, to maintain existing standards until further progress has been
made in economic development. Nevertheless, the achievement of
substantial economic development may itself depend in considerable
measure upon better application of the human resources of the country.

When specific needs are examined, the central question appears
to be, not whether Jamaica can afford to improve these services, but
rather, whether it can afford to do without certain improvements in
them. The increments which additional factories or power plants
may contribute to the national product, and certainly the efficacy of
comprehensive measures for soil conservation, irrigation, or the controlled use of land, will be determined in large measure by the degree
in which the people generally can understand and appreciate the objectives and can apply effective techniques. The dissemination of technical skills and general education, the improvement of nutrition, the
prevention or cure of illness, and the improvement of housing conditions might, therefore, result in substantial improvements in productivity.

Moreover, it must be frankly recognized that conditions conducive
to economic and political progress can be achieved, in a democratic
system, only if the franchise is exercised by an informed citizenry

whose members realize from experience that their own economic well-being as individuals is linked with the prosperity of their country.

Accordingly, a review of existing social services and their possibilities is essential to a comprehensive survey of the potentialities for economic development. In Jamaica, education and health are predominantly responsibilities of government; housing is provided mostly through private enterprise but to a considerable extent with government assistance; and other social services are supplied either directly by government or by government-aided organizations. Consequently, the emphasis in a broad discussion of social services is necessarily upon public programs and policies.

EDUCATION

By all odds, the improvement and extension of education takes first priority among the social services. More education, provided it is of the right kind, can help people to become more efficient, to improve their health, and to develop the civic consciousness and community spirit so essential to cooperative self-help. Moreover, the educational system still falls far short of providing a basic education for all children. Despite the undeniable progress achieved in recent decades, the total enrolment of 210,000 in primary schools in 1950 was only about 75% of the children of school age; and for these the existing schools provided fewer than 150,000 places. In the secondary schools, including the technical institutions, only about 8,000 pupils were enrolled in 1950.

In our opinion the principal goals in the future should be (1) to make the fullest use of available educational facilities and gradually extend them, and (2) to give greater stress to education of a utilitarian character. The academic nature of education has long been criticized in Jamaica, but efforts to change it have met with resistance from both teachers and parents. There is a general tendency, not peculiar to Jamaica, to identify booklearning with knowledge and wisdom. The acquisition of "practical" knowledge emphasizing manual skills is too frequently regarded as inferior. If education is to become a useful tool in acquiring a higher standard of living, this attitude must be overcome. The necessary change in values can be accomplished only if the present intellectual leadership of the island—particularly the teacher-training institutions and the University College of the West Indies—energetically supports the idea that practical education is socially respectable and culturally valuable and that the acquisition of manual skills is a means to a better life. The University College is already directing its medical research facilities and teaching hospital staff to practical health problems of the Caribbean area; through a similar orientation in other fields, it could contribute profoundly to the economic and cultural progress of the islands.

Recommendations

The program of educational improvements we suggest points only to broad objectives. The specific methods of realizing them will have to be worked out by the appropriate educational authorities. With this reservation we outline below the measures which might be taken:

1. *Fuller Use of Existing Facilities*

To provide all the teachers and school buildings needed for universal education at this time would clearly overtax Jamaica's resources. Much better use, however, can be made of the existing facilities and teachers. School attendance is irregular even in the selected urban areas where by law it has been made compulsory. Many pupils drop out before their primary schooling is completed. This entails a wasteful use of both buildings and teachers. It inevitably retards the progress of the brighter students and those who attend regularly. We suggest therefore, the introduction of incentives to regular attendance or strong deterrents to irregular attendance. With effective incentives of this kind, it might be possible to reduce somewhat the duration of primary schooling provided that at the same time special postprimary or intermediate classes were made available for pupils

117

who have demonstrated ability beyond the primary level, but are not old enough for secondary school.[1]

2. *Gradual Expansion of Primary School Facilities*

As a minimum the regular government budget must make provision for an additional enrolment of about 5,000 pupils annually if the proportion of the number of places to the number of school-age children is not to deteriorate. Beyond this we would propose a limited expansion program to permit a modest but steady increase in the percentage of school-age children who can be accommodated in the schools, to ameliorate some of the worst conditions of overcrowding, and to make good some of the depreciation of existing facilities. This would involve a capital outlay of approximately £ 54,000 per year or a total of £ 480,000 during the period 1953-54 to 1961-62 to provide places for about 40,000 pupils, and an additional recurring expenditure for maintenance and operation rising gradually from £ 5,000 in the first year to £ 165,000 in 1961-62. We would suggest also that about £ 15,000 be spent annually for teacher housing adjoining the rural schools in particular. This would serve to protect school property from destruction and loss which has often been costly. It would also help to attract good teachers and fit them better into the school community.

3. *Training in Handicrafts and Skills*

The primary schools need to put more emphasis on the development of manual skills and familiarity with tools. Facilities for prevocational training in handicrafts and other skills should be expanded, a greater variety of training provided and means for more intensive

---

[1] These suggestions are further developed in Annex 31. They will require some reorientation of the present school staff and additions to the supervisory staff. An additional annual expenditure of £ 20,000 might be necessary for strengthening the supervision and inspection of local schools, providing additional expert guidance for teachers, conducting intensive work with parents' groups as well as teachers in order to foster understanding and support of the program, and augmenting the central administrative staff of the Education Department.

training offered to older pupils who demonstrate marked aptitudes for, and interest in, this type of work. More teachers with training in this field will also be required. We recommend, therefore, that the present school program which does provide for a gradual increase in primary school facilities for practical work of a prevocational nature, be accelerated by allocating an additional £ 10,000 a year to pay for more equipment, teachers and materials.

4. *Improvement in Teacher Training*

In line with the above program more teachers will have to be trained and equipped to emphasize practical teaching keyed to local needs. The many untrained teachers now in the school system should be given systematic in-service training. Additional specialized teachers are also needed. The existing liaison between teachers' training colleges and the Kingston Technical School should be extended to the Jamaica School of Agriculture, the Practical Training Centers and similar institutions. Steps should be taken to make effective use of the resources of the University College of the West Indies to assist in the preparation of teachers and supervisors. For the expansion and improvement in training facilities we envisage a capital expenditure of £ 200,000 in the period of 1953-1957 and a related increase of £ 10,000 per year in recurring costs for operation and maintenance. This should make it possible to increase by 40 or more the number of teachers graduated annually.

5. *Technical Education*

We have already stressed the key importance of technical education to industry and agriculture and made recommendations to expand and re-equip the Kingston Technical School, establish four more technical high schools and increase the capacity of the Agricultural School at Hope. Here it might be appropriate to comment at somewhat greater length on the Practical Training Centers now operating at Dinthill, Holmwood and Knockalva. These centers which have a capacity for 300 pupils provide sound practical training in both agriculture and the crafts useful to agriculture. The training is especially valuable in strengthening the capacity of farmers for self-help. For this reason we recommend the establishment of three additional centers with accommodation for about 600 residential pupils. This would entail a capital outlay of £ 200,000 and recurring annual expenditures of approximately £ 50,000 a year when the centers are in full operation. The vocational work of Stony Hill Industrial School should also be continued and strengthened.

6. *Additional Scholarships*

A substantial increase in the number of scholarships now granted would enable more children of better than average ability but inadequate means to finish elementary school and attend a secondary school, technical school or practical training center. We recommend that additional scholarship funds, rising gradually from £ 20,000 in the first year to £ 160,000 in 1961-62, be made available.

Conclusion

In putting forward the above recommendations we wish to stress that they must be carried out as an integral part of the whole program for expanding the country's productive capacity. They represent the maximum which the country can undertake at this time. For some time to come it will be impossible to contemplate universal, compulsory primary education. First priority must be given to improving the quality of schooling for those children whose parents enroll them voluntarily, and second priority to making enough places for those so enrolled. For very much the same reasons we see no possibility in the near future of adopting measures to make secondary education available to all children or to increase significantly the provision for postprimary vocational education for girls. The proposed additional scholarship grants together with the expansion in technical education facilities and teachers' training colleges should open up, however, many more opportunities for postprimary education. The emphasis of the whole program must be upon doing first those things which will make the most substantial and rapid contribution to economic improvement.

HEALTH

During the last three decades, great strides have been made in the improvement of public health. The infant mortality rate has been reduced by one half and the general death rate has sharply declined. The life expectancy of new-born children, now 51-54 years, has increased by some 16 years. There have been no smallpox cases for many years and the incidence of yaws, typhoid and typhus has receded greatly. A significant expansion of medical services and hospital facilities has substantially reduced the toll taken by disease. Health conditions in general compare favorably with those in similar countries.

No one, however, can be wholly satisfied either with the rate or the uniformity of progress achieved. There is still much room for improvement. Health conditions and the incidence of disease vary significantly throughout the island. Diseases such as pulmonary tuberculosis, syphilis, diarrhea, enteritis, nephritis and malaria still take many lives or cause crippling disabilities and dependency. Poor nutrition, unsanitary and crowded living conditions and polluted water supplies account for much illness and debility. There is still only one doctor to 4,000 people and the shortage is likely to persist a long time despite the medical education now afforded by the University College of the West Indies. Many hospitals remain seriously overcrowded, and laboratories are in large part inadequate.

While there is no justification for complacency, the health standard which has been attained does suggest that a substantial general expansion of medical facilities no longer has a high priority claim on Jamaica's limited resources. In our judgment a program for the future should focus primarily on (1) an intensification of efforts directed at the prevention of disease, and (2) an expansion of hospital accommodation roughly in accordance with the growth of population, with some improvement in substandard facilities.

In the future relatively more emphasis will have to be placed on disease prevention; and in projecting health expenditures we have accordingly allowed for a modest increase in this type of work. This

121

implies more attention to public health education, pre-natal and infant welfare clinics, insect control, sanitation, nutrition, dental care and the like.[2] To a large extent success in the prevention of disease will depend on improvements in diet and relief from congested, unsanitary housing conditions which in large part can be realized only as production and standards of living rise. Thus the entire economic development program will supplement the direct and more specific efforts of the government to safeguard and promote good health.

Available hospital accommodations—about two general hospital beds per 1,000 in the population—are close to the standards prevailing in comparable countries although still far below the requirements specified as desirable by professional bodies. Existing overcrowding is due in large part to inadequate utilization and poor geographic distribution of facilities. One hospital, for example, was found to be crowding two or even three patients into a single bed and 24 beds into a ward built for 16 while the private rooms of the institution stood empty. Four hospitals on the north shore—at Port Maria, Annotto Bay, Buff Bay and Port Antonio—have about three beds available for each 1,000 of the population they serve. The rest of Jamaica, outside of Kingston, barely averages one and a quarter bed per 1,000.

The hospital construction and improvements which we believe should be included in the development program are set forth below together with extremely tentative estimates of the capital cost.

Kingston Public Hospital and Victoria Jubilee Hospital
 —various extensions and improvements including
 replacement of blocks for 200 beds, conversion of
 children's wards, extension of the nurses' homes, and
 provision of a new out-patients building for venereal
 disease .... £   780,000

New regional hospital at Montego Bay—450-500 beds ..   550,000

---

[2] More detailed suggestions on the types of preventive work which might be undertaken or expanded are given in Annex 32.

Renovation of mental hospital (and provision of adequate out-patients clinic)	500,000
Expansion of the tuberculosis hospital	120,000
Improvements and additions at other hospitals	150,000
Bacteriological laboratory	80,000
Additional health centers	100,000
Equipment, including diagnostic equipment for tuberculosis	100,000
Expansion of BWI Training Institute for public health personnel	20,000
Building repairs and replacements at various hospitals, clinics, and centers, including Hansen Home	300,000
Total capital outlay	£ 2,700,000

Some comments on this program are in order. The expenditure on general hospitals will make minimum necessary improvements in existing hospital facilities and maintain the present ratio of beds to population. Accommodations may in effect become more adequate if as the result of modern medical practices the patient's average length of stay continues to decline as in the past. The new hospital at Montego Bay is designed to replace the existing overcrowded institution and will be large enough to serve a region which is remote from Kingston. Unfortunately, the erection of a new parish hospital at nearby Falmouth will reduce the area which will be served from Montego Bay. The decision to construct the Falmouth hospital is a reflection of an unfortunate tendency in the past to concentrate on providing many local hospitals rather than regional facilities which could be built more economically and would make possible more efficient utilization of specialized equipment and scarce medical skills. At present Kingston Public Hospital is the only one providing specialist services.

In the interest of economy and full utilization of all facilities, new hospitals should be of simplified design and equipped with semipermanent partitions, adjustable plumbing and wiring arrangements and other features that would insure flexibility in the use of the available space. The continuing advance of medical science makes inadvisable the construction of elaborate and expensive permanent facilities which may quickly become obsolescent.

The needs of the special hospitals cannot be ignored. The tuberculosis hospital at Kingston is seriously overtaxed and the needs of the leprosarium (Hansen Home), while less acute, must also be met. Most urgent of all is the renovation and expansion of the mental hospital which houses more patients than all the general hospitals combined. Many of the buildings and much of the equipment are obsolete, unsanitary and dangerous. A controversy over relocation of the hospital has delayed an attack on this problem. Since it would be more economical to modernize and expand the existing hospital than to erect an entirely new one on a different site, we urge a prompt decision to undertake the necessary renovation and expansion. The burden on the institution might be greatly reduced by preventive measures and proper after-care supervision. An out-patient clinic would facilitate early discovery of incipient illness which, in many types of cases, will result in effective prevention or more rapid recovery. A system of after-care supervision would enable the hospital to release more of the nearly-cured patients and some of those incurable patients whose malady is not dangerous to other people. Both within and outside the hospital more stress should be placed on occupational therapy.

Finally, we would urge a thorough study of the entire question of payment for medical and hospital care. This might focus on (1) the charges to be made for treatment of industrial accident cases and (2) the advisability of proposals which have been made for the adoption of some type of medical care insurance. Since the workmen's compensation law does not make the employer liable for medical or hospital care, the government usually provides such care free of charge. Under this system careful employers help to pay, through taxes, for losses occasioned by the carelessness of others. By charging employers at least part of the cost of treatment an incentive might be given to the adoption of safety devices and practices. With reference to the proposed medical insurance plan, it should be noted that most of the population already receives free or virtually free medical attention at government hospitals and clinics. Its principal effects would therefore be to increase the government's revenue from the medical services and to benefit the middle income groups who may now be unable to afford adequate medical care. While these are real advantages, any study of this proposal should also consider the administrative problem involved and the possibility that the plan might impose additional demands on the limited medical and hospital facilities which could not be satisfied. The institution of medical care insurance will probably have to be deferred until more doctors and more facilities for treatment are available.

HOUSING

In view of the low standard of living it is not surprising that housing conditions are bad. According to the 1943 census half of the dwellings in the Island, and 80% of those in Kingston, consisted of only one room, usually no larger than 10 by 15 feet in size. The average dwelling had 3.8 occupants, and in several parishes the average occupancy was substantially higher. The low-income classes are by no means the only ones suffering from poor housing. In 1951 a survey made in the corporate area of Kingston and St. Andrew revealed that 10,402 "middle and lower middle" income families earning £ 300 to £ 800 a year were crowded into 7,104 houses; of these, 1,904 averaged as many as 8.7 occupants. Overcrowded housing is unquestionably responsible for much crime and disease.

The need is overwhelming. Housing authorities in Jamaica have estimated that about 100,000 of the 325,000 units in the Island are so poor as to require urgent replacement. In addition 5,000 new dwellings or more should be built every year simply to take care of the increase in population. Existing housing programs offer no prospect that these requirements will be met. Government programs may provide about 20,000 units by 1956, and private enterprise perhaps another 12,000.

Until recently the Central Housing Authority has been the principal government organization concerned with housing. It has erected some rental housing in connection with slum clearance projects and has provided assistance for owner-occupier housing, both urban and rural, in organized settlements. To a limited extent it has also guaranteed building society loans in order to enable houseowners to obtain longer-term mortgages. This program involves an expenditure of about £ 1,900,000 most of which has already been disbursed. The Authority's activities have now been dwarfed by those of the Hurricane Housing Organization which was established to repair the serious housing damage caused by the hurricane of August 1951. The first object of the hurricane relief scheme has been to provide small grants to nearly 50,000 householders for building materials to make emergency repairs. The second and more important part of the program was launched only in the spring of 1952 and contemplates the replacement of some 14,000 dwellings which were destroyed or rendered incapable of repair. The cost of the entire scheme which will be completed in 1954 will amount to about £ 2.5 million, of which £ 2.25 million is financed from loans and grants by the United Kingdom. While the program will obviously not provide a net addition to housing accommodations, it should help to improve housing standards.

A broad and comprehensive attack on the housing problem would require expenditures clearly beyond the present capacity of the government, particularly in view of all the other claims on its limited resources. In the period immediately ahead primary emphasis will have to be put on the expansion of productive capacity. With the improvement of employment opportunities and incomes, people will gradually be able to afford better housing. After a considerable increase in production has been achieved the government may be able to devote more of its resources to assisting and supplementing private building.

We have accordingly allowed for only a rather modest government outlay of £ 4 million on housing in the period ending 1961-62.

We have already suggested that £ 2 million of this be spent on rural housing as an integral part of the agricultural development program. The remainder would be allocated to urban housing. Past experience has demonstrated that the construction of rental housing involves the government in substantial losses. The £ 2 million would accomplish more if it were lent to responsible low-income families for the purpose of assisting them in building modest houses of their own. The Central Housing Authority is now in fact concentrating on "owner-occupier" schemes of this type. This program will not meet the needs of the middle or lower income groups. For these groups the government might contemplate underwriting or guaranteeing part of the mortgage funds required. The objective would be to attract more private capital on reasonable terms for middle-income housing. Mortgages are now generally too short in duration, carry rather high interest rates and cover too small a proportion of the total cost. Government mortgage guaranties or insurance should therefore be conditioned on some alteration of the terms in favor of the house-owner. Requirements would also have to be formulated on the specifications to which housing would need to conform in order to qualify for this type of assistance.

The best means of improving the supply of housing should be the subject of continuous study. To this end, the Mission suggests that the government make particular efforts to establish those legal, technological, and financial arrangements which will encourage private investment. Measures to reduce the cost of building sites and of clearing and transferring titles will have to be worked out. The aerial and ground survey we have recommended will have as one of its objectives the establishment and registration of clear title to all property. It will above all be necessary to examine all possibilities of reducing construction costs. These costs are far too high. For example, it has cost £ 400 to £ 500, exclusive of the site, to build modest two-room cottages with a floor space of 240 square feet for workers on sugar estates. A unit of comparable size in a government-sponsored scheme cost £ 250. Experimentation is needed to develop low-cost, standardized construction materials and house plans which can be used safely and economically by persons with little or no knowledge of house-building. Experience with the rather large Hurricane Housing program should point to some of the possibilities. Under one of the schemes, the government will provide up to £ 120 of grants and loans for a one-room rural dwelling unit, an amout which the householder is expected to supplement through self-help. The Hurricane Housing Organization will give much of its help in the form of certain standardized prefabricated building materials. Further efforts on behalf of private housing as well as government-aided housing might well be directed particularly toward the use of abundant native materials in prepared building panels and blocks and toward further standardization of various building components so as to permit quantity production. Such studies might well be made jointly with other territories in the Carribean region, since they are confronted with equally acute needs for additional housing.

OTHER SOCIAL SERVICES

Government expenditures in this field fall into two categories: (1) prisons and industrial schools which absorb more than half of the total; and (2) general welfare activities, including grants-in-aid for services rendered by voluntary societies and parochial governments. In the first category capital outlays of about £ 600,000 will probably be necessary to effect urgent improvements and expansion in the facilities of prisons and industrial schools over the period ending in 1962. The projected relocation or major reconstruction of the general penitentiary, however, will have to be deferred. The steady increase in the institutional population which has been taking place might be retarded somewhat by development of probation methods and introduction of the parole system.

In the second category a small increase in outlays is also envisaged. These expenditures help to provide school lunches, finance the broad range of activities undertaken by the Jamaica Social Welfare Commission and the Juveniles Authority and assist the Child Welfare Association in its program for the distribution of milk to preschool children. In some instances a relatively small grant to a voluntary association relieves the government of larger financial and administrative responsibilities. The Jamaica Social Welfare Commission is particularly deserving of more support. It has done constructive work in fostering cottage industries and organizing community self-help measures which will have to play an increasingly important role if the entire development program is to succeed.

IX.

Financing of Development

To project a large development program without taking into account Jamaica's capacity to finance it would be an idle exercise. We have accordingly given careful attention to this problem. The total public expenditures entailed by the program have been projected and compared with the financial resources potentially available. All of the estimates of expenditures were necessarily based on present prices. Changes in prices must, of course, be anticipated, but they will also affect government revenues. Some consideration has also been given to the private investment outlays required, although in this field it has been impossible to make any quantitative estimates. In assessing the whole problem of financing it has been especially difficult to determine the financial resources which could be mobilized outside of Jamaica. The extent of these resources depends in part on the supply of capital available for investment and in part on the prospective returns of investment in Jamaica. The creditworthiness of Jamaica—i.e., its ability to raise funds—cannot be conceived in absolute terms. It is largely to the country's capacity to utilize these funds effectively so as to achieve a substantial increase in national income.

THE PUBLIC SECTOR

Government expenditures on development and total public expenditures have been projected on two alternative bases. The first assumes that the entire program outlined in preceding sections of this report will be carried out by the end of 1961-62. In our opinion, this should be the goal. We cannot ignore, however, the possibility that obstacles will arise to impede the rate of progress. A second or "reduced" program has accordingly also been drawn up. It anticipates in particular possible difficulties in borrowing abroad and a lag in the accomplishment of the ambitious agricultural development program. It is, of course, impossible to forecast exactly what adjustments might

TABLE 5

DEVELOPMENT PROGRAMS

(thousands of pounds)

	Maximum Program	Reduced Program
Agriculture		
Agricultural Development	9,041	6,800
Production and Development Loans (net)	4,640	2,770
Railway (capital investment)	670	670
Harbors	80	80
Airport	1,200	1,200
Land Survey	650	650
Sugar Factory	2,000	2,000
IDC Development Loans	3,500	3,000
IDC Technical Service	142	142
Rural Housing and Water Supplies	3,500	2,100
Urban Housing	2,000	1,700
Education (capital outlay)	4,401	4,161
Health (capital outlay)	2,700	2,700
Total Expenditures	34,524	27,973
Financing of the Program		
Contribution from Revenue	6,440	4,550
Colonial Development and Welfare Allocations up to 1956	1,860	1,860
Colonial Development and Welfare Grants 1956-61*	3,600	3,600
Government Borrowing	22,624	17,963
	34,524	27,973

* It is assumed that grants will be continued at approximately the same level as in the past. The amounts which will actually be provided is a matter for decision by the Government of the United Kingdom.

have to be made in the light of changing circumstances and prospects.

The expenditures and revenues under each of the two programs are given in Table 5. They are built up from more detailed estimates

TABLE 6

PROJECTION OF TOTAL ANNUAL GOVERNMENT EXPENDITURES
AND REVENUES
(millions of pounds)

| | | Annual Average 1953-54 to 1961-62 | |
	1952-53	Maximum Program	Reduced Program
Ordinary Budget Expenditure			
Development and Welfare[a]	6.03	7.08	6.98
Other[b]	6.61	7.25	6.99
Total Ordinary Expenditure	12.64	14.33	13.97
Revenue[c]	12.29	15.65	15.09
Budget Surplus (or deficit)	—0.35	+1.32	+1.12
Extraordinary Development Expenditures[d]	1.04	3.77	3.10
Balance to be financed by borrowed funds	1.39	2.45	1.98

[a] Includes expenditure on roads, health, education, socal welfare and public works.

[b] Includes net service charges on public debt.

[c] Including Colonial Development and Welfare grants.

[d] In 1952 this is expenditure from loan funds (excluding hurricane loan expenditure but including £ 350,000 for Palisades Airport). After 1952 it covers expenditure on the development programs.

of projected annual expenditures and the impact of such expenditures on revenues. [1] In accordance with existing practice, part of the expenditures in development are included in the regular budget or "ordinary estimates." Even a part of the extra-budgetary expenditure (which are classified in Jamaica as "development estimates") are to be financed out of budget revenues. This is brought out particularly in

---

[1] See the tables in Annex 33.

Table 6 which gives the total of all projected government expenditures over the entire period ending 1961-62 and shows how it is proposed to finance them. The figures in these two tables illustrate what is in our opinion an important requirement—that Jamaica should finance a substantial portion of the development program out of its own revenues. It will be impossible to marshall foreign resources for the program and limit borrowing to manageable proportions unless the Jamaicans themselves pay a large part of the cost out of current income.

The maximum program envisages total borrowing of about £ 22 million; the reduced program, £ 18 million. These estimates in turn rest on the assumption that government revenue will rise substantially. It is necessary both to explain this assumption and to assess the government's capacity to borrow.

Government Revenues

Government revenues will be determined largely by the rise in national income. We estimate that the maximum program will raise net output from a level of about £ 85 million in 1950 to £ 150 million in 1962 and that the reduced program will bring output to £ 136 million. With the larger program, production and income would rise at the rate of 5% a year. This is undoubtedly an unusually rapid increase. It should be remembered, however, that the scale of expenditures envisaged is in itself unprecedented for Jamaica, and it may be expected that these extraordinary outlays, if spent in accordance with the Mission's recommendations, will yield equally unprecedented results. In the recent past, production has risen significantly even in the absence of large development expenditures.

We have assumed that the government will take steps to insure that its revenues will increase in accordance with national income, i.e., at an annual rate of 5%, or at a rate of 4% if production rises more slowly in accordance with the reduced program. It might be argued that national income would not rise as rapidly in the initial years as in the later phase of the program and that a uniform rate

TABLE 7

NATIONAL INCOME
(millions of pounds)

	1943[1]	1950[2]	Maximum Program 1962[2]	Reduced Program 1962[2]
Primary Production	11.4	22.6	33	29
Secondary Production	3.7	9.5	19	17
Transport and Distribution	11.0	26.8	50	46
Government Services	4.2	6.5	12	11
Miscellaneous Services	6.1	13.5	26	24
Housing and Construction	3.5	6.1	10	9
Net Value of Output	39.9	85.0	150	136

[1] At 1943 prices. Source: *National Income of Jamaica,* prepared by the Central Bureau of Statistics. The figures were adjusted to a net output basis by the Mission.

[2] Estimate by the Mission on the basis of 1950 prices.

of growth in revenue cannot therefore be anticipated. We expect, however, that the marked expansion of public expenditures even in the earlier years will produce a considerable increase in money incomes. Insofar as this increase does not stimulate an immediate rise in domestic output, it will be reflected in an expansion of imports. Import duties now account for about 40% of the government's ordinary revenue.

While we do not propose a general increase in existing tax burdens, adjustments in tax rates may conceivably have to be made in order to maintain the present proportion of the total tax yield to national income. The extent and nature of the adjustments which may prove necessary are impossible to forecast. In general, we would advise against increasing significantly the rates of direct taxation which in 1950-51 accounted for a little over 22% of ordinary revenue. Higher direct taxation might easily make it impossible to attract the volume of private capital essential to economic development. In the long run the growth of manufacturing industries and of per capita incomes should increase the relative contribution of direct taxes to government revenues. Any major adjustment for the short term will therefore probably have to be made in indirect taxes, including customs duties[2] and excises. If prices of Jamaica's exports again rise, the government will have an opportunity to impose export taxes with minimum disturbance to the economy. In the immediate postwar period of rising prices it unfortunately did not avail itself of a similar opportunity.

In addition to tax revenues we have anticipated continuation of Colonial Development and Welfare grants from the United Kingdom. These are assured only until 1956 when the Colonial Development and Welfare Act will expire. It seems reasonable to suppose, however, that some provision for grants will continue to be made.

Projected Debt Charges

The borrowing required—£ 22.6 million or £ 18 million, depending on which of the two programs is followed—would mean a substantial addition to the gross public debt which stood at £ 14,056,000 at the end of March 1952. Even a total debt of £ 36.7 million, however, would represent only about 24% of the national income anticipated by 1962 under the maximum program. There should be no serious difficulty in servicing this debt out of rising government revenues. A large part of the expenditures on agricultural and industrial development and all of the expenditures on housing and agricultural credit will be in the form of loans which will be serviced by the recipients. The budget will have to carry probably between £ 12 million and £ 14 million of the debt that would be incurred under the larger program. Annual debt charges against ordinary revenues would rise from

---

[2] It should be noted, however, that customs duties are already high. In 1950-51 customs receipts represented 18.3% of the value of imports in 1950.

£ 576,000[3] in 1952-53 (just over 5% of ordinary revenue) perhaps to £ 1,350,000[4] (about 7.4% of estimated revenue) in 1961-62. Under the smaller program, the increase in the public debt chargeable against ordinary revenue will be about £ 11 million and total debt charges will probably reach £ 1.19 million or 7.05% of ordinary revenue. In the Mission's opinion, the budget should be capable of carrying these charges.

Sources of Borrowing

The government will be able to raise some money in the local market. During the war it borrowed considerable sums locally, but since 1946 the increasing private demand for the limited funds available for investment has made it impossible to raise much more than a million. In the future, savings will presumably rise as development proceeds, and the government should be able to mobilize part of this increase for public investment.

Savings in Jamaica are primarily institutional in form, i.e., they go to insurance companies, building societies, and certain organized groups of agricultural producers who accumulate crop insurance and price stabilization funds. Noninstitutional savings other than business savings have apparently been negligible in recent years. In the three years 1948 to 1950, withdrawals from the government savings bank exceeded deposits. Savings deposits in commercial banks, which were £ 5.5 million in December 1945, fell to £ 4.9 million in December 1948 but recovered to £ 5.7 million by the end of 1951.

If therefore, the government is to raise sums of any size within

---

[3] Although £ 890,000 was voted for debt service in 1952-53, only £ 576,000 of this sum can be regarded as a direct charge on revenue. The remainder is paid by municipal and other bodies as interest and sinking fund charges on funds relent to them by the government.

[4] While the terms on which loans will be raised cannot be accurately forecast, we have allowed for 4½% interest and an annual allocation of 1% to sinking fund. The latter provision is customary for loans raised in the United Kingdom and reflects our assumption that most or all of the borrowing will take place in that country.

the country, it will have to be principally from insurance companies, banks, and to some extent from the assets of certain crop funds. In March 1952 life insurance companies held locally issued government securities amounting to £ 1,881,000, which represented probably about 25% of the assets of these companies attributable to their business in Jamaica. The total value of life insurance policies issued in Jamaica has been increasing rapidly since the war and by the end of 1950 had reached £ 21.4 million as compared to £ 11.4 million at the end of 1945. Since the investment policy of the companies varies, it is not easy to say how much of their assets they will be prepared to invest in the future inside Jamaica. At present their holdings of Jamaican government securities amount on the average to about 25% of their total assets. If the amount of life insurance in force were to increase by £ 1.5 million a year, or somewhat below the recent rate of almost £ 2 million a year, the assets corresponding to the total outstanding at the end of ten years should reach about £ 12.5 million. If it were possible to persuade the companies to invest, say, 35% of these assets in Jamaica government securities their holdings would amount to £ 4,375,000 or almost £ 2.5 million more than at present.

The other important sources of savings which may be tapped by the government are the commercial banks[5] and the various crop funds. In the investment of their resources both of these must pay careful attention to their liquidity requirements. The absence of a ready market in Jamaica for long-term government bonds restricts the amounts which they could purchase. The issue of medium three to five year bonds would go some way to compensate for this situation, and the government would not ordinarily have difficulty in refunding them upon maturity. In March 1952 the commercial banks held almost £ 2 million of government securities, and with the general expansion of their resources which will take place as development proceeds their holdings might reasonably be expected to increase by another £ 1 million. Furthermore, they may be able to

---

[5] A note on the banking system is given in Annex 35.

assume responsibility for a large portion of the short-term crop production loans amounting to £ 3.3 million which have included in the program as government expenditures. At the end of 1951, the banks had outstanding £ 1.6 million in agricultural loans to clients of recognized credit rating, and they may be expected to provide more of this type of accommodation as their resources expand and agricultural production increases. While the commercial banks cannot be expected to grant loans to thousands of small farmers, they may find it possible to extend credit to the Loan Societies Board for production loans granted by the People's Cooperative Banks, provided the government guarantees such credits.

The most important of the agricultural crop funds are the sugar price stabilization fund and the banana industry funds. At the end of 1951 the sugar price stabilization fund had accumulated just over £ 1 million; and it has already offered to lend £ 500,000 to the Agricultural Development Corporation. Unless there is a marked fall in sugar prices this fund may be expected to rise by £ 250,000 to £ 300,000 per year. The banana insurance fund and the banana profits fund which together amounted to almost £1 million were both utilized for the post-hurricane banana rehabilitation scheme. It is expected that they will again reach a total of £ 1 million by the end of 1953 and about £ 1.5 million by the end of 1954, always assuming that there are no further emergency calls upon them. It is perhaps not unreasonable to hope that these various funds might be able to lend £ 1.5 million to the development program over the decade.

Finally, investors other than insurance companies and banks held just over £ 3 million of locally issued government securities in March 1952. Although the opening of other investment opportunities will reduce the amount available for government bonds, it is possible that another £ 500,000 to £ 700,000 may be obtainable over the next ten years from these sources. Altogether, therefore, probably between £ 6 million and £ 8 million should be available locally to finance the development plan. The necessary external borrowing will thus be £ 14 million to £ 16 million for the full program and £ 10 million to £ 12 million for the reduced program.[6]

It is difficult to determine whether amounts of this size can be raised abroad. In view of the uncertain economic situation the ability of the capital market in the United Kingdom to meet domestic requirements as well as colonial development needs cannot be predicted with any accuracy. While we have reason to believe that the external borrowing required by the maximum program may be managed, one reason for contemplating a more limited program is the possibility that all the necessary funds may not be available.

THE PRIVATE SECTOR

The large size of the public investment program is predicated on the reasonable assumption, among others, that private investment is likely to fall far short of development needs, particularly in the field of agriculture. A substantial volume of private investment will still be required, however, in the manufacturing and tourist industries, and, to a somewhat smaller extent, in agriculture and housing. Since domestic savings, even though increasing, will fall far short of meeting these requirements, foreign capital will have to supply a substantial portion of the private investment funds.

In agriculture the private investment needed to supplement the government's assistance program for small farmers should not be difficult to achieve. It can take the form of labor supplied by the beneficiaries of the program themselves. The large farmers and

---

[6] Probably all or almost all of these funds can be raised in the United Kingdom. If borrowing in hard currencies should prove necessary, the foreign exchange required for servicing such loans would have to come from the sterling area dollar pool. Jamaica normally runs a dollar deficit although its dollar earnings have risen from $13.2 million in 1947 to $19.5 million in 1951. Dollar payments dropped from $52.9 million in 1947 to $17.7 million in 1951 but rose again in 1951 to $28.4 million. The development program may be expected to increase direct dollar earnings, particularly from the tourist trade, and to stimulate the production of commodities such as sugar which save dollars for the United Kingdom.

estates will have to rely largely on reinvestment of profits to the extent that they cannot borrow from commercial banks or the agricultural credit institutions. In recent years some large agricultural properties have been bought for development by foreign investors; and the future may witness more of this type of investment as the prospects of agriculture improve.

In housing the building societies and, to some extent, the insurance companies will supply the bulk of private capital. No doubt this will continue to be insufficient in relation to acute housing needs. However unfortunate it may seem, substantial improvement in housing will have to wait until Jamaica has achieved a marked expansion in productive capacity and an accompanying rise in incomes and savings.

With respect to industry we have already commented at length on the conditions necessary to attract foreign capital. If the inducements offered by the government are supplemented by an energetic campaign to raise the efficiency of production, additional foreign capital may well be forthcoming. In recent years the textile mill, the cement factory, and the pre-stressed concrete plant have all been built up largely with foreign capital. There is no reason to believe that the capital required for the expansion of the power industry will not be available.

The tourist industry has demonstrated an increasing ability to attract foreign investment, including American capital. In view of the favorable prospects of the industry, this trend may well be expected to continue, particularly if the government provides assistance along the lines we have recommended.

Residents in the sterling area can make investments in Jamaica without restrictions. Foreign exchange regulations cannot on the whole be regarded as a significant deterrent to dollar investment. Facilities for transfer of income and for ultimate repatriation of capital are granted for any dollar investment approved by foreign exchange control authorities, and approval is normally given for any investment likely to benefit Jamaica. To a very limited extent, residents of dollar areas may also use blocked sterling already in their possession, or acquired at a discount, for new investments in Jamaica. This requires official permission, however, and the authorities in the United Kingdom are understandably reluctant to give their consent for fear that such new investment would be used primarily as a means to evade foreign exchange control. Permission can be obtained in exceptional cases, particularly when the new investment is likely to save or earn dollars for the sterling area. On this basis, the tourist industry offers the most promising prospect of attracting blocked sterling.[7]

INVESTMENT, INFLATION AND THE BALANCE OF PAYMENTS

Many countries which undertake large development programs encounter difficulties arising from inflation and an adverse pressure on the balance of payments. Is it likely that Jamaica will experience problems of this kind in the execution of the program we have recommended?

Inflation can develop only if the supply of money and money incomes increases more rapidly than the availability of goods from domestic production and from imports. The investment program will undoubtedly cause a considerable expansion of money incomes which will in turn produce a demand for more goods and services. The program cannot be carried out, however, unless substantial external resources are obtained for its financing; and the sterling (or foreign) exchange from such capital imports will be available to meet the greater demand for imports. The present arrangements controlling the issue of currency provide assurance that expenditure on the development program cannot exceed the real resources available for its financing. Under these arrangements the Jamaican pound is backed 100% by sterling and complete convertibility with sterling is therefore assured. Any local borrowing by the Jamaican Government is therefore, in effect, the borrowing of already convertible

---

[7] In the last three years permission to use blocked sterling for new investments was apparently given in only three cases, and it is perhaps significant that two of these were for new ventures in the tourist industry.

141

currency so that, if necessary, its expenditure on development could always be matched by increased imports.[8]

In this process adjustments may be required which could exert either an upward or a downward influence on local prices. Rising money incomes will increase the demand for domestic goods as well as for imports. The supply of domestic goods may rise only in response to higher prices or may not respond sufficiently to the increased demand so that the deficiency may have to be met by more costly imports. This will be particularly true in cases where the local price is controlled, for the price of imports will normally be higher than the controlled price. The case of meat at the present time illustrates this possibility. The low price fails to encourage expansion of output and imports cannot be obtained except at much higher prices.

It is also necessary for export production to expand with the rise in incomes. If export production lags, the maintenance of imports will lead to some deflationary movements resulting from a fall in the money supply. The same result would follow from an adverse movement in the terms of trade. These are the sort of adjustments which have to be made continually in all except the most static economies and as the development program should lead to a substantial increase in production both for export and for domestic consumption, we do not expect that the necessary price and output changes will entail any unusual degree of difficulty.

With rising output and productivity some rise in money wages may be expected. So long as it does not run ahead of the increase in labor productivity it should be welcomed as an index of the progress of development.

---

[8] In further elaboration of this point see Annex 34.

X.

Summary and Conclusions

In the preceding chapters of this report a comprehensive development program for a period of ten years has been outlined. We have indicated our belief that this program would increase net output at the rate of about 5% per year. The production of goods and services would rise from an estimated level of £ 85 million in 1950 to approximately £ 150 million in 1962. For the smaller program the increase would be to about £ 136 million. The effect in employment must now be assessed.

In the introduction it was brought out that the increase in population expected by 1962 would make it necessary to find employment opportunities for 100,000 to 110,000 people if the present high percentage of unemployed in the labor force were not to rise still further, and for 180,000 to 210,000 if the proportion of unemployment were to be reduced to 5%. We have estimated that agriculture may offer employment for an additional 35,000. The tourist trade may furnish direct employment for another 8,000. Factory employment may increase by approximately 15,000. In addition, perhaps 10,000 more may be absorbed by the "manufacturing" trades such as dressmaking, shoe-repairing, cabinet-making and similar occupations which employed about 46,000 in 1942.[1] To this total increase of perhaps 68,000 in employment in the so-called primary and secondary industries (agriculture, manufacturing and the tourist trade) must be added the rise in employment in the remaining or tertiary occupations. The extent of this addition is determined by the development of employment in the primary and secondary industries and by the rise in the standard of living. The volume of tertiary employment is extremely difficult to predict, but as incomes rise it may

---

[1] The census of 1943 recorded about 60,000 people in "manufacturing industry" of whom a little over 14,000 were employed in factories as defined by the factories law. By 1951, "factory" employment had increased to 23,000, but other manufacturing employment probably rose much less rapidly.

increase somewhat more rapidly than primary and secondary employment, particularly since there will still be many people seeking full or partial employment in tertiary occupations. We have accordingly estimated this increase at roughly 75,000 which would bring the total additional employment to 143,000. This would represent a very substantial improvement but would still leave a residual unemployment equal to between 8% and 10% of the labor force.

While these estimates are subject to a considerable margin of error, employment will undoubtedly lag considerably behind the expansion in production. This is the primary reason for carrying out the maximum development program we have projected. If targets are lowered to those of the reduced program, the increase in employment will be still smaller than that indicated above. The persistence of considerable unemployment even under conditions of growing prosperity seems quite probable. A further reduction in unemployment can in the end be achieved only through emigration, the possibility of which is limited, and a limitation of population growth.

Most of the expansion of production and employment we foresee will result directly or indirectly from the development of agriculture. Contrary to widely prevalent belief, we are convinced that the potentialities of agriculture in Jamaica are far from exhausted. With proper use of land and water resources a much greater output can be achieved. A vigorous soil conservation campaign is required to rebuild the fertility of the hill lands which have been largely destroyed by reckless, shifting cultivation. In the plains and valleys, irrigation must be extended and part of the swamp land reclaimed. A pasture improvement program should be undertaken and beef prices raised to ensure intensification of the livestock industry. A complete aerial and ground survey is needed to provide the data necessary for proper planning of land use and for carrying out the essential improvement works. The taxation of land on the basis of its unimproved value would give an additional incentive to development. With these measures it should be possible to add about 150,000 acres to the land under cultivation and to enhance yields significantly. This would permit a substantial increase in the production of beef and milk, sugar, bananas, coffee, cacao, citrus, rice and other food crops.

To accomplish all this, energetic efforts must be made to enlist the cooperation of farmers and a comprehensive scheme of grants and loans will have to be launched to provide the necessary inducements. Generous provision should be made for agricultural credit, particularly to enable farmers to establish crops in accordance with approved land use patterns. Some help will also be needed for rural housing and water supply. Rapid and continuing progress with this entire improvement program will be impossible, however, unless in the future the government conditions all forms of assistance to farmers on their cooperation in these development schemes. The government should also be empowered by law to proceed against small minorities who, despite all inducements, refuse to participate in cooperative improvement programs which are imperative in the interests of the country as a whole.

More limited possibilities exist in manufacturing industries. At present about 60% of industry is engaged in the processing of local agricultural commodities and nearly all of the rest in turning out goods and services which by their nature can be most advantageously produced in the market where they are consumed. These branches of manufacturing will undoubtedly continue to expand. In other manufacturing industries Jamaica suffers from a number of serious handicaps and can offer only one potential advantage in the form of a plentiful labor supply. This advantage can be converted into a real asset only if the efficiency of production is greatly improved. Despite the low level of wages, labor costs in industry are generally higher in Jamaica than in the United Kingdom.

Efforts must accordingly be concentrated on raising labor productivity. The inauguration of an appropriate apprenticeship system and expansion and improvement of facilities for technical education will help considerably. The Industrial Development Corporation will have to provide technical and financial assistance on a considerable scale in order to overcome existing deficiences in industrial management and capital equipment. Management and labor must be more ready than in the past to cooperate not only in developing harmonious industrial relations but also in improving efficiency and lowering labor costs. The government program for attracting capital to industry by tax inducements, moderate tariff protection and similar measures is generally adequate. The experience of the past, however, demonstrates the need for vigilance against measures of excessive protection which foster inefficient industry.

Prospects of the tourist industry are promising. While its development can be left largely to private enterprise, the government can stimulate it by making more funds available for an effective campaign to advertise the undoubted attractions of Jamaica and by reorganizing the Tourist Development Board to make it more directly representative of those who have an immediate interest in vigorous promotion of the tourist trade. The government might also supplement the measures it has already adopted to encourage investment in the hotel industry by providing a strictly limited guarantee of investments in hotels, particularly in new areas which might be opened up for tourist development.

The recent development of the island's extensive bauxite deposits has greatly stimulated the mining industry. It will employ, however, relatively few workers in the future, especially in relation to the employment peak attained in the immediate past on the construction of the necessary installations. There is some prospect that other mineral resources will be developed.

In the fields of power and transport certain measures will have to be taken if they are to keep pace with expanding production in agriculture and industry. The supply of electric power in recent years has been barely adequate to the demand but will improve with the expansion now under way. Tentative plans for further expansion of generating capacity may be too conservative and ought to be reviewed in the light of expected requirements. The 40-cycle power frequency is a considerable handicap to industry. In view of the industrial development impending, the time has come to carry out the long-delayed plan to convert the system to 50-cycle which along with the 60-cycle figuring is standard in the world today.

SUMMARY AND CONCLUSIONS

In transport the most urgent requirements is to put the railway on a sound footing. The railway is essential to the island's economy, but the heavy deficit at which it operates imposes a serious burden on the government budget. The existing low freight rates should be raised in order to compensate the railway more adequately for the services it performs. To stimulate efficient operation the railway should be placed under an autonomous administration and enabled to carry out a modest capital improvement program. If these steps are taken, the railway will be able to profit fully from the expected increase in traffic and to eliminate very largely the present deficit.

The existing road network seems adequate for the island's needs. Maintenance, however, has been very poor, and much larger funds must be made available for this purpose if the progressive deterioration of the past is to be reversed. Expenditures on road construction and improvement have been largely wasted because political considerations have been required their distribution over numerous projects. There is little need for entirely new roads, and funds appropriated for improvement and reconstruction should be concentrated on a few roads of key importance to the economy as a whole.

Harbors and ports apparently have the capacity to handle a much larger volume of traffic. In Kingston the primary need is to relieve the serious congestion of the waterfront area, an objective that would be considerably advanced by the replacement of the out-dated Wharfage Act. The airport at Kingston will require improvement and expansion to enable it to accommodate larger and faster aricraft.

It is difficult to determine exactly what provision a development program must make for the social services—education, health and housing. In this general field further improvement in education appears most urgent and most directly related to the development of the productive capacity of the country. Expansion of facilities for vocational and technical education is particularly important. Also urgent is a gradual increase in the number of primary

147

schools which today can provide accommodation for only a little over half the children of school-going age. This should be accompanied, however, by steps to give education a less academic and more practical orientation. Health standards, while hardly ideal, have been improved to such an extent that large expenditures on an expansion of medical and hospital services going beyond the requirements arising from the increase in population would be an unwarranted use of Jamaica's limited resources at this time. Some increase in outlays will be necessary, however, to expand the preventive services, to effect urgent improvements in some hospitals and relieve serious overcrowding in others. In the housing field, the needs are so great that the means available to meet them will for a long time remain wholly inadequate. Over the years immediately ahead the government can afford only a very modest supplement to the hurricane housing program it is currently undertaking. It should be feasible, however, to take constructive steps to facilitate private investment and lower building costs.

The proposed development program will necessitate borrowing up to £ 22 million over a ten-year period. If the money can be found—and we believe that all or most of it will be available—there should be little question about Jamaica's capacity to carry this additional debt. This judgement, however, is subject to the important proviso that the money is wisely spent in such a way that the goals of the program are in fact achieved. This is the responsibility of the government and people of Jamaica. In the past there has been an inclination to consider finance the crucial and even the only obstacle to development. The elimination of this obstacle in other countries has frequently brought to light even more serious difficulties, particularly the lack of sufficient enterprise and energy and of capacity for organization and cooperation. Capital can only supplement and facilitate the work which Jamaicans must themselves devote to the development of their resources. In the last analysis only confidence can sustain the continued flow of capital from abroad, and this confidence can be created only if the people of

Jamaica evince a determination to lift themselves by their own efforts.

The program will demand of the government and people a degree of singlemindedness and cooperation which has not hitherto been evident. This condition can be achieved only if the people understand the program and rally behind it. The people must know what the program is, what it will do for them and what it will require of them. A publicity campaign on a large scale will be necessary to disseminate this knowledge. It must enlist the participation of the press and radio and of all groups and organizations—the churches, the teachers, and the farmers associations—who are in intimate touch with the people. If the people understand the program they will realize more readily the advantages and obligations of wholehearted participation and will be less likely to tolerate any diversion from its fundamental objectives.

Jamaica today is at a crucial stage of its political and economic development. In the near future important steps in the direction of complete self-government will be taken. The success of this venture may well be jeopardized unless economic progress can also be assured. Jamaica can support its population under conditions of political and economic stability only if an imaginative, farsighted development program is vigorously prosecuted. In this task the people of Jamaica face a great challenge.

Annexes

Selected Statistics

1. Total Population

1943	1951	1961
1,237,063	1,443,699[a]	1,700,800[b]

[a] Provisional.

[b] Estimate by G. W. Roberts, *Population Trends in the British Caribbean.*

2. Labor Force

1943	1951	1961
514,000	600,000	730,000

Note: The labor force in 1951 and 1961 has been estimated by assuming it to be the same proportion of the age-group 15-64 as shown in the 1943 census. There are some indications that the population estimate for 1961 may be on the low side and the labor force may be as high as 738,000.

3. Gainfully Occupied Population

	1943
Agriculture	221,376
Manufacturing	59,229
Construction	34,149
Trade	38,540
Services and Unspecified	106,897
Total	460,191

Note: The difference between the gainfully occupied population and the labor force is accounted for by some 54,000 persons under the age of 25 who stated they were seeking a job but had never found one.

4. External Trade

	Total Imports	Domestic Exports
	(£ thousands)	
1938	6,485	4,926
1946	12,452	8,575
1947	18,943	9,939
1948	19,681	11,150
1949	19,225	11,843
1950	22,379	14,663

SELECTED STATISTICS

	Import Price Index	Export Price Index
1938	100	100
1948	326	319
1949	314	290
1950	330	321

PRINCIPAL COMMODITIES EXPORTED
(£ thousands)

	1947	1948	1949	1950
Sugar	2,656	3,482	4,702	5,934
Rum	2,569	2,043	1,292	1,559
Bananas	2,049	2,321	2,270	2,116
Citrust & Citrus Products[1]	289	476	537	564
Tobacco, cigars	906	502	385	564
Ginger	119	125	130	341
Pimento	155	223	405	291
Coffee	138	129	131	341
Cocoa	143	351	204	204

[1] Citrus pulp, grapefruits, limes and lime oil, oranges and orange oil.

TRADE WITH PRINCIPAL COUNTRIES
(£ thousands)

	United Kingdom		Canada		United States	
	Value	% of Total	Value	% of Total	Value	% of Total
1938						
Imports	2,109	32.6	1,014	15.6	1,359	20.9
Exports	2,939	58.5	1,316	26.2	203	4.0
1948						
Imports	7,762	39.5	3,595	18.3	3,826	19.5
Exports	8,388	74.0	1,902	16.8	390	3.4
1949						
Imports	8,669	45.0	2,483	12.9	3,174	16.5
Exports	7,505	62.0	3,141	25.9	450	3.7
1950						
Imports	9,600	43.0	2,230	10.0	3,193	14.3
Exports	8,592	56.7	3,951	26.1	782	5.2

5. *Primary Production*

SELECTED COMMODITIES 1943 AND 1950

Commodity	Unit	Production 1943[a] Quantity	Production 1943[a] Value (£)	Production 1950[b] Quantity	Production 1950[b] Value (£)
Bananas	Stem	11,700,00	858,400	7,700,000	1,447,000
Cocoa	Ton	3,060	136,000	2,100	197,600
Coconuts	Nut	158,000,000	583,400	102,000,000	556,400
Coffee	Ton	3,348[c]	140,600	2,020	181,000
Corn	Ton	12,000	130,500	17,300	426,000
Oranges, sweet	Field box	450,000	90,000	725,000	200,000
Grapefruits	"	525,000	105,000	700,000	170,000
Eggs	Dozen	1,500,000	112,500	1,800,000	247,500
Fresh beef	Lb.	13,000,000	365,100	18,400,000	844,000
Fresh pork	Lb.	3,600,000	96,200	3,930,000	153,000
Poultry, etc.	Lb.	549,000	25,200	600,000	75,000
Fish	Lb.	5,600,000	164,000	5,800,000	300,000
Fresh Cow's Milk	Gallon	5,000,000	328,000	7,000,000	725,000
Rice	Ton	2,340	106,700	4,450	225,000
Ginger	Ton	1,142	91,100	1,326	356,400
Pimento	Ton	2,600	214,200	1,973	172,400
Sugar Cane	Ton	1,800,000	1,621,000	2,568,000	4,130,200
Tobacco Leaf	Lb.	2,000,000	140,000	2,000,000	280,000
Tomatoes	Ton	5,000	115,000	6,960	123,400
Total			£ 5,422,900		£ 10,809,900

[a] From 1943 National Income estimate.
[b] Estimate by Central Bureau of Statistics.
[c] Probably too high. Census shows amount harvested in 1942 as 2,640 tons.

Notes: The total value of primary production in 1943, according to the National Income estimate, was £ 12,699,000. The commodities listed above were 43% of the total. The most important items omitted are root crops, pulses and vegetables.

From the above data the following indexes can be calculated based on 1943 = 100.

Volume Index 1950 (Base weights) = 112.3
Price Index 1950 (Current weights) = 177.5

6. Secondary Production
SELECTED COMMODITIES 1943 AND 1950

Commodity	Unit	Production 1943			Production 1950
		Quantity	Factory Value (£)	Net Output (£)	Quantity
Aerated water	000 gal.	750	209,000	138,950	2,087
Beer, etc.	" "	346.5	104,100	48,860	797
Boots and shoes	doz. pairs	1,682	25,500	9,000	8,467
Bread, bis- cuits, etc.	Ton	32,322	1,600,000	730,000	39,062
Cigarettes	000	385,000	450,000	147,000	427,500
Condensed Milk	Ton	2,043	109,800	44,900	5,313
Copra	"	18,422	423,000	13,000	7,500
Cornmeal	"	4,259	64,200	10,000	4,931
Edible Oil	000 gal.	1,104	230,700	40,360	561.3
Margarine, lard, butterine	Ton	2,679	243,400	63,280	2,221
Electricity	000 kwh	30,090	242,200	198,200	76,038
Ice	Ton	74,000	102,000	87,000	105,100
Matches	000 gross bxs.	1,812	92,800	26,160	2,125.5
Meal, feed, etc.	Ton	3,180	82,000	67,000	3,900
Rum	000 liq. gal.	1,933.1	418,000	298,000	2,127.3
Soap	Ton	4,320	237,700	80,930	5,712
Sugar	"	177,770	2,352,500	367,700	271,582
Total			£6,986,900	£2,370,340	

Note: Data for 1943 are from the National Income estimate and those for 1950 are by the Central Bureau of Statistics. Net output is equal to factory value less cost of materials and, in some cases, excise duty.

From these data an index of the rise in net output may be derived using the net output per unit 1943 as weights. From the data as given above this index equals 149 (1943 = 100). This result is somewhat on the high side owing to some duplication in the figures particularly in regard to electricity. If the consumption of electricity for industrial uses is subtracted from the totals shown, the index is reduced to 147.

THE ECONOMIC DEVELOPMENT OF JAMAICA

7. *Consumption*

ANNUAL PER CAPITA AVAILABILITY
OF CERTAIN COMMODITIES, 1943 AND 1950

Commodity	Unit	Total Supplies Per Capita	
		1943	1950
Bread	Lb.	57.9	62.4
Flour & meal of wheat	”	32.4	33.9
Cornmeal	”	7.5	7.9
Beef	”	10.5	13.4
Pork	”	2.8	2.8
Fresh fish	”	4.5	4.1
Codfish	”	7.2	7.2
Mackeral	”	3.6	4.4
Butter	”	0.8	1.1
Eggs	Dozen	1.2	1.3
Sugar	Lb.	53.8	80.0[a]
Cigarettes	No.	513.0	480.0[b]
Aerated water	Gallons	0.6	1.5
Beer	”	0.5	1.0[b]
Soap	Lb.	7.7	9.4
Boots and shoes	Pairs	0.5	0.8
Electricity	kwh	2.6	8.2[c]

[a] No adjustment made for sugar used in manufacture of confectionery, condensed milk, etc.

[b] Per capita persons aged 15 and over.

[c] For domestic use.

156

Land: Utilization, Distribution and Tenure

LAND UTILIZATION

The census of 1943 remains the basic source of information regarding land utilization. A sample survey made in 1950 has made it possible, however, to revise the census data to some extent.

The total area of the island is 2,823,000 acres of which only 570,000 acres or 20% are flat, consisting of alluvium, marl (limestone) and swamps. The area used for agricultural purposes in 1950 is estimated at 1,018,000 acres, of which 423,000 acres are arable land and orchards, and 595,000 acres, permanent meadows and pastures. Of these pastures, only 57,000 acres (10%) have been improved by good agricultural practices; and of the total agricultural area, only 41,400 acres are irrigated (35,400 acres arable land and 6,000 acres pastures).

Of the rest of the island, some 500,000 acres (18%) is considered forest land. About 312,000 acres (11%) are not used for any purpose but are considered potentially productive; this area is partly under shifting cultivation, and 2,000 acres are in process of reclamation. Moreover, there is a vast area of 878,000 acres (31%) of permanent wasteland, in which are included 5,300 acres of swamps, 175,000 acres of alienated[1] wasteland and 650,000 acres of unalienated lands of low productivity, which have never been surveyed and are not under forest. Finally, the area used for buildings, roads, railways, etc. is estimated at 115,000 acres.

DISTRIBUTION OF LAND

The 1943 census, supplemented by the sample agricultural survey of 1950, is also the principal source of information about the number and size of farms, and forms of ownership and management.

The basic data supplied by the census may be summarized as follows:

---

[1] *I.e.*, transferred from Crown property to private property.

(a) Total population in 1943: 1,237,000

    Rural population 1,013,000

        Number of people on farms 362,200

        Operators of farms and members
           of operators' families 104,600
        Regular employees 59,600
        Temporary employees 47,400

(b) Number of farms 66,200

    Number operated by:

        Owners 38,300
        Managers 600
        Tenants 6,900
        Part owners and part tenants 20,400
        Number of holdings comprising farms 138,000

(c) Total area[2] 2,823,200

    Area in farms 1,793,700
        Area under cultivation 383,000
        Area operated by owners 1,071,100
        Area operated by tenants 114,200
        Area operated by managers 608,300

(d) Number of plots other than "farms"
    producing some crops 146,500
    Number classified as "backyards" 46,500

The census defined a "farm" as land directly farmed by one person which had either an area of at least one acre or had a production in 1942 valued at £15 or more. A farm may consist of more than one "holding." The 146,500 plots smaller than "farms" covered, according to figures of the Collector General, an area of 69,000 acres or an average of about half an acre.

Of the 66,000 farms, 61,000 are of the mixed type. Only a small number of them specialize in one crop. The census counted

---

[2] All area figures are in acres.

1,000 banana farms, 1,500 sugar cane farms, 900 root crop farms, 600 livestock farms and small numbers of other one crop farms.

Census data on the size of farms are given in the following table:

FARMS CLASSIFIED BY SIZE (1943)

Class		Acreage (in thousands of acres)	Number of Farms (in thousands)	Percentage of Area		Legal Position		
				Under Cultivation	In Pasture	Owned	Rented	Managed
						(in thousands of acres)		
1-2	acres	10	8	77	6	6	4	—
2-3	"	23	10	71	7	15	8	0.2
3-4	"	27	8	64	10	19	7	—
4-6	"	54	12	55	13	42	12	—
6-10	"	83	11	45	18	71	12	0.1
10-25	"	172	12	31	24	152	19	1.0
25-50	"	99	3	21	30	87	9	2
50-100	"	71	1	16	36	61	6	4
100-200	"	67	0.5	16	35	52	4	11
200-500	"	120	0.4	16	36	85	4	31
500-1000	"	146	0.2	18	42	73	5	68
over 1000	"	921	0.3	15	37	407	24	491

It will be noted that farms of four to 25 acres account for little over half the total number. In area, however, they comprise less than a fifth of the total and a little less than one third of that under cultivation. The smaller farms have a larger proportion of their area under cultivation, the proportion of land devoted to pasture increasing steadily with the size of the farm. Most of the rented land is in the smaller farms. Only the larger farms are operated by managers.

From the sample survey made in 1950 it was concluded that some 30,000 farms changed in size since 1942. Approximately 15,000 small farms of less than 10 acres increased in size, while 7,000 other small farms diminished. In the group of medium-sized farms of between 10 and 50 acres nearly 2,700 increased, and more than 3,700 decreased in size. Nearly 800 of the larger farms increased in size, and more than 2,000 of these had a smaller acreage in 1950. Altogether, 18,000 farms "grew," while 12,000 diminished over these eight years. As the net result of these changes, the number of medium-sized farms was greater, and the number of large units smaller, in 1950.

The sample survey of 1950 also indicated that some 12,000 new holdings, including 4,000 in Land Settlements, had been created since 1942. On the other hand, 8,000 holdings were absorbed by other units, so that there was only a net increase of 4,000 in the total number. Since a farm generally consists of two holdings, the number of farms rose by only 2,000.

Changes in the number of farms classified by size are shown in the following table:

NUMBER OF FARMS

	1942	1950
1-4 acres	33,200	32,000
5-9 "	16,000	16,950
10-24 "	11,500	13,300
25-49 "	2,970	3,360
50-99 "	1,070	1,140
100-199 "	490	440
200-499 "	380	390
500 and more	532	495
Total	66,142	68,075

LAND TENURE

According to the 1943 census, there were only 7,000 tenants and 20,000 part-tenants out of a total of 66,000 farmers. Of the entire area in farms—1.8 million acres—only 114,000 acres were rented. Tenancy is a much greater problem, however, than these figures suggest. First of all, a large proportion of the smaller farmers rent all or part of their land. Secondly, rented land accounts for a higher percentage of cultivated land than of the total area in farms. Finally, and most important of all, land is generally rented for only a short period, so that the tenant has no incentive to farm it well and improve it. Tenancy is responsible for much of the shifting hillside cultivation which has been so destructive of land in Jamaica.

In 1940 a committee was appointed to draft a new Tenancy Law. This draft was published in 1942 and endorsed by the Agricultural Policy Committee in 1945. In that year legislation, largely along the lines drawn by the tenancy committee, was enacted, as the Agricultural Small Holdings Law of 1945. This law, which covers farms of less than 50 acres, provides for compensation for improvements made by tenants, and for disturbance of tenants by landlords. The minimum duration prescribed for tenancy—only 18 months—is, however, much too short. It should be lengthened, and the tenant should at the same time be given the right to prolong the contract as long as he follows satisfactory agricultural practices.

The size of farms, however, is more important than questions of ownership and tenancy. Many farms are too small to support a family. The trend toward middle-sized farms should be fostered as far as possible. Among the measures which might be adopted to this end, the following are the most important:

(a) The use of a considerable portion of the new land made available for cultivation by the agricultural development program to increase the size of existing small farms rather than to create new farms;

(b) Bringing a large percentage of the area of the smaller farms under cultivation to the extent consistent with proper soil conservation practices;

(c) Allocation of Land Settlement holdings forfeited by default to deserving settlers on neighboring farms.

Forest Lands and Timber Supply

Although three centuries ago virtually the whole of Jamaica was covered with trees, only 486,000 acres out of a total area of 2,823,000 acres is now classified as forest. Most of this deforestation was unavoidable as a growing population required ever more land for agriculture, housing, transport and other purposes. Part, however, is traceable to the habit of shifting cultivation and other careless practices. Reckless deforestation has rapidly accelerated soil erosion, increased the incidence of damaging floods and made the island desperately short of timber and firewood.

The present situation is illustrated by the following data for 1950:

	Acres
Total forest land	486,000
State forest	269,000
of which production[1] forest	48,000
protection[2] forest	190,000
unreserved forest	31,000
Private forest	217,000
Planted state forest April 1, 1949	3,638
State forest planted in 1949	650

The timber supply position in 1950 was estimated as follows (in thousands of cubic feet):

Domestic sources	
State forest reserves	68
Private production marketed through	
Department of Commerce and Industry	96
Private production sold directly to consumers	96
Imports (value £ 318,000)	805
Total Supply:	1,065

---

[1] Forest used for the primary purpose of producing lumber.

[2] Forest designed primarily to protect the soil and its capacity to absorb water.

Domestic production thus accounts for less than one quarter of the island's timber requirements. Domestic supplies are so short that licensed cutters now have to work on short-boled and inferior trees growing in remote places.

Apart from cuttings for timber, much wood is also extracted for firewood and charcoal and an unknown quantity is lost by uncontrolled or inadequately controlled fires.

Crops: Acreage and Production

The only report covering virtually all crops is contained in the census of 1943. For later years data on some products (sugar, citrus, bananas and milk) have been collected by commodity associations, and information on others was obtained in 1950 through a sample survey made by the Department of Agriculture. The census figures are unfortunately not expressed in uniform units, and for a number of commodities they cover only the production on farms over one acre. Moreover, later investigations have given rise to some doubts about the reliability of the census data, especially as to production. For this reason production figures for the year 1942 are given here only for those crops for which the information could be checked.

With the cooperation of the agricultural economist of the Department of Agriculture, it was possible to compile fairly complete data for 1949 and 1950. For those commodities for which no new information has become available since the census, the 1942 figures are assumed to be still true. These include principally rootcrops, pulses, cacao and coffee.

All figures must be treated with great caution. Only the production of export crops can be estimated with a fair degree of accuracy. The output and acreage of locally consumed food crops are subject to a very wide margin of error. All data in the table must be considered only as rough indications of general magnitudes.

ACREAGE AND PRODUCTION

	Acres Harvested in 1,000 Acres			Production in Metric Tons		
	1942	1949	1950	1942	1949	1950
Maize	33	35	58	7,000	18,000	17,000
Rice (paddy)	0.5	8	5.4	550	5,800	4,450
Sorghum	0.3	0.3	0.3		126	120
Potatoes	0.8	1.6	1.6		2,000	1,300

	A1	A2	A3	P1	P2	P3
Sweet Potatoes and Yams	38.7	38.7	38.7		62,700	62,700
Cassava	11.6	11.6	11.6		16,500	16,500
Breadfruit[1]		23	23		61,500	61,500
Beans		4.8	4.8		1,125	1,125
Cowpeas }	12.4	2.4	2.4		550	550
Congo Beans }		5.4	5.4		1,318	1,318
Other Beans	0.9	0.6	0.6		140	140
Groundnuts	0.1	0.6	0.6		120	122
Soybeans	0.2	0.1	0.1		19	17
Coconuts[2]	132	100	123	84,000	60,000	60,000
Sweet Oranges }	13.4	16	20		50,000	30,000
Manderins }		1.4	1.1		3,800	6,300
Grapefruit	4.7	5.2	6.4		22,000	23,000
Lemons }	2.7	0.4	0.4		660	1,500
Limes }		3.2	5.0		2,450	7,000
Tomatoes		—	1.3		—	6,960
Mangoes[3]		9.1	9		76,200	71,000
Sugar Cane	102	92	116.4	1,868,690	2,426,000	2,567,850
of which for sugar	84	80	104.8	1,856,050	2,306,000	2,474,800
Bananas	94		65 }	140,000		98,000
Plantains	2		3.7 }			7,000
Tobacco	2.8	2.8	2.8		1,000	900
Cocoa[4]	12.4	12.4	12.4		2,000	2,100
Coffee	17.4	17.4	17.6		2,000	2,020
Pimento[1]		52	47		1,696	1,973
Ginger	1.6	1.6	2.3		1,100	1,350
Sisal	1.1	2	2.5		240	249

[1] Calculated at 40 trees per acre.
[2] Bearing coconuts were estimated to cover 98,000 acres in 1949 and 77,000 acres in 1950.
[3] Calculated at 100 trees per acre.
[4] Calculated at 200 trees per acre.

Source: 1942 figures from Census of Jamaica 1943; 1949 and 1950 figures from Department of Agriculture.

ANNEX 5

Fisheries

Locally caught fish contribute only about 15% of the protein-value of fish consumed in Jamaica. The rest has to be imported, mainly in the form of salted dry fish, from Canada and Newfoundland. Fish imports were 25 million pounds in 1949 and 22 million pounds in 1950, and cost on the average £ 1 million per year.

In 1945, sea fishing employed approximately 7,500 men of whom 3,500 were full-time fishermen. They caught about 12 million pounds of fish which were valued at £ 0.6 million. Prices are now roughly double those of 1945 so that the retail value of the sea fish catch may now be estimated at £ 1.2 million (2 shillings per lb.).

The continental shelf of Jamaica is already being fished to the limit. The development of sea fisheries depends mainly on the result of experiments on the Pedro banks and on research studies on the migration of fish. Prospects do not appear bright, but cannot be definitely ascertained until completion of a survey of the Caribbean Seas such as the one discussed at the Conference of Fisheries Experts recently sponsored by the Caribbean Commission.

Fresh water fisheries, which up to the present have yielded only a negligible output, offer more possibilities for development. Following the reports of Mr. Thompson[1] and Mr. Hickling,[2] the Government in December 1949 appointed a full-time fisheries officer who has since made a thorough study of the pond fisheries in the Far East. The reports and the study concluded, quite rightly, that it is possible to breed half a ton of fish per acre annually under Jamaican conditions.[3] All experts agree that there is room for 10,000 acres of fishponds scattered all over the island—along the coast and in the mountain

---

[1] *The Fisheries of Jamaica*, by E. F. Thompson, Bulletin No. 18, Development and Welfare in the West Indies, June 1945.

[2] *The Fisheries in the British West Indies*, by C. F. Hickling, Bulletin No. 29, Development and Welfare in the West Indies, August 1950.

[3] In Java, the yield of a hectare (2.471 acres) of fish ponds is two tons of fish and from Palestine yields of one and a half to two and a half tons to the acre are reported.

areas. If these areas were in production, the catch might be of the same magnitude as the present output of sea fisheries. This catch would have a food value equal to three million pounds of imported, dried fish which now cost about £ 150,000.

This shows clearly the importance of encouraging more fishponds, though with some caution as to the financial results. A catch of half a ton of fish may be sold by fishermen at 1 shilling per pound, or for £ 55, an amount comparable to the yield of an acre of food crops. Clearly, therefore, it would be uneconomic to invest much money in the construction of an acre of fishponds. However, the authorities are satisfied that there are many places along the coast and at sugar estates, cattle pens and bauxite mining sites where cheap ponds can be arranged. All those opportunities should be utilized insofar as costs permit. The development of pond fishing has one distinctive advantage over sea fishing: ponds can be made close to the centers of consumption so that marketing will not be a difficulty.

Marketing and distribution of sea fish is still done in a very primitive manner. Cooperatives need to be organized to improve marketing and supply fishermen with their requisites. The reorganized Loan Societies Board should provide such cooperatives with adequate funds for working capital.

Cattle Breeding

Jamaica has made considerable progress in developing good types of beef and dairy breeds suitable to tropical conditions. By the introduction of a small proportion (about one eighth) of Zebu (i.e. Brahman or Indian) blood into European milk or beef breeds it has been possible to produce heat-tolerant types which are a credit to the island.

Years of selective breeding since 1910, carried on mainly by Cousins and Lecky, have resulted apparently in a true ecotype breed of dairy cow recently named "Jamaica Hope." The herd is now on irrigated pastures at the Bodles agricultural station and nearly £ 50,-000 is to be spent on its further improvement and expansion. It will still be necessary to breed and cull under the guidance of a man with an eye for a good bull and a good cow.

New beef herds which have been developed will also probably be registered. These include breeds produced from Aberdeen Angus with Zebu; from Red Poll with Zebu; and a Zebu herd. The Zebu cattle are a large type and are generally used as work animals on the sugar estates. Pedigreed cattle of all these types will be in increasing demand in the Caribbean countries and South America.

It will undoubtedly prove worthwhile to carry on additional work on the breeding of productive, heat-tolerant cattle. Of interest for this purpose are the studies on heat tolerance of different types of animals carried out under controlled conditions at the Beltsville station in the United States. There the Zebu type used is the small Red Sindhi. In the United States the Holstein, which admittedly suffers more from higher temperatures and humidity, is still generally preferred over the Jersey for crossing with a heat-tolerant type, simply because of its high milk yield.

The important task now is to use the new and improved herds for upgrading the cattle generally used throughout the island. While there are some excellent private herds, the average dairy cow is a very poor animal. The Livestock Division of the Department of Agriculture in cooperation with the Livestock Association and the Jamaica Agricultural Society should work particularly to assist the small farmer to improve his cattle. Good bulls and facilities for artificial insemination are available.

Pasture Experiments

NATAL

Before the war, work was done at Umbogintwini on Elephant, Bermuda and Kikuyu grasses. It was shown that the protein content of Bermuda grass (known in Jamaica as Bahamas grass), which is normally about 12%, could be increased to over 20% by means of fertilizer applications. Moreover, fertilizer treatment of this grass over five years stepped up the annual yield of dry matter per acre from 1700 pounds to between 7000 and 8000 pounds. Fertilizer applications on Kikuyu grass, another important tropical grass, produced six to seven tons of dry matter per acre, with a content of 18% protein. One pound of nitrogen produced up to 25 pounds dry matter of high-grade food. The grass provided grazing for one and a half beasts per acre throughout the year. Other grasses not as productive as those grown in Jamaica carried a beast to the acre under conditions much less favorable than those in Jamaica.

GEORGIA AND FLORIDA (UNITED STATES)

Important work has been carried out in the Suwannee River valley in Florida and at Tifton in South Georgia.

In the Suwannee River valley, where the soil is virtually pure sand, fertilizer applications have resulted in grass yields averaging five or six times those in the control plots—and often higher. In these experiments 400 pounds of nitrogen (in the form of ammonium nitrate) together with phosphates and potash were applied to the acre. On the average, one pound of nitrogen produced from 25 to 30 pounds (dry-weight) of grass or more than the amount required (18 to 20 pounds dry-weight) to increase the weight of an animal by two pounds per day. At the Suwannee Experimental Station, however, no grazing experiments have been carried on.

At Tifton grazing trials have been conducted and some work done on the economics of pasture fertilization. There fertilizer was applied to a new and vigorous type of Bermuda (Bahamas) grass which had been developed. On this grass it was possible to graze two and a half beasts to the acre for six months and to produce enough hay to feed them during the balance of the year even though much grass was wasted owing to lack of proper management. The profitability of fertilizers was demonstrated, the profits rising steadily with the first few hundred pounds of nitrogen. Where 400 pounds of 6/8/6 fertilizer ($N/P_2O_5/K_2O$) and 400 pounds of sulphate of ammonia were applied, the net profit was $100 per acre with dairy cows and $70 with beef cattle. Even larger quantities of fertilizers are recommended today.

JAMAICA

1. *Fertilization Trials in St. Ann, St. Mary and Portland (1946-48)*

Experiments were carried out on a total of 23 small plots (15 by 15 feet) over a period less than two years. Results were adversely affected by unusually low rainfall. Response to phosphates and potash were generally not particularly marked, but when nitrogen was added, yields in terms of dry matter virtually doubled in most cases. The crude protein content of the grass—about 7%—was not materially affected by fertilizers. Higher nitrogen applications (only four cwts. of sulphate of ammonia per acre were used) would probably have produced substantially greater yields. The report on the experiments concluded rather prematurely: "Tall tropical fodders cannot be regarded as sources of high protein feed. Fodder grasses alone are not suitable for providing adequate protein . . . Compared with standards in temperate climates the feed value of the fodder grasses is very low."[1]

2. *Experiments at Orange River and Oxford*

These experiments were carried out only on Napier grass during 1947 and 1948. At Orange River where the soil was said to be extremely deficient in nitrogen but not markedly lacking in phosphates and potash, the application of four cwt. of sulphate of ammonia per acre over one year increased the dry matter yield on two plots

---

[1] Department of Agriculture, *Bulletin No. 41.*

by 68% and 52% respectively. At Oxford, where the soil was reported to have a more nearly normal nitrogen status but to be deficient in phosphates, potash and lime, the use of nine cwt. of sulphate of ammonia produced an increase of only 13-14% in terms of dry matter. At Oxford, however, the crude protein content was raised by 20%; at Orange River only 1-7%. Phosphates (four cwt. 18% super-phosphate) increased dry matter yields by 8-10% and 7-13% at Oxford and Orange River respectively. Potash and lime gave responses only at Oxford where soil analysis was reported to show deficiencies in both elements. It was concluded that application of nitrogen to fodder grasses would generally prove profitable although in large parts of the island where soil types are markedly deficient and acid conditions prevail, nitrogen would have to be used in conjunction with other fertilizers.[2]

These varied results can hardly be regarded as conclusive. Not only was rainfall abnormally low, but the experiments were not carried out on a sufficiently comprehensive scale, with enough variations in the timing, quantities and combinations of fertilizer applications. They were conducted on planted grass rather than established pastures. Sulphate of ammonia was applied after each cutting, although, as is indicated by experience in other countries, the application of part of the nitrogen shortly before each cutting (perhaps a week) might well have raised the protein content. If, as was indicated, nitrogen hastened the maturity of the grass, the soil must have been extremely deficient in nitrogen and more nitrogen should have been applied, for it is well known that nitrogen delays the maturing of grasses. The small response to nitrogen at Oxford was undoubtedly due to the marked deficiency in potash revealed by the increasing response to potash attained over two years. The decrease in protein content resulting from potash applications at Oxford also demonstrated that carbohydrate production had been limited by lack of potash.

The experiments showed that yields in the dry months November-March dropped sharply. Undoubtedly mulching combined with fer-

[2] Department of Agriculture, *Bulletin No. 43.*

tilization would have maintained the yields at a much higher level. Sugar cane, which is, after all, a grass, is kept green and growing well throughout the dry season by fertilization and mulching.

A further experiment to determine the effect of increasing quantities of nitrogen on both Napier and Guinea grass was laid down in 1946 at Orange River. Nitrate of soda and sulphate of ammonia were also compared in this experiment. The response to nitrogen in 1948 was more in accordance with results obtained in other countries. With increasing quantities of nitrogen (three cwt., six cwt. and nine cwt. of sulphate of ammonia), yields were progressively increased from 22 tons to 33 tons, 38 tons and 41 tons of green matter. The response might well have been still greater if potash and phosphates had also been applied. Previous experiments had shown the use of these fertilizers in conjunction with nitrogen to be essential. It was concluded that four to six cwt. of sulphate of ammonia per acre would be the most economical application. The crude protein content of the grass remained remarkably low—about 4.5%—which is strange in view of the success other countries with poorer soils have had in growing higher protein grasses.

One grazing experiment with Napier grass, carried out in 1949, is worth noting. Two sets of 12 heifers each were grazed on fertilized plots at intervals of both six and eight weeks. It was found that the carrying capacity with six-week intervals was higher. With six week grazing intervals one acre carried two and a half heifers per acre for nine months, and produced a live-weight increase of 294 pounds per animal, or 700 pounds per acre.[3] This result was remarkable in view of the average increase of about 100 pounds per acre for Jamaica as a whole. Yet much better results could be achieved. The green grass yield was only 25 tons; yet the Department of Agriculture *Bulletin 41* records an instance of Napier grass in St. Mary yielding 90 tons per acre. It was reported that 20% of the pasture was trampled and a further quantity fouled by droppings which apparently were not scattered by harrowing. The animals ate only the leaves and succulent portion of the grass, owing evidently to

---

[3] Department of Agriculture, *Bulletin 47*.

its low protein content. It was observed that the animals preferred Bahamas grass even when abundant succulent Napier fodder was available. This preference must have been due to the higher protein content of the Bahamas grass which is the chief grazing grass in much of the tropical world. Yet the conclusion was not drawn that this grass might be grown in place of Napier.

3. *"Commons" Pasture Grazing Trial*

This experiment was begun on "commons" pasture near the Groves Place Agricultural Station in 1948-49. The commons contained nearly 50% crab grass, and most of the remaining species of grass were inedible. According to local testimony, the carrying capacity of such pasture was one beast to three acres.

The experiment was laid down to determine the stock carrying capacity and beef production of "commons" both with and without fertilizer. The fertilizer application was four cwt. sulphate of ammonia and one and a half cwt. of muriate of potash per acre each year. On both the fertilized and unfertilized areas, each of which was 24 acres, 20 steers were grazed; and particular care was taken to insure that the animals, whose water consumption doubles in the dry period, had enough water at all times. Rotational grazing was applied. The cattle were to be weighed monthly and if their weight increase fell below a "standard" of one and a third pounds per day, a beast was taken off the area.

The results were striking. In the first year of this five-year experiment the fertilized plots carried a beast to 1.2 acres from May to December and a beast to 2.4 acres in the driest period. Beef production per acre was 116 pounds. Even the unfertilized plots yielded 73 pounds per acres, reflecting apparently the results of better management.[4]

Conclusion

All countries that have tried intensive pasture work with fertilizers have found it paid handsomely, but only on the basis of beef prices

---

[4] *Ibid.*

much higher than in Jamaica. In Jamaica some of the experiments show promising effects on yields, but much better results could have been achieved had the conditions of some of the experiments been altered. Much more work should be done under varying conditions which would, among other things, combine the use of fertilizer with better management practices such as the mulching of row grasses. The object should be to increase yields and to provide a supply of fodder which will insure as uniform a level of nutrition as possible the year round. The economics of pasture improvement should also be given much greater attention.

Irrigable Areas

Parish	Estimate of Area Irrigated by Gravity in 1951	Estimate of Area Which Could Ultimately Be Irrigated by Gravity	
Kingston and Pt. Royal	30	30	
St. Andrew	700	1,000	
St. Ann	2,700	3,200	
St. Catherine	20,000	30,000	
St. Elizabeth	200	1,500	
St. James	800	1,000	
St. Mary	1,400	2,000	
St. Thomas	2,500	3,500	
Clarendon	15,000	35,000	
Hanover	2,000	2,200	
Manchester	—	—	
Portland	30	50	
Trelawny	500	1,500	
Westmoreland	1,300	1,500	
Total	47,160	82,480	129,640

Irrigation Projects

Priority	Project, Location and Type	Acres to be Irrigated	Estimated Cost of In- vestigation
*	Minor projects — Probably 150 minor projects scattered over the island under the Minor Irrigation Scheme.	20,000	£ 30,000
1.	Area in eastern St. Catherine between Spanish Town and Bushy Park irrigated by:		
	(a) Gravity flow from Harker's Hall Dam on the Rio Pedro. A large part of the cost might be charged to flood control and some to power. If the Harker's Hall project is found to be impracticable, the following might be considered as alternatives;	8,000	30,000
	(b) Gravity flow from Rio Cobre when in spate, three months per year for short-term crops;	(2,500)	(1,500)
	(c) Bore-holes in several areas.	(1,500)	(1,500)
2.	Area in St. Dorothy Plain, St. Catherine, near Old Harbour, irrigated by pumping water from Cockpit River up about 120 feet to a high-level canal about four miles long.	4,000	2,500

* Since these represent a large number of projects of varying importance, no over-all priority rating can be given.

Priority	Project, Location and Type	Acres to be Irrigated	Estimated Cost of Investigation
3.	Area in Clarendon between Denbeigh, Four Paths, York Pen and Bullards, irrigated by lifting water from bore-holes 200 feet to high level canal.	3,000	£ 2,500
4.	Areas in St. Elizabeth provided power becomes available:		
	(a) east of Upper Black River Morass, irrigated by pumping from river or bore-holes;	3,000	1,500
	(b) lower Pedro Plains, by bore-holes;	2,000	2,500
5.	Area in Queen of Spain's Valley, Trelawny, by overhead irrigation from bore-holes if power becomes available in the area;	2,000	2,000
6.	Area in St. Thomas, near mouth of Plantain Garden River, by pumping from river or from bore-holes for short-term irrigation to increase yields.	4,000	1,000
7.	Experiments with overhead irrigation, using various combinations of equipment on:		
	(a) Sugar cane, 200 acres;		14,000
	(b) bananas, 100 acres		6,000
	(c) mixed crops, 50 acres at Bodles Agricultural Station		5,000
		46,000	£ 97,000

178

Reclamation Projects

Possible reclamation projects are listed below according to the priority with which they should be investigated. The total area which might be reclaimed is 20,000 acres, and the total cost of surveying the projects is estimated at £ 20,000.

Priority	Project

1. *Lower Cabaritta River in Westmoreland*

   This project would require levees (or bunds) along the river and probably along other sides of the swamp, pumps for dewatering and gates for controlling the flow of water on the land. The land reclaimed could probably be used for growing rice. If landowners cannot agree on a comprehensive scheme, some legislation may be required. Probable reclaimed area, 1,500 acres.

2. *Coastal Areas in St. Catherine from Duhaney (Salt) River to Old Harbour*

   This project would start at the eastern border of St. Catherine and extend through the Salt Pond District, north of Healthshire Hills to Old Harbour. Most of the lands in the area are now saline. The projects envisage bunds or levees, drainage canals and pumping and, where necessary, flooding, to assist in de-salting. At the eastern end, the Caymanas Estate has already reclaimed about 700 acres of swamp land by these methods. The areas in the project include:

   (a) 500 acres east of the mouth of the Rio Cobre and south of the Spanish Town Road. The area reclaimed might be irrigated by water from the Ferry River;

   (b) 500 acres southwest of the mouth of the Rio Cobre to Port Henderson Hill including the Port More area. Surplus water from the Rio Cobre and drainage from the

Priority	Project

irrigation system on United Fruit Lands to the north might be used for de-salting and irrigation;

(c) 1,500 acres in the Salt Pond area. Salt might be leached out with drainage from irrigation systems to the northwest;

(d) 2,000 acres along Town Gully and Salt Island Creek. By discharging surplus water from the Rio Cobre into Town Gully, the lands might be flooded for de-salting and the same water might be used after land is de-salted for irrigation;

(e) 1,500 acres in Bushy Park-Galleon Harbor area. The reclamation of this area would depend on the extension of irrigation to the north, as it would have to depend on drainage from such irrigation for de-salting and irrigation operations. The land is probably good, but water supply may be a problem.

3. *Coastal Areas in Clarendon from Clarendon Gully to West Harbour*

About 4,000 acres in this area might be de-salted by the use of water from the cockpit canal system for 100 days per year when Monymusk Estate is not using water. Later the area might be irrigated from the Cockpit Canal system plus drainage from irrigated lands above it. Consideration might also be given to closing the entrance to West Harbour by a levee and de-watering the area by pumping.

4. *Upper Black River Morass in St. Elizabeth*

It is possible to drain the upper Black River Morass and reclaim about 4,000 acres of land, but the quality of the land is unknown and a soil survey would be required to determine it. The reclaimed land would need irrigation by pumping from the river.

Priority	Project

5. *Coastal Area Southwest of Morant Point, St. Thomas*

About 1,000 acres of coastal swamps in this area might be reclaimed by drainage canals and pumping. It is probably good land.

6. *Negril Swamp, Hanover and Westmoreland*

The drainage of the Negril Swamp is impracticable because of the enormous cost of the works required and the amount of pumping required to keep it de-watered. Even if it were de-watered, there is no assurance that salt water would not infiltrate through fissures in the limestone bottom.

Strips of land along the border of the swamp, however, might be drained by better drainage channels sufficiently to permit the growing of rice. Such areas might amount to as much as 2,500 acres.

7. *Martha Brae Swamp, near Falmouth, Trelawny*

The drainage of this swamp is likely to require levees and pumping. The land is probably poor and the area would be only 1,000 acres in extent. The project has more merit as a health measure for Falmouth than as an agricultural project.

ANNEX 11

Economic Feasibility of Irrigation and Reclamation Projects

Expenditures on irrigation and reclamation projects will be justified only if they are profitable to the individual beneficiaries who in the last analysis must be expected to bear the cost and if by their impact on national income and employment they measurably benefit the economy as a whole. While a final judgment can only be made after the detailed investigation of every project which we have recommended elsewhere, it is possible even at this time to marshall some evidence to support a prima facie case in favor of an extensive program of irrigation and reclamation.

The relationship between costs and returns should be such that the direct beneficiaries will be able to bear the capital and operating charges of the projects. To determine whether such a relationship could be established for irrigation projects we gathered some instructive data on crops grown under irrigation on the government farm at Twickenham Park. While conditions on this farm are somewhat different from those of privately-owned estates, we have reason to believe that its costs are roughly comparable with those elsewhere. At Twickenham Park the total cost of irrigating one acre of sugar cane in 1951 was a little over £ 11, broken down as follows:

1) Cleaning of canals	£	4. 7.6
2) Application of water		1.14.8
3) Cost of water		5. 0.0
Total cost	£	11. 2.2

Production per acre was 36 tons of cane which brought £ 72. After allowing for all costs, a profit of £ 4.14.0 was made per acre. With bananas grown under irrigation the results were much more favorable. There the total costs of irrigation were only £ 7.17.6 and all costs £ 78.5.2, leaving a profit of £ 36.6.1.

If costs on newly irrigated land are comparable, there is little doubt that irrigation will pay. The results will depend, of course, on what the land is capable of yielding without irrigation. If the land affords only a little pasture or produces only a poor food crop, the gross yield will be no more than £ 5 or £ 30 per acre respectively. Under such conditions the net return is almost certainly to be less than that on irrigated land. If, however, rainfall is sufficient to produce cane or bananas but with rather low yields, the question is whether irrigation can increase yields sufficiently to warrant irrigation. We estimate that an increase in yields of nine tons of sugar cane and 23 count bunches of bananas would be sufficient to cover the cost of irrigation.[1] In places where rainfall is barely adequate to permit the growing of cane and bananas, irrigation is likely to produce much larger increases in yields.

All these calculations assume that costs, including irrigation costs, will be about the same as those at Twickenham Park. There is no reason to believe that costs of planting, cultivation, harvesting, maintaining canals and applying water will be substantially different. The real question is whether the cost of water will be comparable considering the capital outlay required for new irrigation works. If water has to be supplied exclusively from bore hole wells in about the same amount as at Twickenham Park,[2] the cost of water per acre of sugar cane may be in the neighborhood of £ 7 to £ 8. Even at this price it would still be very profitable to grow bananas under irrigation, and it might pay to grow sugar cane, depending on the yields that would be achieved. Where a significant quantity of water can be

---

[1] After deducting, on the basis of experience at Twickenham Park, 13s. 1d. in harvesting and transport costs, one additional ton of cane per acre would fetch 27s. or, conservatively, 25s. Nine additional tons of cane would therefore yield 9 x 25s. or £ 11.5.0 (cost of irrigation £ 11.2.2). An additional count bunch of bananas would bring a farmer 7s. 10d. or 7s. after making a generous allowance for cost of harvesting and transport. Thus 23 count bunches would yield 23 x 7s. or £ 8.1.0 (cost of irrigation £ 7.17.6). In each case the additional production per acre would not, of course, increase costs of planting and cultivation.

[2] The cost of water from new borehole wells recently added to the Cobre irrigation scheme is said to be £ 3.4.0 per cubic yard per acre per annum, which would mean £ 6.8.0 per acre of sugar cane.

derived from rivers, the cost of water would be lower and the profitability of irrigation would be correspondingly greater.

The extension of irrigation would also make important contributions to national income and employment. Dry land used only for a little grazing or a "catch crop" would at most have a gross yield of £ 5 and £ 30 per acre respectively, while the same land when irrigated and devoted to sugar cane would produce 36 tons of sugar cane, equivalent to four tons of sugar, having a total value of £ 117.14.4. Two thirds of this increased amount would probably be spent on wages for cultivation, harvesting, transport and processing. Irrigated land under bananas would almost certainly produce 200 count bunches valued at £ 126 of which perhaps half would be spent on labor. Both bananas and sugar would help to expand the island's exports.

It is therefore likely that the irrigation of land suitable for bananas and sugar cane would be advantageous both to the producer and to the economy as a whole. The same would probably be true of land which can be reclaimed at costs not much higher than the cost of irrigation. Whether it would be worthwhile to irrigate or reclaim land for rice growing is somewhat more doubtful. The indicated gross yield of an acre is only about £ 30. Since rice matures within six months as compared with 18 months for sugar cane, any comparison with cane must, of course, take into consideration the possibility of producing at least one other crop in combination with rice. For the farmer rice has the advantage of a labor cost that is apparently somewhat less in proportion to gross yield than in the case of cane. From the point of view of the national economy, on the other hand, it would be more advantageous to grow the most labor-intensive crops.

Agricultural Credit

Credit is extended to agriculture both by the regular commercial banks and by the Peoples Cooperative Banks which were specially founded for this purpose. The first had £ 1.6 million in agricultural loans outstanding on March 31, 1951. This total, however, also includes loans to processors and handlers of agricultural produce. In general only the larger producers such as sugar estates have sufficient credit standing to qualify for commercial bank loans. All others must rely principally on the Peoples Cooperative Banks and money lenders. The Cane Farmers Association and Citrus Growers Association have each made about £ 25,000 to £ 30,000 available for loans.

The resources of the 120 Peoples Cooperative Banks, which have 75,000 members, are very modest. Their members save little, so that the banks must obtain nearly all their funds from the government through the intermediary of the Loan Societies Board. The government has not committed large sums, partly because of other claims on its limited resources, partly because of lagging repayments by many of the Peoples Cooperative Banks and their members. The inability of many farmers, owing to deficient titles, to put up their land as security has also reduced the effective demand for agricultural credit.

In view of these factors it is hardly surprising that the volume of lending by the Peoples Cooperative Banks has remained very small. Table 1 gives data on the amount of new loans extended by these banks other than for post-hurricane rehabilitation. It will be noted that in the six-year period, April 1, 1945 to March 21, 1951, the banks lent a total of about £ 786,000 or an average of only £ 131,000 per year and received total repayments amounting to £ 542,000. Despite rising prices in the immediate postwar years the volume of new loans has tended to shrink.

TABLE 1

Loans of Peoples Cooperative Banks to Farmers
(£ thousands)

Type of Loan	1938 New loans	1938 Repayments	1945-46 New loans	1945-46 Repayments	1946-47 New loans	1946-47 Repayments	1947-48 New loans	1947-48 Repayments	1948-49 New loans
General Purpose	20.4	14.1	102.6	54.8	101.1	62.1	112.7	66.4	98.0
Dairy Cattle	—	—	3.9	1.5	6.9	1.9	4.7	2.7	5.7
Banana Extension	—	—	7.8	1.1	3.9	1.0	2.3	3.9	0.1
Food Production	—	—	7.1	13.1	9.0	8.5	5.9	8.5	0.6
Irish Potatoes	—	—	4.6	4.6	4.9	4.7	0.1	0.4	x
Special Food Production	—	—	—	—	—	—	—	—	—
Rice	—	—	—	—	—	—	—	—	2.4
Cane	—	—	—	—	0.4	—	2.0	—	—
Citrus	—	—	0.4	x	0.3	—	x	x	—
Farmers Housing	—	—	7.7	0.2	9.4	0.9	12.3	2.1	9.1
Total	20.4	14.1	134.1	75.3	135.9	79.2	140.0	84.0	115.9
Excess of New Loans over Repayments		6.3		58.8		56.8		56.0	

x means very small amount

— means zero

Source: Loan Societies Board. The 1938 data cover the calendar year; postwar data in each case cover the fiscal year April 1 to March 31.

TABLE 1 (Continued)

LOANS OF PEOPLES COOPERATIVE BANKS TO FARMERS
(£ thousands)

Type of Loan	1948-49	1949-50		1950-51		Totals for 1945-46 to 1950-51		
	Repayments	New loans	Repayments	New loans	Repayments	New loans	Repayments	Excess of loans over repayments
General Purpose	72.6	108.6	85.0	101.4	89.3	624.4	430.2	194.2
Dairy Cattle	3.4	4.0	3.7	1.9	4.0	27.1	17.2	9.9
Banana Extension	1.6	—	1.6	—	1.1	14.1	10.3	3.8
Food Production	6.9	0.5	5.8	—	3.6	23.1	46.4	−23.3
Irish Potatoes	0.2	x	0.3	—	0.1	9.6	10.3	− 0.7
Special Food Production	—	7.1	0.8	2.2	2.5	9.3	3.3	6.0
Rice	x	4.6	2.1	3.5	2.4	10.5	4.5	6.0
Cane	0.2	10.8	1.0	7.1	5.9	20.3	7.1	13.2
Citrus	x	—	—	—	—	0.7	0.05	0.6
Farmers Housing	3.0	4.7	4.1	3.1	3.4	46.3	13.7	32.6
Total	88.0	140.3	104.5	119.2	112.3	785.5	543.3	242.2
Excess of New Loans over Repayments	27.9		35.8		6.9		242.2	

x means very small amount
— means zero

Source: Loan Societies Board. The 1938 data cover the calendar year; postwar data in each case cover the fiscal year April 1 to March 31.

187

Approximately 80% of the loans made by the Peoples Cooperative Banks have been for general purposes, *i.e.* for "the encouragement or promotion of the agricultural or pastoral activities of the island." Terms of repayment on these loans are not uniform but if a rather high average of three years is assumed, annual repayments beginning with 1948-49 should have amounted to about £ 100,000. Actually they lagged considerably behind this total. Loans for other purposes except housing have been very small indeed. In most of these cases, too, part of the repayments have fallen in arrears.

Aside from these credits regularly extended by the Peoples Cooperative Banks, special funds have been made available to them from time to time for post-hurricane rehabilitation loans. Table 2 gives the total of such loans made by the Loan Societies Board up to April 1, 1951. Repayments on all of these loans except those for the rehabilitation of coconut plantings and buildings are considerably in arrears.

TABLE 2

Post-Hurricane Rehabilitation Loans to the Peoples Cooperative Banks
(£ thousands)

Type of Loan	Period of Repayment	Issued	Balance Outstanding
1944 Rehabilitation for:			
Bananas	3 years	81	9
Coconuts	20 years	22	9
Orchard crops	10 years	6	2.5
Food crop	2 years	36	10
Mixed Cultivation	3 years	33	12
Buildings	20 years	653	405
	Total	831	448
Loans before 1944		181	10

Special credit arrangements have also been made for farmers on land settlements who generally have not yet obtained title to their land and thus cannot qualify for loans requiring landed security. Under such arrangements the government has from time to time advanced funds through the Loan Societies Board to the Commissioner of Lands to enable the latter to make loans for food production and repair of buildings. The repayment record on these loans is particularly poor. Information supplied by the Commissioner of Lands discloses:

(1) In September 1951, £ 2,800 out of a total of £ 6,728 in two-year production loans made in 1940 had still not been repaid; 701 settlers were in default;

(2) At the end of 1950, out of £ 8,059 in two-year crop loans granted in 1944 to 1,200 settlers, £ 5,627 remained unpaid; only 319 settlers had completed repayments;

(3) At the end of 1950, £ 2,110 were still outstanding from a total of £ 3,346 advanced in 1944 for repair of buildings in the form of five-year loans.

In general it may be said that the volume of agricultural credit has been insufficient but that at the same time many farmers have lacked the capacity and willingness to repay even the modest loans which have been extended. To meet this situation we have recommended that loans in the future be granted only for specific purposes within the framework of the over-all development program. Farmers can be expected to repay only if the money they have borrowed is definitely used to enhance the productivity of their properties. Security should as far as possible be taken in the form of crop liens, and to this end cooperative marketing ought to be encouraged. Where land is taken as security, there must be a determination to enforce payment, if necessary through foreclosure of the mortgage. No system of agricultural credit can flourish unless there is strict insistence on repayment of loans.

Some settlement will also have to be made with respect to these loans which are now in arrears. In the case of loans to farmers on land settlement it would be desirable to consolidate remaining re-payments with installments still due on the land and to make both of these charges on the land. In the event of future defaults, the settler should forfeit his land. This suggestion is in accord with recommendations made by the Commissioner of Lands in 1951.

Finally, certain changes need to be made in the existing credit machinery. We have recommended that the Loan Societies Board be transformed into a cooperative central bank of which the local Peoples Cooperative Banks and future marketing and credit societies would be members. At present the Board is in essence a quasi-govern-ment institution which distributes government funds and audits the books of the loan societies. The farmers and many directors of the loan societies do not regard the board as their own central bank and therefore often do not have a strong sense of obligation to repay loans within the stated period. When the board is converted into a cooperative bank steps should at the same time be taken to amalga-mate some of the smaller Peoples Cooperative Banks. A number of these are so small that they cannot employ a full-time, well-trained manager. On March 31, 1950, only four societies had a balance out-standing of more than £ 10,000; 67 had between £ 1,000 and 5,000; and 32, less than £ 1,000.

Borrowing Capacity of Farmers

In proposing an ambitious program for agricultural credit we have considered whether the individual farmer will be able to repay out of his gross receipts the amortization and interest charges on all the loans he may receive. To find a wholly satisfactory answer to this question it would be necessary to project the incomes, debt charges and other expenses for an extremely large number of farms with many variations in size and an almost infinite number of production patterns. This would manifestly be impossible. Instead, we have tried to estimate the debt-carrying capacity of a number of typical small farms on the basis of certain assumptions.

A typical small farm might have five to seven acres in production. We have assumed that the pattern of production on a hillside farm of this size would provide both for quickly maturing cash crops and for longer maturing tree crops. Thus it might have one half to one acre under coffee or cacao (or a combination of the two), mixed with bananas (especially while the trees are still small), and the rest of the acreage in food crops and citrus, approximately evenly divided. In other cases, particularly on the gentler slopes, sugar cane and bananas might be the principal crops, and there might be some pasture. On the flat areas, the farm might produce such crops as sugar cane, tobacco, rice, pineapples or tomatoes and might also have an acre of pasture land. The gross yield of such a farm might range between £ 300 and £ 350 annually at prevailing prices, depending upon the pattern of production. The higher figure would be attained by farms with more tree crops, bananas and sugar cane, and the lower figure by farms with a larger proportion of pasture and food crops.

In estimating this gross return we have assumed the following yields per acre:

Coffee: 750 pounds
Cacao: 750 pounds
Root crops: 5-7 tons
Rice: 1200 pounds

Beans and peas: 900 pounds

Citrus trees: 200 boxes in the first years of production, increasing to 300 and 400 boxes when trees are in full production.

Bananas: 200 count bunches

Sugar cane: 20 tons

Tobacco: 800 pounds

Tomatoes: 9 tons

Improved pastures; beef and milk at a value of £ 40 (much higher than the present average yield because of potentialities for improvement).

These yields in turn reflect the assumption that the farmer would participate in all the government schemes for soil conservation, pasture improvement and planned land use and would also borrow to buy necessary fertilizers, seeds, insecticides, etc. The gross return of £ 300 to £ 350 per farm would compare with that of perhaps £ 100 to £ 150 on an unimproved farm.

On the basis of the patterns of production outlined above the farmer might contract total loans of between £ 100 and £ 200. These figures assume that farmers would contract

(1) short-term crop loans or advances at 50% of the expected money yield;

(2) longer-term development loans on tree crops at 50% of establishment costs;

(3) longer-term soil conservation loans of £ 3 per arable acre;

(4) longer-term pasture rehabilitation loans at £ 4 per acre of grassland;

(5) longer-term cattle loans at £ 25 per acre of grassland.

Debt charges have been computed on the assumption that farmers would be carrying all these loans simultaneously, which in practice may seldom be the case. After deducting the short-term crop loans, which in essence are crop advances, from the gross return and averaging repayments on other loans over a five-year period, we come to the conclusion that the remaining debt charges, with interest at 6%, would amount to between £ 20 and £ 30 per year.[1] The charges would thus compare with an increased return of around £ 150 attributable to the farmer's participation in the development schemes. Even allowing for a considerable margin of error in these calculations, we consider that the small farmer would clearly be capable of contracting the indebtedness implied in the development program.[2]

The larger farmer who has to rely wholly or largely on hired labor to carry out the development work will be at a disadvantage as compared with the small farmer. He will need larger financial resources of his own and may therefore have to proceed more slowly with the development of his property and rely more on quickly maturing crops.

---

[1] These amounts do not include, of course, charges on loans which the farmer may have contracted in the past. Such charges, however, should be easier to carry if the gross return on the farm is substantially increased by the development program.

[2] It should be noted that the development program contemplates much more financial assistance to the farmer than is implied in these loans. Under the soil conservation and pasture rehabilitation schemes, he would receive a grant of three times the amount of the loan per acre.

Land Settlement

The land settlement program was conceived to provide employment and satisfy the well-nigh universal longing for a "piece of land." It was started in 1929 but did not receive a real impetus until the political disturbances of 1937-38. The Lands Department, which had hitherto been a part of the Surveys Department, was then made a separate agency although it has never been made a statutory body. The program was considerably accelerated and the terms on which settlers could buy plots were repeatedly liberalized. In the years 1938-41 no less than 79 properties were purchased and distributed to settlers. Altogether the government has acquired about 150,000 acres of which 115,000 acres have been used to establish 144 land settlements consisting of 24,000 allotments. The government paid nearly £ 1 million or an average of about £ 6.4 per acre for these properties and, after spending an additional £ 536,000 for their development, particularly on the construction of roads, sold the land for allotments at an average price of £ 8.5 per acre.

The program has now been virtually halted. Although instrumental in increasing somewhat the total area under cultivation, the program has been far from successful. Among its conspicuous deficiencies, the following may be cited:

1. *Poor land.* Much of the land purchased was derelict and sold to the government only because the owners had no use for it. In most cases it could be made fertile only at considerable expense which was not undertaken.

2. *Inadequate size of allotments.* About 9% of the holdings (plus the majority of so-called house lots) are under two acres, and two thirds are between two and six acres. The cultivated acreage is even smaller in most cases.

3. *Poor selection of settlers.* Many allotments were given to people with little or no farming experience. One survey disclosed that 2,500 out of 14,600 purchasers did not even till the land themselves. Another, covering 4,400 resident purchasers, showed that

550 had no experience in agriculture and 2,900 were former agricultural laborers. The generally poor quality of the settlers is also demonstrated by the large proportion of land remaining uncultivated. Of the 14,500 holdings in 1949, only 8,600 had more than half of their acreage in cultivation. Altogether only 37,000 acres of a total cultivable area of 68,000 acres were actually cropped.

4. *Failure to enforce terms of payment.* Although the price charged for land can hardly be regarded excessive and settlers were given 25 years to pay, half of the settlers were in arrears on their payments in 1949. Of these, half again were more than one year behind in their payments. Only in very few cases did the government proceed against defaulters.

5. *Insufficient amenities.* Inadequate provision was made for housing and water. Failure to provide assistance for housing was undoubtedly largely responsible for the fact that only about 3,600 purchasers out of 14,000 surveyed lived with their families on their holdings. On all of the 144 settlements there are only 50 entombed springs, 101 ponds, 40 catchment tanks, 13 wells and 15 pipelines.

6. *Poor agricultural practices.* The development and cultivation of the land was largely left to the settlers. The Lands Department has not had sufficient expert staff or funds to enable it to insist on soil conservation and the adoption of other good agricultural practices. The field extension staff of the Department of Agriculture has not been concerned with the land settlements. Under these circumstances, much of the land has rapidly deteriorated. This has unquestionably been the most serious defect of the program.

Many of these deficiencies were apparently due to the great political pressures which gave rise to the program and which have since impeded its efficient execution. Fortunately, there has been a growing awareness of this fact. The future may therefore offer an opportunity to put the existing land settlements on a sounder basis and to carry out any new settlement along better lines.

We suggest one important change in the administration of the existing land settlements. The Department of Agriculture should be requested to include these settlements within the scope of the activities of its field extension service. This would make more and better agricultural advice available to the settlers. No special agricultural rehabilitation program need be undertaken on the land settlements. The farmers on these settlements should qualify for assistance under the general agricultural development program on the same basis as all farmers.

Under our proposal the Lands Department would in the future limit itself to the administration of the settlements, particularly to the collection of instalment payments by the settlers. We urge that it be empowered to proceed against delinquent farmers. Settlers in arrears on their payments should be given a specified period to meet overdue payments, and future defaults should then be penalized by forfeiture of the land. On the other hand, those who are up-to-date in their payments ought to be given provisional title to their land in such a way that they can use it as security for obtaining development loans.

In addition to the land settlements described above there are two so-called cooperative settlements at Lucky Hill and Grove Place. Each of these properties is tilled as a unit by a group of settlers working under a manager. The settlers are paid wages and share in any profits which may be earned during the year. Most of them are not fully satisfied with this arrangement since they prefer to have their own land in freehold. It will be a long time before they are ready to operate these farms as true cooperatives. Community operation of these properties under an efficient manager does, however offer an opportunity for the application of better agricultural practices and the achievement of more balanced cooperation. We urge, therefore, that these experiments be continued.

Note on Other Crops

In the text of the main report the Mission has commented on most of the principal crops in connection with the program for increasing agricultural production. Here we note briefly the remaining crops of significance to the island and discuss the possibility of introducing certain new crops.

Ginger has long been an important crop to small farmers. It is grown in small patches and requires a considerable amount of labor for its cultivation and the curing and peeling of the root. In 1950 about 2.6 million pounds, valued at £ 340,000, were exported. While not as good as the ginger of southern China, which is exported in syrup and fetches high prices, Jamaican ginger enjoys a good reputation. Unfortunately the growing of ginger on hillsides without precautions for soil conservation has played an important part in destroying the fertility of the area north of Christiana.

The sharp drop in ginger prices over the last year has greatly agitated the growers and led to urgent demands for relief. After rising precipitately to 500 shillings per hundredweight in June 1951, the price dropped successively to 195 shillings in June 1952. Even that price is still four times as high as prewar. To prevent dumping, the government recently reintroduced licensing of exports. In the end only the organization of cooperative marketing will help to stabilize prices. It should be realized at the same time that any attempt to raise prices to the excessively high levels of 1951 would severely curtail the consumption of ginger. Cooperative marketing might well be supplemented by efforts to improve yields through the use of fertilizers and soil conservation practices. It is doubtful that the processing of ginger in Jamaica would help materially to raise prices. The grinding of ginger and the production of ginger extract are relatively simple processes requiring little labor.

In *pimento* or "all-spice" Jamaica has a virtual monopoly. Pimento trees used to grow almost everywhere in the island, but a leaf rust has killed those in the higher altitudes. In 1950 about 4.6 million pounds valued at £ 291,000 were marketed abroad, in large part in the dollar area. There is no reason to extend the cultivation of this crop, but research on the possibility of increasing yields may prove worthwhile.

The production of *tobacco* and the manufacture of cigars were greatly stimulated during the war and immediate postwar years when the shortage of dollars compelled the United Kingdom to curtail severely its import of Cuban cigars. Imports of Jamaican cigars rose rapidly until 1947 when much higher duties on all forms of tobacco were imposed. Part of the subsequent sharp drop was undoubtedly due to previous stocking in anticipation of the higher duties. While the consumption of cigarettes was hardly affected by the new duties, that of cigars fell off markedly. In levying these new taxes the government found it impossible on administrative grounds to discriminate between cigars and cigar tobacco on the one hand and cigarettes and cigarette tobacco on the other hand. In 1950 Jamaica exported cigars and tobacco to a value of £ 564,000. More recently the United Kingdom resumed modest imports of Cuban cigars under a new trade agreement which aroused considerable indignation in Jamaica where it was characterized as the "Black Pact." The very fact, however, that most British consumers still prefer Cuban cigars indicates the need for a further improvement in the quality and uniformity of Jamaican cigars. More work must also be done on the cultivation and curing of tobacco. In addition, it would be desirable to explore the possibilities of growing more cigarette (Virginia) tobacco for which there is a large market in the United Kingdom. Some is now being grown for the local manufacture of cigarettes. The work now being carried on by the Tobacco Development Corporation ought to be expanded with the help of outside experts in order to determine whether enough suitable soils are available for the cultivation of Virginia tobacco and what methods of cultivation and curing should be used to produce a high-grade tobacco.

In the drier areas a number of minor crops are grown. Among these are *lime trees*, cultivated primarily for lime oil which in 1950 contributed £ 89,000 to the value of Jamaica's exports. The yield from such trees is not high enough, however, to justify their cultivation in areas which can be irrigated. *Cashews* are widely grown, but until a good mechanical method of shelling the nuts without breaking them is developed their exploitation on a commercial scale will not be feasible. *Guavas* also do well in the dry areas, and the possibility of producing guava jelly and tinned guava on a commercial scale may merit investigation.

Eventually it will be desirable to experiment with a number of new crops, although for the time being other work has a higher claim on the attention of the Department of Agriculture. Among possible new crops are sorghums, African oil palms, cotton, ramie, raisins and spices.

In a country where tropical conditions make the cultivation of wheat impossible, *sorghums* are well worth consideration. They are an excellent cattle feed and are also used in some countries to make a nutritious "porridge" for human consumption. Since sorghums are drought resistant, they can be grown in drier areas and in drier seasons than would be suitable for maize. Experimental plots of several varieties of sorghums might be tried in order to test their value under conditions prevailing in Jamaica.

Cotton, which is grown in Texas with a rainfall of less than 20 inches, may do well in the dry southern coastal plains of Jamaica. "Tree" cotton now flourishes in the area and is apparently free from serious pests. The fear of pests has in the past discouraged commercial growing of cotton. The development of new insecticides and of new varieties of cotton has created new conditions which warrant experimentation with cotton growing under the guidance of a recognized expert. Cotton would not, however, be able to compete with other crops in irrigated areas.

Ramie is now being grown on a commercial scale in British Honduras by the Colonial Development Corporation. There it is harvested mechanically after defoliating the plants by spraying a weedkiller from the air. If experience with ramie in that country proves satisfactory, the Department of Agriculture might try the crop in Jamaica.

Some *oil palms* have been grown in Jamaica for many years. They require a heavy well-distributed rainfall and a deep soil—conditions which can be found in certain parts of Jamaica. They yield a valuable edible oil, rich in vitamin A, and in a volume far greater than that produced from coconuts. Trials should be made, however, only with the best seed obtainable from Nigeria or Malaya.

Raisins might be successfully produced from grapes grown in the drier areas of the south. Grapes need to be treated with a potash solution and then dried in the sun. The requisite technical information is obtainable from Victoria, Australia or from Cyprus where raisins have become an important industry although until a few years before World War II no raisins at all were produced.

The growing of *spices* might also be considered. Spice importers in the United States are interested in developing a closer and more secure source of supply for such products as nutmegs, cloves, vanilla, cinnamon and aromatic bay leaves and would be willing to assist Jamaica in trying to grow them. In particular there is a reliable demand for black pepper which the United States obtains exclusively from the Far East.

The Use of Fertilizers

Jamaica lags far behind the United States and European countries in the use of fertilizers. It consumed only about 19,000 tons of fertilizers in the year 1951-52. Of this, about 15,600 tons (13,000 tons of sulphate of ammonia) was taken by the sugar industry. Even this industry, which is the most advanced in the application of fertilizers, uses only about half the amount applied per ton of sugar in Hawaii.

Fertilizer consumption elsewhere in Jamaican agriculture is negligible. On bananas less than 2,000 tons or .5 cwt. per acre were used in 1951-52. Consumption is expected to rise to 6,000 tons in 1952-53 but will still be far from the optimum which is probably in the neighborhood of one ton per acre. On citrus applications average only about 30 pounds per acre although probably at least 10 times that figure should be applied to small trees and much more to older trees. A survey of citrus orchards in 1947-48 disclosed that 90% of them showed clear symptoms of deficiency in the major plant nutrients. The highest proportion—85%—were deficient in nitrogen; 78.5% were deficient in potash and 64.5% in phosphates. Food crops such as yams and corn are not fertilized at all except in the parish of St. Elizabeth where the use of fertilizers on a limited scale has long been general.

Fertilizer consumption per acre should be high in Jamaica for two principal reasons:

(1) It has been demonstrated that in the wet tropics poor soils, if well fertilized, are capable of producing large crops.

(2) Much of the land has lost its topsoil through erosion so that generous quantities of fertilizer are needed for the rapid restoration of fertility.

Much more work on fertilizers needs to be done. Only the sugar industry has employed the staff necessary to carry out experiments. The Department of Agriculture should devote a considerable portion of its resources to an experimentation program designed to determine not simply the fertilizer requirements which would give maximum yields but also the applications which would be profitable to the farmer. Fertilizer experiments of this kind ought to be carried on in combination with other desirable agricultural practices such as soil conservation and mulching. They should be conducted on a wide range of crops including Lacatan bananas, yams, cacao, coffee, citrus, rice, tobacco, tomatoes and pineapples.

In encouraging the use of fertilizer the Department of Agriculture has placed a disproportionate emphasis on liming and phosphates. Under the Farm Improvement Scheme, for example, subsidies are granted only for the application of lime and phosphates. In the wet tropics such as Jamaica, soils frequently require far more nitrogen than phosphates. While experiments may show that the use of small quantities of lime is justified under certain conditions, recent research and practice have demonstrated that liming in the tropics is generally unnecessary. In British Guiana, for instance, even though the acidity of cane and rice soils is far greater than in Jamaica, it has not paid to use lime.

Phosphates are particularly necessary for beans and peas and for legumes as a whole. It is generally claimed that most soils in Jamaica "fix" phosphates, *i.e.*, make them unavailable to plants. This belief undoubtedly accounts in large part for the fact that only about 1,000 tons of imported superphosphates and less than 1,000 tons of the local dicalcium phosphate were used in 1951-52. Quite possibly the problem of "fixation" can be overcome by applying more phosphate and by placing it in the root zone in a granular form rather than broadcasting it. Water-soluble phosphates are more readily "fixed" than the less soluble forms such as bonemeal and dicalcium phosphate. The latter are "fixed" slowly since they must first be dissolved, and in the slow process of dissolution a larger proportion is taken up by the plants over a longer period of time. This has become increasingly recognized. In South Africa, for example, all water-soluble phosphates must be mixed with rock-phosphate.

The amount of potash used in Jamaica—only 2,600 tons in 1951-52—is also very small considering that many of the soils are deficient

in, and very responsive to, potash. Potash is the principal requirement of such crops as cassava, sweet potatoes and other carbohydrate
root crops, but it must be used in conjunction with phosphates and
nitrogen. For most crops in the wet tropics, such as sugar cane, rice,
maize and citrus, nitrogen is the primary requirement. To bring the
best results, each plant food must, of course, be used in proper balance
to other nutrients required by the soil.

Without doubt, a far more generous use of fertilizers would make
farming more profitable and greatly enhance the total value of agricultural production.

Factories and Factory Employment in 1951

	Number of Establishments		Number Employed	
All Manufacturing		*627*		*23,098*
Vegetable Products		*384*		*15,937*
Aerated and mineral water	20		443	
Beer, wine distilleries, etc.	9		494	
Bread, biscuits, etc.	205		2,961	
Coffee	36		586	
Sugar	23		6,809	
Fruits	14		2,246	
Copra	15		605	
Meal, feed, etc.	43		200	
Tobacco, cigars, etc.	3		1,407	
Other vegetable products	16		186	
Animal Products		*9*		*138*
Butter, cheese, etc.	1		70	
Meat products	2		10	
Other animal products	6		58	
Leather Products		*21*		*428*
Boots and shoes	11		324	
Tanning	10		104	
Textile Products		*23*		*1,406*
Cordage, rope, twine	4		87	
Men's and women's furnishings	19		1,319	
Wood and Paper Products		*122*		*2,209*
Furniture manufacturing, etc.	39		429	
Printing, publishing, etc.	26		1,092	
Saw and planing mills	51		606	

FACTORIES AND FACTORY EMPLOYMENT IN 1951

	Number of Establishments	Number Employed
Other wood and paper products	6	82
Iron Products and Repair	*31*	*1,445*
Automobile and bicycle repair	13	411
Railway work shop and repairs	1	434
Other iron products	17	600
Chemical Products	*9*	*1,018*
Soap and toilet preparations	3	494
Other chemical products	6	524
Miscellaneous Products	*28*	*517*
Brick, tile, etc.	10	239
Nonferrous metal products	1	14
Other miscellaneous products	17	264

Source: Labor Department data on factory registration.

Wages and Labor Productivity

INTRODUCTION

In every industry the level of labor costs is of great importance. In export industry using imported raw materials, it is, however, the crucial factor. For this reason the Mission tried to gather as much information as possible regarding labor costs in manufacturing industries based largely on imported raw materials. Labor costs are determined by the relation between wages and labor productivity. Both subjects are discussed below.

WAGES

Little reliable information is available to compare wages in manufacturing industry in Jamaica with those in similar occupations in other countries. The published statistical data do not compare exactly the same kinds of work. Moreover, the wage level in Jamaica is much less uniform than in countries which are industrially more developed. Especially as a result of increases during the last few years, wages in some branches have increased more sharply than in others. For these reasons we have used two different ways of comparing wages.[1]

The first method is to compare wages in 15 occupations in Jamaica and the United Kingdom as shown in the *Yearbook of Labor Statistics*. These figures can only be used to obtain a general impression about the relative level of Jamaican wages. They are insufficient for an investigation of Jamaica's competitive position because they relate almost exclusively to occupations in industries catering to the domestic market.

Broadly speaking the situation revealed in this table can be summarized as follows:

1) Wages for unskilled labor in Jamaica were approximately one

---

[1] For the greater part the comparison is made with the United Kingdom; the growing manufacturing industry in Jamaica will in the first instance have to compete with industry in the United Kingdom.

Hourly Wage Rates in 15 Occupations in Jamaica and United Kingdom

(October 1946)

	Jamaica Kingston		United Kingdom Manchester	
	s	d	s	d
Bakers	0	8	1	11.5
Cabinetmakers	1	0	2	4.5
Upholsterers	1	0	2	4.5
Hand Compositors	1	2	1	3.6
Bookbinders	1	8	1	3.6
Unskilled Laborers in Printing	0	10.5	1	10.47
Fitters and Turners	1	4	2	2.04
Unskilled Laborers in Machinery Manufacture	0	8.5	1	9.96
Bricklayers and Masons	1	3	2	6
Painters	1	3	2	6
Plumbers	1	3	2	6
Unskilled Laborers in Construction	0	9	2	0
Electric Fitters	1	8.5	2	3.61
Unskilled Laborers in Electric Light and Power	0	10	1	11.41

half to one third of those for comparable labor in the United Kingdom.

2) Wages for skilled labor were approximately three quarters to one half of the United Kingdom levels.

The second way to which the Mission tried to arrive at comparative wage figures was to gather information relating particularly to those industries which, either by export or by import, compete with other countries, from a number of businesses engaged in the same kind of work outside Jamaica. This investigation led to the following broad conclusions:

1) Wages for unskilled labor in manufacturing industry in Jamaica are roughly one half of those in the United Kingdom.
2) Wages for skilled labor are approximately 20-25% lower than those in the United Kingdom.

These two sets of conclusions are significantly different. At the end of 1946 wages for skilled labor were 50-75% lower than in the United Kingdom. By the beginning of 1952 they were only 20-25% lower. Wages for unskilled labor were 50-65% lower in 1946 and 50% lower in 1952. The obvious inference that, since the end of 1946, wages have increased more rapidly in Jamaica than in the United Kingdom, is confirmed by the figures published by the Statistical Office of the United Nations regarding *Earnings in Manufacturing*.[2] From 1946 to 1951, the increase given for the United Kingdom was approximately 33% while for Jamaica it was approximately 55%.

LABOR PRODUCTIVITY

The term "labor productivity" sometimes gives rise to misunderstanding. In general, it refers to the quantity of output produced by one worker in an establishment. But it is clear that productivity in this wide sense is the outcome not only of the laborer's individual capacity, but also of many other factors. In the course of its investigations, the Mission gained the impression that in Jamaica the laborer is often held responsible for low output in cases where other factors play an important—in some cases a more important—role. For an analysis of labor productivity, insofar as it is determined by the laborer himself, it is essential to eliminate the influence of these other factors. They have nothing to do with the laborer as such, but with the circumstances under which, or the equipment with which, he works. Among the most important are: the quality of management, the equipment in the factory, the scale of production, and the variety in the production program.

---

[2] Supplemented by figures from the Central Bureau of Statistics in Jamaica.

The fact, for instance, that in some cases the production program is frequently altered in order to cater to the variety demanded in a small market, often causes a considerable loss of time. This necessarily lowers output per head but the individual worker is in no way responsible.

The Mission's investigations into relative labor productivity (again based on comparison with the United Kingdom) under similar circumstances regarding management, equipment, scale of production, etc., lead to the conclusion that labor productivity in Jamaica in manufacturing industry is on the average something like 20 to 25% lower than in the United Kingdom.[3] Although the basis for this conclusion is quantitativily small, it was obtained from sources well qualified to judge.

It is worth while to discuss some of the possible reasons for this difference. It seems probable that the workers' *diet* is not adequate for heavy work in manufacturing industry. In many cases, the Mission was informed, the Jamaican laborer had trouble on this score, especially when doing steady heavy manual labor. Even in occasional heavy work, the Jamaican laborer is in general not equal to his counterpart in more industrialized countries.

Insofar as comparative material is available, the physical condition of the workers appear to be generally lower than that of workers in more developed countries. In several cases where a selection system similar to those used in more industrialized countries was practised, the number of workers rejected was exceptionally large, some 50%. The chief disabilities were high blood pressure, hernia, and physical deformities.

Lack of experience in manufacturing may have a great influence upon labor productivity. As Jamaica still has little industry, knowledge of industrial working methods and experience with machinery and equipment is generally low. Several employers told the Mission that in training workers they had much better results with those who

---

[3] To avoid possible misunderstanding it should be said that in many cases the actual difference in labor productivity is considerably larger, especially if one includes the influence of the factors here eliminated.

had already learned to handle simple tools as craftsmen or artisans. This opinion is confirmed by reports of the wartime experience of American industries in employing Jamaican workers. One reason why the American worker could be trained more quickly than his Jamaican colleague was that the American unskilled laborer, without ever having been employed in industry, was not completely new to industrial working methods, machinery, etc.

It goes without saying that a higher level of general education will have a beneficial influence upon labor productivity.

Another important factor influencing labor productivity may be the *insufficient feeling of responsibility* on the part of the worker. The Mission realizes that this subject is a difficult and somewhat speculative one. But because manufacturing industry depends to a high degree upon the sense of responsibility of the worker, we do not want to let it go entirely undiscussed. The quality and the necessary uniformity of the industrial product demand from the worker a sense of responsibility for his equipment and a feeling of pride in the product. Too often these attitudes are wanting in the Jamaican worker. At present the average worker requires a comparatively large amount of supervision. In many cases the Mission noted that the women employees seemed to have a greater sense of responsibility than the men. The reason for this might be that in Jamaica the woman is often largely responsible for the family. Probably the gradual evolution of a more stable family life would go far towards developing a sense of responsibility in all workers. In Jamaica there are a large number of so-called common-law marriages and, although they may constitute a fairly strong tie between the parties concerned, it is reasonable to suppose that in a formal marriage the husband would feel greater responsibility for his family and would consequently be more anxious to enlarge his income. There is in fact some evidence for the belief that labor productivity is higher among those workers who are formally married.

The *training of labor* is, of course, of the greatest importance in the attempt to increase the productivity of labor. This is discussed in Chapter IV and Annexes 19 and 20.

As mentioned before, Jamaican workers tend to require much supervision. In many instances, the amount of supervision required may even be double that necessary in the United Kingdom. It is not easy to determine exactly why this is so, but it is clear that the quality of the supervisor is an important factor. The Jamaican generally cannot supervise as many workers as foremen from industrialized countries. For example, in some cases in the building trades foreign foremen supervise two and a half to three times as many workers as Jamaican foremen. As would be expected, the Jamaican worker requires considerably less supervision when he is familiar with the work than when he is partly or completely unfamiliar with it.

It is of interest to compare the Mission's findings in this field with the conclusions of a survey made by the U.S. Bureau of Labor Statistics of the productivity of Jamaican workers employed in the United States during the war.[4]

In the last year of the war a little over 12,000 Jamaicans were employed in manufacturing industry in the United States. In order to assess their productivity, as well as to investigate the problems connected with the employment of foreign workers, representatives of the Bureau of Labor Statistics visited 60 factories. These employed more than 60% of the Jamaicans working in manufacturing industry, mostly as general laborers. In about one fifth of the factories visited the Jamaicans did semiskilled work. In practically all factories supervisors of Jamaicans received special instructions in relation to their background and characteristics and in a few cases the workers received extra supervision.

The investigators could not obtain sufficient information to compare productivity, but in 37 factories some general information could be obtained regarding the capacity of the Jamaican laborer. According to this information their productivity was highest when doing light work. "It was observed in a number of cases that they work more slowly, but somewhat more steadily than domestic laborers; almost two thirds of the companies reported that the output per

---

[4] See *Wartime Utilization of Jamaicans in United States Industrial Establishment*, Monthly Labor Review, November 1945.

worker for Jamaicans compared favorably with that for other employees. A minority of the establishments reported that the Jamaicans were excessively slow and that their output fell below that of domestic workers. It was apparent that greater success in obtaining satisfactory production from the Jamaicans was achieved when more effort had been devoted to fitting them into their new working environment by means of special attention to orientation, training and supervision."

In cases where the Jamaicans had to do production work, they required more intensive training than was normally given. Almost all the companies laid this slowness to learn factory work to lack of industrial background. Several of these companies, two of which had organized extensive training courses, said that the majority of the Jamaicans "were naturally apt and quick" and "very capable workmen after a period of adjustment to factory routine and discipline." It is notable that "in almost half of the companies visited, the Jamaicans received the same supervision as native workmen; in the remaining half extra supervision was necessary." In the cases where extra supervision was necessary the plant officials blamed this on lack of experience on the part of the Jamaicans and on their general unfamiliarity with factory work. In most cases where sufficient attention and patience were given to adjust the Jamaicans to their work, it became apparent that the supervisory requirements were the same or only slightly higher than those of domestic workmen. It is remarkable that companies sending representatives to Jamaica or to disembarkation ports to select the workmen themselves, usually did not report special requirements as to supervision. A closer investigation into the factories reporting serious difficulties with the supervision of the Jamaicans in many cases led to the conclusion that this was the result of "poor personnel practice or neglect on the part of the supervisors themselves."

As far as their capability is concerned, the report stated that, with a few exceptions, the Jamaican laborers were not well able to do continuous heavy work requiring physical strength. "In almost all plants where Jamaicans had been assigned to lighter, unskilled or semiskilled work, their job performance was satisfactory." About one third of the companies visited stated that the average output per work for Jamaicans was roughly the same as that for the American workers which were engaged during the war, but it was below the output of the experienced prewar worker. More than two thirds of the factories visited characterized the Jamaicans as being "conscientious, steady workmen, eager to learn and with a good attitude towards their work."

LABOR COSTS

As already stated, wages for skilled labor in Jamaica are roughly 20% to 25% lower than in the United Kingdom, and those for unskilled labor are roughly 50% lower. Taken together with the information on labor productivity this means that, as far as skilled labor is concerned, labor costs in manufacturing industry in Jamaica are, roughly speaking, about the same as in the United Kingdom. For unskilled labor they may be some 25% lower. In considering these figures, account should be taken of the fact that in Jamaica workers who are only semiskilled are often classified as skilled.

These conclusions have only a general significance. Circumstances differ in every branch of industry. For instance, in spite of low wages in the building industry, nonresidential construction costs about the same as in the United Kingdom, even when the same equipment is being used and the management is the same.[5] For some tasks labor costs were even higher than in the United Kingdom.[6] But it is true that in the building industry the range of variation in individual capacities may be large. Nevertheless information obtained from industries where the pace is set more by the process and by the type

---

[5] Information from two cases.

[6] Another company had a similar experience, but in this case the comparison is with the United States. With a labor productivity about 25% lower than in the United States, the company paid wages amounting to about 20% of United States wages for unskilled labor. The result was that labor costs for work requiring much unskilled labor were somewhat lower. On account of the comparatively high wages for skilled labor in Jamaica, costs for work requiring much skilled labor were higher.

and quantity of the machinery used, led to similar conclusions. In one such case, for example, productivity appeared to be roughly 25% lower and wages 20% lower than for a comparable establishment in the United Kingdom. In another factory in a totally different branch of industry labor productivity was about 20% lower, wages for skilled labor about 15% lower and wages for unskilled labor about 50% lower than the United Kingdom levels. As a result of the structure of the labor force, the labor costs came to about the same as in the United Kingdom.

Apprenticeship System

Legal provisions for apprenticeship are contained in the Apprenticeship Law of 1881. The primary purpose of this act is not to promote apprenticeship, but to eliminate and prevent abuses. It is thus insufficient for the present phase in the economic development of Jamaica. In 1942 an Apprenticeship Committee was established "to advise after consultation with the representatives of employers and workers in the various trades concerned, as to the possibility of establishing by voluntary agreement or otherwise:

(1) Uniform conditions of apprenticeship and learnership;

(2) Minimum or standard rates of payment;

(3) Arrangement for the continued adequate and technical training of apprentices and learners."

The Committee finished its report at the end of 1943. Its recommendations led to the drafting of a bill in January, 1951, which is "designed to provide for the establishment of uniform and improved conditions of apprenticeship and in particular for the institution of proper systems of theoretical and practical training of apprentices, maximum working hours, standard rates of pay, and adequate living facilities for apprentices."

This bill contains the following provisions affecting labor training:

A. Contract

1. All contracts of apprenticeship have to be in writing.

2. They must be made at least the duration of the apprenticeship period set by the Apprenticeship Board which the bill would establish.

3. A copy of the contract must be sent to the Apprenticeship Board.

4. An employer is allowed to enter into a contract only if he is an "approved" employer and if the apprentice in question meets the age and educational standards set for the trade.

B. Obligation of the Employer

The employer is obligated:

1. To provide for the prescribed method of practical and theoretical training and to put this method into operation;

2. To provide for adequate living accommodation and proper supervision if, because of the location of the employer's business the apprentice cannot live at home; however, the apprentice should contribute a reasonable amount towards the costs involved;

3. To supervise the apprentices and report annually to the board on their progress;

4. To pay the apprentices wages which are not lower than the minimum wages fixed for the branch of industry in question.

C. Obligations of the Apprentice

The apprentice is obliged "to serve his employer faithfully in the trade in which he is engaged and to carry out his lawful orders."

D. Organization

1. An Apprenticeship Board will be set up for the purpose of "securing the administration of the law and the regulations made thereunder."

2. "The Board may make representations to the Governor in Executive Council on any matters relating to apprenticeship and in particular, but without prejudice to the generality of the foregoing they may, after consultation with existing general and vocational educational authorities or institutions, make representations as to the measures which in their opinion should be taken for the guiding of young persons into suitable vocations."

3. The board can classify as an "approved employer" for the purpose of the law anybody who, in the opinion of the board, is in a position to give adequate training in the trade in which he is engaged.

4. A register is to be kept by the board in which will be recorded:

216

(a) The names of the approved employers and the number of apprentices employed by them;

(b) The names of all apprentices;

(c) The reports on their training.

5. Officers serving on the board and anybody authorized by the board may enter the premises where an apprentice is working and, in the case of an apprentice living away from his home, the premises where he lives, for the purpose of investigating and reporting on the working and living conditions provided for apprentices.

6. The board can make regulations necessary to carry out the law. In particular it may prescribe minimum ages, standard of education, system of theoretical and practical training, period of apprenticeship, minimum wages, maximum hours, and reports to be sent in by the employers. These regulations must be approved by the Governor in Executive Council, who can alter, amend and add to such regulations.

E. CERTIFICATE

1. After termination of the apprenticeship period the last employer informs the board accordingly and reports upon the standards attained by the apprentice.

2. After the board has made sure that the apprentice has served the prescribed period of apprenticeship, a certificate is given to him.

Many objections were made against this bill and it was decided to draft a new one. Apart from certain technical objections, two substantial objections were put forward. In the first place it was argued that the apprentice would be given excessive protection in that penalties could be visited on the employer for isolation of his obligations but no provision was made for corresponding sanctions against the apprentice. The second objection was to the burden that the obligation to give theoretical training might impose on employers. Under the bill in its present form the board could make regulations relating to theoretical training which many employers, lacking the necessary instructors and equipment, would find hard to carry out.

Technical Schools

Kingston Technical School is responsible for practically all technical preparatory education in Jamaica. This school has about one thousand registered students, approximately half of them enrolled in daytime classes. It consists of four departments: domestic science, commercial, technical, and trade, the last two being particularly concerned with education for occupations in industry. The technical department trains "technicians," and the trade department craftsmen and artisans. The program of the technical department aims at a more or less "general education together with training in the scientific principles underlying modern engineering and industrial practices." In this department the students seldom handle tools. The program in the trade department is more "to provide definite and direct trade training for boys who wish to secure employment as apprentices or artisans in various branches of industry."[1] This department provides courses for machine shop engineering, automobile engineering, electrical engineering, cabinet making, carpentry, and joinery. In contrast to the technical department, the trade department emphasizes practical work.

The buildings as well as the equipment of the school are inadequate and in poor condition. As a result comparatively few of the annual applicants can be admitted. In September 1951 the technical and trade departments had 599 applicants and only 56 vacancies.[2] Even if a large proportion of the applicants, say 50%, were unable to meet the qualifications for entrance the picture is not very bright. It would still mean that roughly four out of every five eligible applicants would have to be turned down because of insufficient room and equipment. In reality the situation is more serious. Because inadequate machinery makes it difficult to expand the trade department, many applicants who should have gone into that department could only be

---

[1] Prospectus and Time Table (Session 1950-51), Kingston Technical School.

[2] The commercial and domestic science departments had 357 and 330 applicants, respectively, against 51 and 34 vacancies.

accepted for the technical department. In these circumstances the number of young people turned out for employment in industrial occupations is not large. In 1949, 1950 and 1951 the technical department turned out 28, 30 and 23 pupils, respectively, and the trade department 26, 13 and 10.

The practical instruction given in the trade department is more useful than the instruction given in the technical department. Apprentices turned out by the trade department usually find work immediately, while those from the technical department have more difficulty and often end up in jobs for which the education given in the trade department would have been more suitable.

The unsatisfactory situation led to the appointment of a Technical Education Exploratory Committee in October 1948. Its terms of reference were to advise "on the aims, scope and type of the proposed new technical school and of technical education in Jamaica." The committee reported on January 26, 1949. It advised that technical education in Jamaica "should aim at technical high school training, trade or vocational training, and ultimately full technological training. It should also provide facilities for the preparation of students for entrance to the Universities." In order to achieve this, the committee suggested:

1. "That there should be established in Kingston (or nearby) a Technological Institute;

2. "That subsidiary Technical High Schools be established either as complete units or as departments of other secondary schools at convenient centers near industrial or occupational areas, at, say, Montego Bay, Savanna-la-Mar, May Pen or Mandeville, Spanish Town, Morant Bay, and further, since they will serve as feeding institutes for the Technological Institute, that direction of these schools or departments should be referred to the Principal of the Technological Institute."

In its report the committee quite rightly emphasized the great importance of establishing an apprenticeship system. It regarded the courses at the Technical High School as preparatory to apprenticeship. "Thus equipped, the Technical High Schools should provide prevocational, *i.e.* pre-apprenticeship training as well as a further three years part-time or evening training during the apprenticeship period." The task of the Technological Institute would be "to provide general and then specialized training reaching to universally accepted standards."

The committee recommended a program along the following lines:

1. TECHNICAL HIGH SCHOOLS

In addition to the one in Kingston, new Technical High Schools would be established in different parts of the island. These would accommodate 100-150 pupils and the new school in Kingston would be considerably enlarged. The Technical High Schools would offer complete three-year courses, and, in addition, part-time and evening courses for further education. The accommodation and equipment at the new schools would include classrooms, rooms for the teachers, rooms for the commercial and domestic science departments, as well as drawing offices, a general science laboratory, a combined carpentry and woodwork machinery shop, a combined metal work bench and machinery shop, a mechanics laboratory incorporated with the electrical engineering laboratory, sanitary offices and fittings, and an industrial art and design room.

2. THE TECHNOLOGICAL INSTITUTE

The institute would cover nine branches of study: commerce, domestic economy, mechanical engineering, architecture and building, electrical engineering, printing, applied science, industrial art and design, and navigation. Naturally the equipment of the Technological Institute would have to be very extensive. At the time the cost was estimated to be £ 180,500 capital outlay (to be spread over six years) and £ 59,000 recurrent annual expenditures after the institute was fully in operation.

Labor Management Relations

Trade-unionism in Jamaica is relatively young; not until 1939-40 did labor union organization assume importance. Expansion since then has been rapid and accompanied in many instances by growing pains. The growth of unionism is illustrated in the following table.

TABLE 1

LABOR UNION ORGANIZATION

Year Ending March 31	Total Wage Earning Labor Force as of March	Union Membership	
		Number	% of Total Wage Earners
1919	199,300	80	.04
1926	208,600	120	.06
1934	245,500	80	.03
1938	261,700	1,080	.41
1939	266,300	8,500	3.19
1940	270,900	12,600	4.65
1941	275,500	10,700	3.88
1942	280,100	24,000	8.57
1943	284,600	35,000	12.29
1944	289,200	46,000	15.90
1945	293,800	56,400	19.19
1946	298,400	57,700	19.34
1947	303,000	64,200	21.18
1948	307,300	67,700	22.03
1949	313,100	68,100	21.75
1950	319,400	67,400	21.09

The development of trade-unionism was accompanied by many conflicts between employers and employed but even during its early days some results were obtained by negotiation where both employers and workers were organized. The first important results of collective

221

bargaining were achieved in 1941 and 1942. At that time the most important agreement was between the Sugar Manufacturers Association and the All Island Cane Farmers Association on one side, and the Bustamante Industrial Trade Union on the other. Among other things, this agreement laid down regulations covering wages, working hours, payment for overtime, and the like. Since then trade-unionism has continued to spread to other industries, as shown in Table 2.

TABLE 2

DISTRIBUTION OF ORGANIZED LABOR ACCORDING TO MAJOR INDUSTRIES, MARCH 1950

Industry	Estimated Wage Earning Labor Force	No. of Wage Earners Organized	% of Organized Wage Earners in Respective Industry
ALL INDUSTRIES	*319,400*	*67,400*	*21.09*
Agriculture	120,000	36,174	30.15
Quarrying and mining	400	117	20.25
Fishing, hunting & forestry	2,600	151	5.81
Electricity, gas and water	1,400	362	25.86
Manufacturing	*25,000*	*5,239*	*20.96*
a) Baking	2,100	1,294	61.62
b) Printing	4,100	658	16.05
c) All others	18,800	3,287	17.48
Construction	30,900	3,214	10.40
Transportation	11,300	7,107	62.89
Trade	12,100	1,524	12.60
Finance, insurance & real estate	800	—	—
Services	*82,600*	*6,173*	*7.47*
a) Business & recreational	1,100	117	10.64
b) Professional	8,200	699	8.52
c) Public administration	11,400	4,303	37.75
d) Personal	61,900	1,054	1.70
Unspecified	32,300	7,339	22.72

The frequency of conflicts between employers and employees led to the establishment of a Committee of Industrial Relations which published an interim report in October 1943. The Committee's terms of reference were:

"To consider and make recommendations on:

a) Means for ensuring a permanent improvement in the relations between employers and workers;

b) Methods and machinery for securing that, in the future, wages and working conditions in agriculture, industry and commerce should be systematically reviewed by those concerned;

c) Means for a speedy settlement of trade disputes and strikes;

d) The position with regard to trade unions, employers and the non-unionist workers; and

e) Present trends in trade union legislation and organization."[1]

The principal recommendations of this committee were:

1) The establishment of Central Trade Boards and a Central Agricultural Board with local Advisory Committees to make a systematic and continuous review of wages and working conditions and "to provide efficient machinery in cases where existing voluntary negotiation arrangements" are inadequate.

2) The establishment of an Arbitration Court.

---

[1] With these instructions the field covered by the Trade Disputes (Arbitration and Enquiry) Law of 1939 also became a subject of investigation by the Committee. The Trade Disputes Law provided for the foundation of an Arbitration Tribunal and a Board of Enquiry in connection with trade disputes which had to make provisions for the settlement of such disputes. The main contents of the law are: (1) a trade dispute can be brought to the attention of the government by one of the parties; (2) if the government considers it suitable and both parties agree, the conflict can be referred to an Arbitration Tribunal; and (3) if a trade dispute is not brought to its attention, the government can instruct the Board of Enquiry to investigate and report. Under this law, 17 disputes have been referred to arbitration. The real influence of the law has been greater because, since this method of settlement was established, many cases have been settled through arbitration without invoking the provisions of the law.

3) Adoption of the following general procedure in dealing with disputes:

(a) On notification of a dispute or if a dispute threatens the Labor Adviser shall take action and, in the case of failure to arrive at a settlement, shall take the progressive steps outlined below:

   (i) Endeavor to bring the parties together in conformity with the terms of any existing collective bargaining agreement;

   (ii) endeavor to secure agreement to have the matter considered and settled by discussion either directly between the parties (with or without the assistance of the Labor Department's conciliation officers) or by the Central Trade Boards or the Central Agricultural Board;

   (iii) refer to the Arbitration Court within 10 full working days after the date of receipt by the Labor Department of particulars from either party setting out the matters in dispute.

(b) The Award of the Court shall have effect for at least three months from the date thereof, after which the matter may be reopened by either party; provided, that the Arbitration Court may, on the application of either party for good cause, reopen the matter during this three-month period.

(c) The Arbitration Court may, at the discretion of the Chairman, adopt methods of mediation, voluntary arbitration or compulsory arbitration. The Award of the Court shall be published as expeditiously as possible.

(d) In all cases of disputes, whether apprehended or notified, it shall be within the discretion of the Labor Adviser, whether in consultation with the Chairman of the Arbitration Court or not, to intervene at any stage with a view to effecting a settlement.

(e) The testing of this procedure for a period of one or two years, with provision for reconsideration if it is found during that time to create any hardship to disputants.

4) Institution of a "cooling off" period in all cases of disputes affecting any branch of agriculture, industry and commerce during which strikes and lockouts shall be prohibited and machinery for promoting settlement put into operation.

5) The establishment of Departmental Councils to deal, in the first instance, with negotiations and disputes affecting workers that are not in the regular civil service, but employed by government, quasi-government, municipal and parochial authorities.

6) The drafting of a comprehensive Industrial Relations Law.

7) The cooperation of the police in insuring recognition of Trade Unions' rights to peaceful and proper picketing.

8) The acceptance of a Fair Labor Code for the guidance of employers and employees and their representatives in matters affecting industrial relations.

The recommendations made by the Committee have not been carried into effect, a circumstance which caused the Board of Enquiry into Labor Disputes between Trade Unions appointed in 1950 to state in its report: "It was felt by members of the Board—and this view received general support—that, if Government had implemented the recommendations of the Committee on Industrial Relations which reported in 1943, the chaotic conditions created by the current spate of labor disputes between trade unions would not have arisen, as the comprehensive industrial relations law recommended by the Committee would have provided adequate machinery for settlement."

As the idea of organized negotiations between employers and employees gradually took effect, labor-management relations gradually improved. The number of industrial disputes, which during the first postwar years was very high, decreased markedly in 1948 and 1949, as shown in Table 3.

In 1950 a new complication arose. This stemmed from the close relationship between the large political parties and certain of the trade unions. In the beginning of 1950 the union connected with

TABLE 3

INDUSTRIAL DISPUTES INVOLVING STOPPAGE OF WORK ACCORDING TO INDUSTRY

Industrial Group	Year	Disputes	No. of Strikes Beginning in Year	Workers Involved			Man Days Lost		
				Number	% of Total	Average Per Strike	Number	% of Total	Average Per Strike
All Industries	1945	154	97	11,619	100	120	91,655	100	945
	1946	110	76	15,605	100	205	238,540	100	3,139
	1947	27	25	13,414	100	537	258,700	100	10,348
	1948	23	19	3,185	100	167	10,347	100	370
	1949	7	7	356	100	51	2,656	100	379
Agriculture	1945	59	41	6,189	53.3	151	61,280	66.8	1,494
	1946	38	29	9,229	59.2	318	104,699	43.9	3,610
	1947	12	12	11,560	86.2	963	245,540	94.9	20,462
	1948	7	6	1,603	50.3	267	3,866	37.4	644
	1949	3		175	49.2	58	12,363	89.0	788
Manufacturing	1945	48	28	2,526	21.7	90	14,207	15.5	507
	1946	33	21	1,262	8.1	60	3,012	1.2	143
	1947	7	7	884	6.6	126	11,967	4.6	1,710
	1948	11	8	1,177	37.0	147	2,170	21.0	271
	1949	3		61	17.1	20	173	6.5	58
Construction	1945	6	5	203	1.7	41	1,986	2.2	397
	1946	7	6	1,573	10.1	262	6,317	2.7	1,053
	1947	1	1	206	1.5	206	69		69

TABLE 3 (Continued)

INDUSTRIAL DISPUTES INVOLVING STOPPAGE OF WORK ACCORDING TO INDUSTRY

Industrial Group	Year	No. of Strikes		Workers Involved			Man Days Lost		
		Disputes	Beginning in Year	Number	% of Total	Average Per Strike	Number	% of Total	Average Per Strike
Construction	1948								
	1949								
Transportation and Communication	1945	30	17	2,081	18	122	9,347	10.2	550
	1946	13	10	2,028	12.9	203	68,913	28.9	6,891
	1947	1	1	427	3.2	427	427	.2	427
	1948	2	2	191	6.0	96	3,680	35.6	1,840
	1949	1		120	33.7	120	120	4.5	120
Trade	1945	2	2	200	1.7	100	1,800	2	900
	1946	4	2	160	1.0	80	1,096	.5	548
	1947	1	1	45	.3	45	405	.2	405
	1948								
	1949								
Services	1945	8	4	420	3.6	105	3,035	3.3	759
	1946	15	8	1,353	8.7	169	54,503	22.8	6,813
	1947	4	1	292	2.2	97	292	.1	97
	1948	3	3	214	6.7	72	931	6.1	210
	1949								

the minority party started a forceful campaign to attract more members. Among other things it demanded recognition in several cases from employers who, until then, had negotiated with the other large union. In these jurisdictional issues the strike was used as a weapon. The result was a sharp increase in the number of strikes. In 1947 the number of workers involved in strikes was 13,744, of whom 10,533 struck on account of wages, working hours and other working conditions, 369 on account of recognition, and 2,842 on account of sympathy and unlawful dismissal.[2] In 1948 a total of 3,158 workers went out on strike, 2,768 of them on account of wages and the like, and 390 for other reasons. In 1949 the number was even lower, namely 356, of whom 315 were striking for wages and 41 for other reasons. In 1950, however, the picture changed completely. In that year 161 conflicts originated, sixty of which led to strikes. In these strikes 12,705 workers were involved and 75,212 man-days were lost. Of these workers, 4,952 struck on account of wages, 2,312 on account of jurisdictional disputes and union-recognition, and 5,441 for other reasons. Of the lost man-days, 33,694 were caused by strikes based on jurisdictional disputes.

As a consequence of these developments, the government appointed a Board of Enquiry into Labor Disputes between Trade Unions. Its terms of reference were "to enquire into the present position in regard to labor disputes between trade unions and to make recommendations for the provision of machinery for the settlement of such disputes." The board reported on October 6, 1950.

The board conducted a very thorough and extensive investigation. It came to the conclusion that the jurisdictional disputes were actually caused by the political situation. Whereas during the period 1943-1950 only four or five of such disputes had arisen, the number had increased sharply since the beginning of 1950 as a result of the outcome of the general election. The board also stated that these disputes were partly caused by the sharp increase in living costs. "It

---

[2] There is a slight difference between these figures and the ones contained in Table 3. This is probably caused by strikes overlapping from one year to the next.

must be admitted," said the report, "that the workers had genuine grievances which they sought to rectify by affiliation to the combination which appeared to be more powerful." The board found much criticism of the close link between union and political parties. "It was suggested that the unions were the pawn of the parties and that the workers who constituted the membership of these unions were being used merely to enhance the prestige and position of the parties." However, the board thought that not much could be done about this state of affairs. "This situation, desirable or undesirable, is now a *fait accompli* and must be accepted."

The board made the following recommendations:

1) "The machinery and procedure recommended for the settlement of representational disputes should be given statutory force by the enactment of legislation implementing the recommendations detailed below." The general opinion was that there existed no organization and working method to settle the disputes quickly and effectively. The Trade Disputes Law had "proved a totally inadequate instrument for settling these representational disputes."

2) "The Labor Advisor should be designated as the appropriate authority for the settlement of disputes—provisions being made for the setting up of an Industrial Court which could be the final arbiter on all points in disputes." The board advised that he work 'under a clearly defined code setting out methods and procedures to be adopted.

3) The following procedure should be used:

   a) Dispute to be reported to the Labor Adviser by the trade union claiming representational rights or by the employer involved in the dispute.

   b) The Labor Advisor to call a conference of the parties to the dispute as early as possible but not later than 30 days after receipt of notification to decide:
   —the appropriate bargaining unit;
   —data from which the voters' list should be compiled;
   —the date of poll.

   c) The Labor Advisor to prepare a voters' list from an agreed payroll to be supplied by the employer. Copies of the proposed voters' list to be sent to each of the unions involved for scrutiny and approval or objection as the case may be.

   d) In case of objection a further meeting to be called by the Labor Advisor to hear objections and to arrive at agreement.

   e) Posting of voters' list at employer's place of business.

   f) Polling of voters in secret ballot.

   g) Certification of union gaining representational rights (bargaining agent) by the Labor Advisor.

   h) Commencement of negotiation of collective bargaining agreement within 14 days of certification.

   i) Collective bargaining agreement to be filed with the interested parties.

4) "All disputes in respect to procedure or the application of the provisions of the recommended legislation which cannot be settled by reconciliation methods should be referred by the Labor Advisor to the Industrial Court to be set up, for final settlement."

5) "The appropriate authority should determine the appropriate unit of employers in respect of which bargaining rights should be granted to a trade union." It appeared that on this point fundamental differences of opinion existed between the several parties heard by the board. The different suggestions "varied between all-island units for island-wide industries such as sugar, regional units, individual units consisting of each place of business, factory, estate or other establishment, to craft units which would embrace only workers of a skilled trade or occupation." The board arrived at the conclusion that it would be advisable to consider as a unit the "individual plant, place of business, factory, estate or other establishment except where there are well defined craft units which would embrace all workers of a particular skilled occupation in establishment

in a wide area." The Board noted at this point: "Workers' organizations of this type are nonexistent in the island at present. Indeed the two big unions, whose membership comprises the great majority of organized workers, may be described as 'blanket unions,' as they include workers of widely varying status and occupations in their membership." From this observation it was not to be inferred, however, "That it is proposed to create segmentation in industry by recommending individual units. The value of island-wide bargaining is fully appreciated."[3]

6) "The organization of workers to whom the rights of bargaining agent should be given in respect of an appropriate bargaining unit should be decided by secret poll of the workers in the unit. Any trade union gaining a simple majority of the votes polled should be awarded bargaining rights."

7) "A list of persons qualified to vote in a secret poll to determine the bargaining agent in respect of an appropriate unit should be prepared by the appropriate authority in accordance with certain principles laid down in the report."

8) "The request for a new poll to determine the bargaining agent for a unit in respect of which a bargaining agent had already been determined should be made not later than two months prior to the date of expiry of the existing collective bargaining agreement. In cases where there is no recognized bargaining agent or where a trade union which enjoyed bargaining rights has ceased to function, request for a new poll may be made at any time."

9) "The bargaining agent determined in accordance with the statutory provisions, should be awarded sole bargaining rights in respect of the over-all collective bargaining agreement. This agreement would cover the general matters affecting all workers such as wages, hours of employment and working conditions. The minority union or unions should however have the

---

[3] As appears from the report, the Mission is of the opinion that in general industry-wide bargaining should be encouraged.

right to represent their membership in matters affecting individual workers such as discipline, promotion and dismissals.

10) "The collective bargaining agreement between an employer and the duly determined bargaining agent on behalf of the workers in a unit should remain in force for a minimum period of one year and a maximum of two years." The view that an agreement between employer and a "duly determined bargaining agent" should remain in force for at least one year was unanimous.

11) "The principle of the 'closed shop' is considered undesirable and should be outlawed. The union shop principle is, however, permissible."

12) "Strikes and lockouts should be prohibited in any place in respect of which the prescribed machinery for the settlement of disputes has been set in motion."

13) "The institution of penalties for breaches of any statutory provisions for the settlement of disputes is not at present advisable." The two leading trade unions especially stressed this point. They were of the opinion that there was no reason for such penalties because in practice no flagrant violations had occurred in reaching agreements regarding the procedure. In their opinion one could always wait and see whether these would occur in the future, and take measures accordingly. Against this viewpoint some employers' organizations argued that it should be possible to penalize persons directly or indirectly causing a "lightning strike or lockout."

These recommendations have not been completely carried out. In the meantime, however, a procedure has developed which is similar in several respects to that recommended by the Board of Enquiry.

Government Regulations to Promote Industrial Development

PIONEER INDUSTRY LEGISLATION

In order to encourage industrial development special concessions have been granted to certain branches of manufacturing industry. In general, these concessions allow capital expenditure to be deducted from income in cases where it would not normally be allowed for income tax purposes. These concessions are granted to specific industries: the textile industry, the cement industry, the manufacture of buttons and a group of industries which are considered "pioneer industries."

The most important regulation is the one contained in the Pioneer Industries (Encouragement) Law, 1949, which is due to expire at the end of 1952. This law aims in particular "to encourage the establishment and development of new industries in Jamaica." By the terms of this law the Governor in Executive Council can, if he considers it to be in the general interest, designate as a "pioneer industry" an industry which until that time was not carried on to a substantial extent. Manufacturers who wish to establish a "pioneer factory" can qualify for the concessions under the law.

The following concessions are granted to a pioneer manufacturer: (1) during the first five years he may import the building materials and equipment needed for his factory free of duty and tonnage tax; (2) he may, in each of any five of the first eight years, set off against income arising from the manufacture of the relevant pioneer product, a sum equivalent to one fifth of the permissible capital expenditure.[1] No allowance, however, can be made in respect of any year of assessment later than the eighth year after the year of assessment in which the capital expenditure was incurred; (3) if the pioneer manufacturer

---

[1] The normal writing-off for buildings is 2.5-3%, for machines 2.5-10%, for vehicles 20% of the written down value.

is a limited liability company it is entitled, within two years after the end of the year of assessment in which any sum is set-off, to distribute sums so set-off to the shareholders or debenture holders as capital monies free of income tax and surtax.

Special regulations for the textile industry have been set forth in the Textile Industry Encouragement Law of 1947. In 1949 similar regulations were extended to manufacturers of buttons.[2]

Applications for the following pioneer factories have already been approved: byprocrete building units (25);[3] gypsum products such as plaster, boards, planks, blocks and panels (220); cocoa powder, cocoa butter, breakfast chocolate and bakers' chocolate covering (130); laundry blue (20); tool handles; salt and by-products (350); carbon dioxide gas (20); sulphuric acid (20); linstone—a mixture of sawdust and bagasse, sand, cement and lime—for the production of wall blocks, wall panels, etc; wirebound box shooks, packages and sanitary spoons (90); wire nails; cast-iron pipes; jelly crystals and pudding powders (50); bottles and window glass; paper; anhydrous alcohol (50); metal containers (70); plastic products (18); pre-stressed and poststressed concrete (50); synthetic detergents (87); mechanical decoration of glassware (40); the assembly of radio receiving sets, fluorescent lamps, and the manufacture of transformers (20); ice cream cones; and hand-blocking of fabrics.

Of the industries declared pioneer industries, 15 establishments were in operation at the time of the Mission's visit. These stated at the time of application that initially they would employ 562 laborers but that upon completion of their plans a little over 1,000 would be employed.

---

[2] The Cement Industry Encouragement and Control Law of 1948 provides that the Governor in Executive Council can issue licenses for the production of cement, inserting arrangements regarding setting-off against profits of such sums as may be specified in the license. In conjunction with the system used for the other laws, he can also specify that, in case of a company, it may distribute any sum so set-off to shareholders or debenture holders as capital monies free of income tax and surtax.

[3] The figures between brackets indicate the number of employees.

OTHER LEGISLATION

Under the provisions of the *Cement Industry Law of 1948* a number of specific licensing regulations have been issued, some of which tend to create a monopolistic position for the industry.

The Cement Act provides, among other things, for the following:

(1) The manufacturer concerned is given an exclusive license for the manufacture of cement for a period during which the whole factory may be written off, or for 12 years, whichever is shorter.

(2) The manufacturer is entitled to import free of customs duty and tonnage tax—

(a) the equipment and building materials necessary for building and furnishing his factory;

(b) all fuel oil, diesel oil, or other fuel except gasoline, used in the manufacture of the products;

(c) all drums, barrels, bags and other containers of the type in which cement is commonly sold; and

(d) all raw materials used in the manufacture of cement.

(3) (a) Each year, as long as the license is valid, the manufacturer is allowed to set off for income tax purposes against its chargeable income (*i.e.* insofar as it is obtained from cement production in Jamaica) the whole or such portion of its chargeable income as he sees fit, until the total of the amounts so set-off is equal to the amount of the capital expenditure.

(b) Irrespective of the above he can do the usual writing-off.

(4) The company may within two years after the end of the year of assessment during which any amount as described in (3) (a) above has been written off, pay these amounts to the shareholders, debenture holders or income stock holders as capital monies free of income tax and surtax.

(5) During the time the license is valid the manufacturer is exempt from payment of royalties for the mining and transportation of minerals (whether vested in the Crown or not) necessary for the production of cement.

235

(6) He is also exempt from payment of duty or tax on exporting cement.

(7) After production is underway, a ceiling is imposed on the importation of cement and a license is necessary to import it.

(8) The maximum price of cement manufactured in Jamaica is the total of the following prices and costs, minus 30 shillings per ton during the first period[4] and 40 shillings per ton during the second period:

    (a) United Kingdom trading price,

    (b) Marine freight,

    (c) Marine insurance,

    (d) Any customs and tonnage tax which would have been paid on imported cement,

    (e) Wharfage which would have been paid, and

    (f) Any excise duty.

The first maximum price fixed in Jamaica under the terms of this license was £ 9-8s-8d per ton ex factory. This was based on an average price in the United Kingdom of £ 5-4s-4d per ton.

The *regulations for oils and fats* date from 1939. In connection with Jamaica's defense regulations, import restrictions were imposed at that time upon products competing with domestic coconut products. The result of this policy was that the import of edible oils and fats was practically eliminated, and that of laundry soap severely limited. The industry was granted an arrangement for 10 years[5]—on condition that it would conduct its business efficiently —which provided for the following:

(1) Protection against competitive imports;

(2) Price regulations for copra and products manufactured therefrom to the extent that the profits earned from their manufacture would amount to about 5% of the turnover.

---

    [4] The first period expires at the end of the year "in which the difference between the permitted capital expenditure and the total of the possible set-off shall first reach the sum of £ 470,000 or until the seventh anniversary of the appointed date, whichever shall be earlier."

    [5] These regulations remain in force.

(3) No new licenses to be issued for the manufacture of edible oils, soap, margarine, lard compounds, or substitutes thereof, or for the manufacture of coconut products other than copra, charcoal and fiber;

(4) No licenses to be issued for the building of factories manufacturing the products mentioned under (3) above;

(5) No licenses to be issued for the import of machinery other than that essential for replacement and spare parts for the factories in operation.

The *Safeguarding of Local Industries Law* covers the manufacture of matches, condensed milk and milk powder, and cornmeal and whole meal. In several respects it, and the Coconut Industry Law as well, provide for license regulations like those under the Cement Law. The most important of these are the License Conditions for the Jamaica Milk Products Limited. In this case also, an almost complete monopoly has been created, both for production and transportation. The following provision of the License Conditions is worth noting:

"The Governor in Executive Council may, from time to time, fix the prices at which the licensees shall sell condensed milk, manufactured by them, to the wholesalers and to the retailers in Jamaica or its Dependencies. In fixing these prices, which shall be subject to adjustment as conditions, including the cost of production and selling, vary, the licensees shall be allowed a gross profit of 4 shillings per case. In arriving at any price adjustment any fractional part of 1 shilling per case of any increase or decrease of costs shall be disregarded. Any change of costs shall be met by a variation in the price of 2 shillings or some multiple of 2 shillings per case of 48 tins so that the new price shall as nearly as practicable result in a gross profit of 4 shillings a case."

The Capital Structure of Manufacturing Industry

One of the obstacles to the development of industry is the shortage of capital. It is of interest therefore to see how industry is at present financed and particularly how the expansion of recent years has been made possible.

The Mission attempted to collect statistics concerning the capital structure of manufacturing industry in Jamaica. It was not possible to obtain complete information and what follows relates to the larger concerns which could make data available.[1]

In 1950 the capitalization of 25 concerns, distributed over different industries, showed the following picture:

Share Capital and Reserves

Paid in share capital		£ 1,199,565	
Reserves		195,858	
Undistributed profits		318,060	
	Total		£ 1,713,483

Loans and Credits

Long-term loans		£ 541,080	
Short-term credits		171,513	
	Total		£ 712,593
	Grand Total		£ 2,426,076

From the above figures it appears that the proportion of loan capital to total capital is low. Probably this is chiefly due to the traditional preference of investors for real estate or commercial loans as against industrial enterprises and also to the fact that the

---

[1] Figures concerning the sugar industry are not included because it was not possible to isolate that part of the capital which was invested in the processing of sugar cane.

average manufacturing firm is too small in many cases to justify the cost of a credit appraisal.

The means by which the expansion of industry has been financed are illustrated by the following figures for the period 1948-50. During these years the total capital of the same 25 concerns increased by £ 455,584, distributed as follows:

Share Capital and Reserves

Paid in share capital	£	278,145		
Reserves		62,647		
Undistributed profits		40,648		
Total			£	381,440

Loans and Credits

Long-term loans	£	101,346		
Short-term credits		27,202		
Total			£	74,144
Grand Total			£	445,584

Total capital increased from £ 2,426,076 to £ 2,881,660 or by approximately 19%. This was made possible by a 22% increase in share capital and a 10% increase in loan capital and short-term credits.

The firms contributing the above data show a statisfactory rate of profit during the last few years. In 1948, 1949 and 1950 the average return on the capital invested (including reserves and undistributed profits) was 18-19%. With the exception of one branch of industry which had difficulties owing to exceptional circumstances, the rate of profit was statisfactory both for industries processing agricultural products, and for those based on imported raw materials.

Jamaica Government Railway

The financial results of the railway's operations are given below:

TABLE 1

RAILWAY DEFICITS

Year ending March 31	Revenues	Expendi- tures	Operating Balance	Interest and Redemption	Total Deficit[1]
1938-39	£301,265	£287,728	+£ 13,537	£104,981	£ 91,444
1945-46	545,518	673,561	—128,043	99,776	227,819
1946-47	390,473	593,349	—202,876	105,530	308,406
1947-48	359,831	545,497	—185,666	115,723	301,389
1948-49	356,467	550,474	—194,007	116,090	310,097
1949-50	335,172	607,925	—272,753	91,323	364,076
1950-51	326,619	637,446	—310,827	94,443	405,270
1951-52	397,407	706,636	—309,229	94,525	403,754

[1] Does not include depreciation.

Information on the volume of traffic and receipts is contained in the following table:

TABLE 2

RAILWAY TRAFFIC AND RECEIPTS

Year	Tons of Goods	Thousand Ton Miles	Number of Pas- sengers	Receipts in £		
				Goods	Passen- gers[1]	Miscel- laneous[2]
1938-39	336,256	12,134	420,084	238,459	28,480	35,326
1945-46	346,192	12,575	1,395,784	343,874	164,236	37,408
1946-47	308,206	n.a.	957,663	244,307	113,214	32,952
1947-48	322,034	n.a.	612,844	214,220	77,415	58,196
1948-49	307,831	n.a.	600,488	223,305	67,941	65,221
1949-50	326,890	11,521	734,485	216,647	69,150	50,375
1950-51	332,976	12,351	791,418	196,843	75,126	54,650
1951-52	376,849	13,158	804,080	233,763	84,808	78,836

[1] Including mail.
[2] Including wharf receipts.

The comparatively low level of ton-mile revenues in recent years is illustrated by the figures in Table 3:

TABLE 3

AVERAGE REVENUE FROM GOODS HAULED

Year	Goods tonnage	per ton	Revenue per ton-mile	Total Goods Revenue
1938-39	336,256	14/2.2d.	4.65d.	£238,459
1950-51	326,619	11/9.7d.	3.80d.	196,843
1951-52	376,849	11/9.2d.	4.21d.	233,763

Table 4 indicates that, except for bananas, average revenues per ton-mile are very low:

TABLE 4

AVERAGE REVENUE PER TON-MILE FOR PRINCIPAL COMMODITIES

Commodity	1950-51	1951-52
Dyewood	3.32 d.	3.25 d.
Sugar	2.00 d.	2.00 d.
Canes	3.57 d.	3.60 d.
General Merchandise	4.76 d.	4.50 d.
Citrus	3.28 d.	2.77 d.
Bananas	9.00 d.	9.00 d.
All other traffic	2.46 d.	3.35 d.
Average	3.80 d.	4.21 d.

Table 5 shows that the freight rates charged on sugar cane and raw sugar over specified distances are still below prewar levels.

TABLE 5

PREWAR AND POSTWAR FREIGHT RATES ON CANE AND SUGAR

Stations	Mileage	Prewar Rate per Ton	Prewar Rate per Ton Mile	1950-51 Rate per Ton	1950-51 Rate per Ton Mile
To Sevens From:		*Rates on Sugar Cane*			
Suttons	6	2/–	4.0d.	1/10	3.7d.
Chapelton	9	2/6	3.3d.	1/11	2.5d.
Front Hall	16	3/4	2.5d.	2/–	1.5d.
To Kingston From:		*Rates on Sugar*			
Sevens	37	11/10	3.8d.	6/6	2.2d.
New Yarmouth	40	11/10	3.8d.	6/6	1.9d.
Worth Park	24	9/–	4.5d.	4/10	2.4d.
Bybrook	21	7/10	4.4d.	3/9	2.1d.

Recommended Road Program

The road program which the Mission recommends for adoption is set forth below. This program contemplates reconstruction and improvement of the main arterial road in the order of priority shown below. All single lane bridges on these roads should be replaced by two lane bridges and the roads and bridges should be built to sustain the heaviest vehicles anticipated to be permitted for general use in the Island.

Proposed Program

Priority	Route	Mileage
1	From Kingston via Spanish Town, Linstead, Ewarton and Moneague to St. Ann's Bay, with the section from Kingston to Spanish Town constructed as a four lane highway	57
2	From Montego Bay via St. Ann's Bay, Ocho Rios and Oracabessa to Annotto Bay, with a new section of road along the coast from Port Maria to Annotto Bay	96
3	From Spanish Town via May Pen, Porus, Mandeville and Black River to Savanna la Mar, including a by-pass at May Pen	117
	Total Mileage	270

At present day prices the program, including new bridges, widening and the improvement of grades where possible, would cost about £ 7,000,000. It should be considered a long-term program within the framework of which annual appropriations would be available.

The Public Works Department

The director of the Public Works Department is required by law to construct and maintain roads,[1] bridges, schools, hospitals, public buildings, and lighthouses; to maintain and operate the Rio Cobre irrigation canal; to construct small irrigation schemes in cooperation with small landowners; to construct and maintain water supply systems for small communities; and to undertake engineering, architectural and construction work for other government departments. In addition, the department does some work for private concerns such as sugar mills, steamship lines, agricultural societies, and hotels.

To administer its field work the Public Works Department has established three divisions, the Eastern, Central and Western Divisions, each comprising four to five parishes. In each parish there are several substations. The head office, including the administrative and technical staffs, is located in Kingston at Half Way Tree. In April, 1952, the field and head office staffs totaled 2,684, exclusive of casual labor. In 1946 they totaled 2,102.

The department operates a workshop for repair and maintenance of its machinery and equipment and that of other government departments, a storehouse for its supplies and materials and a concrete pipe manufacturing plant.

The Mission did not make a detailed study of the organization and functional operation of the department, but it did have an opportunity to see the workshops and look at the administrative procedures, cost accounting, annual reports, in the light of the over-all responsibilities of the department.

In the opinion of the Mission, the responsibilities of the Public Works Department for the construction and maintenance of schools, hospitals and public buildings should be transferred to the various government departments concerned and whenever possible the con-

---

[1] The Governor is empowered by law to designate any road a main road.

struction work should be carried out by private contractors on a competitive bid basis. Each department should provide its own maintenance staff. This would make it possible to handle the work of maintaining a large number of buildings and making numerous minor repairs to pushbuttons, doors, windows, floors and miscellaneous plumbing fixtures more expeditiously and more cheaply and would eliminate a burdensome load of paper work. The work undertaken for other government departments should be held to a minimum and unless it is clearly of the type which the Public Works Department is equipped to handle, such as airport work, it should be referred to private contractors by the departments concerned.

Under the present procedures, the Public Works Department has little or no voice in programming its work except that relating to the maintenance of roads, bridges, lighthouses and the Rio Cobre Canal. Even with regard to roads, the Public Works Department cannot formulate and carry out a program of construction of new roads or reconstruction of existing roads because it can only undertake new road work for which a specific appropriation has been made. No appropriations are made for road programs, only for road projects of a very specific nature. The work involved for schools, hospitals, public buildings, prisons, police stations, and other departments is all programmed by them with little regard to the volume of work or staff required for the principal responsibilities of the Public Works Department for roads, bridges, irrigation and water supplies. The cost of the work, however, is defrayed from the Public Works Department's annual appropriations.

Administration of the department is hampered by entirely too much correspondence, especially between the Colonial Secretariat and the department, regarding minor matters. Innumerable "minutes" are written about problems involving small expenditures, such as extra per diem allowances for employees in the field, which the department ought to have authority to decide for itself. The entire concept of the relationship between the Public Works Department and the Secretariat should be reviewed in order to simplify the time-consuming procedures that have grown up over a long period of time. The department should be given much more autonomy with regard to employment, allowances, and other purely clerical and administrative matters. It should also be allowed to make small purchases without going through the Crown Agents.

The cost accounting procedures now in use are of little value to the Director or any of his senior assistants as there is apparently no way in which he can promptly obtain cost figures on any project which include all overhead and other indirect charges. For example, there is no method of distributing equitably the cost of operation (which should include maintenance) of vehicles and other equipment among the jobs on which they work. If, for instance, a vehicle happens to be working on a project and it breaks down, the repairs are charged to that project although it may have worked equally as long on other projects; no means exist by which the cost of the workshop can be allocated to various projects. Many more illustrations could be cited to indicate that no cost accounting is carried out by the department. Records are kept primarily for the purpose of showing what expenditures have been made under the various appropriation headings. In the published records of such expenditures the item of unallocated stores is included as an expenditure. An examination of the breakdown of this item reveals that it includes not only expenditures for stores but the value of stores in stock at the end of the fiscal year.

In the opinion of the Mission the entire cost accounting and auditing systems of the department should be discarded and there should be substituted dependable systems which would reflect the true cost of projects and the status of expenditures. If necessary, a firm of consultants should be employed to install the systems.

The published annual reports of the department give only meager details of the work accomplished and are dominated by a mass of figures which merely show under what vote or appropriation heading the expenditures were made. These are of little value to anyone in or out of the government, especially as many of the headings are so brief and uninformative that they convey no idea of the purpose of the expenditure. Examples of such items are: "Loan Works,"

"Miscellaneous Part I," "Miscellaneous Part II," "Rehabilitation Works," "Subventions." The annual reports should present an intelligible picture of the year's activities, forecast future operations, disclose plans for continued improvements and in general should be links in a chain of cumulative and informative data showing what has been accomplished and what is planned for the future. Figures should illustrate, not dominate, the reports.

In the observation of the Mission, the Director and his senior assistants are so burdened down with unnecessary correspondence and detailed administrative matters that they have little time for their more important duties of supervising the work in the field. The Mission also noted in the annual report that records are kept of the number of pieces of correspondence handled, the number of drawings and prints made, the consumption of native cedar shingles by the department, the quantities of native corn used and many other unrelated bits of information which must require many man-hours of clerical time to compile. This time could surely be used to better advantage.

The Kingston Workshops were established in their present location on the waterfront about 26 years ago (1926) for the maintenance of the comparatively small amount of road machinery and automotive equipment then in use and to handle miscellaneous repairs to equipment and buildings. In size, the workshops remain unchanged, but the volume of work they have been called upon to handle has increased enormously. Some machine tools have been added but they have had to be crowded in, resulting in very limited working space for machine operators and materials handling. Lack of any provision for lifting materials and transporting them by mechanical means also makes for inefficiency. Most of the 40 machine tools in the shops are over 20 years old and three are over 50 years old. The power tools are driven from a single overhead shaft. Not only is this an outmoded system and wasteful of power but the belts from the shaft are unguarded and constitute a danger to the operators.

The woodworking shop, the foundry, the blacksmith shop and the sheet metal shop are all inadequately equipped and poorly located for a proper flow of materials. The space allocated for the storage of tools and supplies makes it difficult, if not impossible, to keep accurate records of the tools and supplies issued, and no space whatsoever is provided for a stock of materials. The workshops are not permitted to keep any appreciable amount of materials or spare parts and must therefore either draw materials and parts from Central Stores, or purchase them in small quantities in the open market. The workshops open at 7:00 a.m. but the Central Stores do not open until 9:00 a.m.

There is no space for parking vehicles awaiting repair within the shop area and vehicles are parked on the street without protection from pilferage or the weather.

The accounting procedures are totally inadequate as the clerical staff to perform the accounting work is too small and the records kept are poor. The supervisory staff lacks proper authority to take prompt disciplinary action and as a consequence the labor is inefficient and morale is low.

No action has been taken to rectify these deplorable conditions because for some time plans have been afoot for moving the workshops to a more suitable location. In the opinion of the Mission thousands of pounds will continue to be wasted annually as long as the shops remain in their present location. If the Public Works Department plans to add to its mechanical and automotive equipment each year (as it should), adequate shops should be provided for its maintenance. Until sufficient shop capacity is provided, no further mechanical or automotive equipment should be ordered. In the present circumstances it is the height of folly to give the Public Works Department any new equipment.

In summary, the Mission recommends that (1) the Public Works Department be relieved of responsibility for all work other than roads, bridges, irrigation reclamation, water supplies and lighthouses, (2) the department undertake no work for other government departments except that closely related to its own work, and (3) the workshop capacity be increased and both the workshops and Central Stores moved to more suitable locations. In addition, the cost accounting and auditing procedures of the department ought to be thoroughly revised. Within the framework of the changes recommended, there should be a thorough reorganization of the Department in order to establish a more efficient distribution and flow of work and to determine personnel needs for the work remaining. The Mission recommends the employment of a firm of management consultants to effect the reorganization.

Regulation of Road Traffic

In general the law regulating road traffic in Jamaica follows the pattern of the road traffic legislation in the United Kingdom. The law, which was based on a study prepared by a Transport Commission in 1935, was enacted in 1937.

The law provides for the establishment of an Island Traffic Authority, subordinate regional Traffic Area Authorities, and a Licensing Authority. It makes the Island Traffic Authority responsible for regulation and control of road traffic and for enforcement of the provisions of the law.

Mr. C. E. Rooke, C.M.G., M. Inst. T., who was retained in 1945 to investigate all forms of transport, made a detailed study of the Road Traffic Law of 1937 and concluded that the law needed clarification and amendment with respect to the following subjects: jurisdiction of the Island Traffic Authority over the Licensing Authority; licensing procedures; terminology; registration of vehicles; safety requirements; limitations on area of operations; and overloading.

The Mission has studied Mr. Rooke's report and concurs in his findings. It is our understanding that none of his recommendations have been implemented. The Mission recommends that the Road Traffic Law be amended to eliminate the deficiencies which Mr. Rooke pointed out and to place responsibility for the control of traffic on the roads and the enforcement of the law in the hands of the police. The law at present does not give the Island Traffic Authority any means or personnel for carrying out these provisions.

The Mission also recommends that the law be amended to provide for the staggering of the examinations required for a certificate of fitness for a license to operate vehicles. Such inspections are required once each year. Each year, towards the end of the period, great congestion occurs at the inspection offices and vehicle owners lose a great deal of time waiting in line. If examinations of vehicles were related to expiration dates of their insurance policies, which are spread rather evenly over the year, this congestion would be eliminated and the work of the inspection officers simplified.

Recommendations have already been made that insurance policies be issued only to applicants producing a certificate of fitness dated not more than 30 days prior to the application. For vehicles not insured, examinations could easily be spread throughout the year.

The load limits on vehicles provided in the law are unrealistic. Virtually all freight-carrying vehicles operating for hire or for their owners' account exceed the established load limits and little or no attempt is made to enforce the limits set forth in the law. If the law were strictly enforced, most of the commercial vehicles would be forced out of business. The law therefore should be changed to bring the limits up to date and in line with present day vehicle capacities. The heavier vehicles however should be restricted to routes with roads and bridges capable of sustaining the loads. The Mission recommends a thorough review of the load limits and the establishment of new limits which are both safe and reasonable. Once this is done, scales should be installed at various points and the new limits strictly enforced.

Ports

NUMBER AND REGISTERED TONNAGE OF VESSELS IN JAMAICA

| Year | Total Arrivals | | Sailing Vessels | | Steam and Motor Vessels | |
	No.	Registered Tonnage	No.	Registered Tonnage	No.	Registered Tonnage
1937	1,510	4,641,300	53	4,567	1,457	4,636,733
1938	1,403	4,279,017	70	6,641	1,333	4,272,376
1939	1,287	3,937,859	58	5,870	1,229	3,931,989
1940	838	1,883,922	60	6,565	778	1,877,357
1941	737	1,426,803	58	8,199	679	1,418,604
1942	375	613,516	53	6,384	322	607,132
1943	362	257,053	95	8,729	267	248,324
1944	370	387,163	28	3,097	342	384,066
1945	359	584,402	22	1,965	337	582,437
1946	524	1,129,766	21	4,428	503	1,125,338
1947	642	1,498,807	22	8,836	620	1,489,971
1948	772	1,715,239	12	2,052	760	1,713,186
1949	771	1,961,134	4	1,066	767	1,960,068
1950		2,000,000[1]				

[1] Estimated.

Tonnage of Cargo Discharged and Loaded at Ports of Jamaica

Year	Grand Total	Kingston			Ports			
		Total	Discharged	Loaded	Total	Outports Discharged	Outports Loaded	
1937	1,219,121	799,717	522,436	277,281	419,404	26,748	392,656	
1938	1,192,670	792,333	522,877	269,456	400,337	50,189	350,148	
1939	1,209,004	853,835	568,548	285,287	355,169	22,979	332,190	
1940	878,046	731,589	484,472	247,117	146,457	11,851	134,606	
1941	864,255	673,494	484,522	188,972	190,761	7,411	183,350	
1942	527,228	416,130	308,928	107,202	111,098	7,233	103,865	
1943	567,927	428,766	278,858	149,908	139,161	12,610	126,551	
1944	642,427	474,411	371,253	103,158	168,016	17,877	150,139	
1945	619,027	471,194	344,615	126,579	147,833	35,767	112,066	
1946	707,213	462,523	384,076	78,447	244,690	31,594	213,096	
1947	774,325	546,353	431,602	114,751	227,972	19,881	208,091	
1948	801,976	515,364	436,736	78,628	286,612	19,269	267,343	
1949	731,213	532,654	410,386	122,268	198,559	11,474	187,085	
1950	1,100,000[1]	909,579	644,317	265,262	190,500[1]			

[1] Estimated.

Power Licenses

Licenses to supply electricity are issued by the Governor in Executive Council under authority of the Electric Lighting Law, Chapter 258. Some licenses have been issued for an indefinite term with the option given to the local authority to purchase at the end of 42 years at its fair market value the property of the supply company within the area included in the license. If the option is not then exercised, the license runs for successive terms of 10 years with the local authority having the option to purchase at the end of each period. Other licenses are issued for definite terms such as 20 and 30 years and, latterly, temporary licenses have been issued for the period of only one year pending the development of a model license now under preparation by a commission appointed by the government.

The first electric license was issued in 1892 to the Jamaica Electric Light and Power Company, Limited, for the supply of electricity in the then city and parish of Kingston, exclusive of the town of Port Royal. In 1907 this license was transferred to the Jamaica Light and Power Company, Limited, of Canada and, in 1923 to the Jamaica Public Service Company, Limited.

At the present time Jamaica Public Service Company, Limited, operates in 11 of the island's 14 parishes under authority of the licenses listed below:

LICENSES IN PERPETUITY

Rio Cobre Electric License	1898
St. Andrew Electric License	1909
St. Andrew Electric License	1929
Kingston Electric License	1892
St. Catherine Electric Licenses	1927
Clarendon Electric License and St. Catherine Electric License Extension	1930

TERM LICENSES

Port Maria Electric License	1934

POWER LICENSES

St. Elizabeth Electric License	1935
Hanover Electric License	1935
St. Ann Electric License	1935
Trelawny Electric License	1935
St. Mary Electric License	1939
Brown's Town Electric License	1940
St. Ann and St. Mary Electric License	1940
Port Antonio Electric License	1930
St. Ann Electric (J.P.S. Co. Ltd) License	1945

TEMPORARY LICENSES

St. Mary Temporary License	
May Pen Electric License	1929
Palisadoes Temporary License	
Trelawny Temporary License	
Port Antonio Temporary License	
St. Ann Temporary License	
St. James Temporary License	

The Jamaica Public Service Company, Limited, has by its licenses the authority to operate within the entire parishes of

Kingston
St. Andrew
St. Catherine
Clarendon
St. Ann
St. Mary
Trelawny
St. James

and in the capital towns of the parishes of

Hanover
St. Elizabeth
Portland

Operation of Jamaica Public Service Co.

INSTALLED AND EFFECTIVE CAPACITIES OF POWER PLANTS, MAY 1952

Station	Type	Cycle Fre- quency	Installed Capacity kw	Effective Capacity kw
Gold Street	Steam	40	9,500	9,000
Bog Walk	Hydro	40	1,050	500
Upper White River	Hydro	40	3,600	1,950
Lower White River	Hydro	40	4,750	3,200
Roaring River	Hydro	40	4,050	3,600
Vernam Field	Diesel	40	2,333	2,283
Montego Bay	Diesel	60	1,415	1,415
Port Antonio	Diesel	60	298	298
Black River	Diesel	60	40	40
Falmouth	Diesel	60	119	119
Lucea	Diesel	60	64	64
Total			27,219	22,469

H T TRANSMISSION LINES, MAY 1952

59 Miles of pole lines   66,000 volts
45 Miles of pole lines   33,000 volts
227 Miles of pole lines   12,000 to 6,600 volts

OPERATION OF JAMAICA PUBLIC SERVICE CO.

GENERATION, PEAK LOADS AND LOAD FACTORS

Year	Total Generation kwh	Generation 40 Cycle System kwh	Peak Load 40 Cycle System kw	Load Factor 40 Cycle System
1938	16,891,000	15,750,580	4,350	41.5%
1939	19,020,700	17,998,170	4,000	51.4%
1940	25,707,900	24,649,830	5,500	57.0%
1941	28,590,300	27,445,670	6,500	48.3%
1942	30,071,500	29,051,910	6,600	50.4%
1943	27,924,100	26,947,910	5,860	52.5%
1944	33,456,300	32,363,100	6,760	54.6%
1945	36,075,500	34,741,730	7,500	53.0%
1946	45,282,400	43,024,500	8,600	57.0%
1947	50,630,400	48,090,630	10,200	54.0%
1948	53,970,700	51,236,780	10,900	53.8%
1949	65,035,300	61,762,550	13,450	52.3%
1950	74,591,700	71,278,720	14,430	56.5%
1951	86,045,100	82,491,940	16,150	58.3%
1952	96,129,000	91,880,000	21,000	50.0%

Proposals Relating to
Primary School Education

The Mission has indicated, in general terms, its conclusion that the primary school system does not attain full effectiveness. This is mostly because many children are not enrolled at all. Partly also it is due to the irregular attendance of many of those who are enrolled, which frustrates teachers' efforts to pursue a systematic schedule of studies.

Irregularities in attendance are impressive. For example, average attendance in all primary schools in the month of January, 1951 —55,000 pupils—was 50% higher than in the preceding month. Even in the compulsory education areas attendance in January was 35% higher than in December. In the rest of the island it rose by 64%. In October 1950, average attendance was 13,000 less than in September. Moreover, the days of the week and even the hours of the day show wide fluctuations. Tuesday and Wednesday bring good attendance; Friday and Monday are very poor. School bells may ring at 9 o'clock, but the call of the roll is delayed until 9:30 when many more pupils will be present to respond.

Probably very little of the irregularity is either wilful or defiant. In part it arises from economic and social factors—the lack of extra clothing, or the parents' need to have children fetch water or run errands, help prepare crops for market, or attend younger children. At some seasons, heavy rains discourage or may actually prevent school attendance, at least in the country. Poor attendance on Fridays leads teachers to relegate to that day the subjects that do not interest them and probably will not interest the children, with the inevitable result that attendance on Fridays is still further discouraged.

An important underlying factor within the schools themselves has been characterized by a responsible authority as "the rigidity of a curriculum which is not only often divorced from the realities of a child's life but in many instances has not even the prospect of any new learning to hold out to a child who has passed the age of 12." It is notable that, in those schools which have introduced practical activities such as elementary woodwork and home economics, pupils' interest has increased and attendance has correspondingly improved.

Fluctuations in enrollment pose another serious problem. Each succeeding generation of children shows a sharp rise in school enrollments at the ages of seven to nine, a peak at the age nine to 10, and then a rapid decline which accelerates sharply after the age of 12. For many children, therefore, a primary school career consists of three or four years of intermittent attendance. It is to these children that the classroom work is inevitably adjusted, so that the regular attendant over the standard eight-year period allotted to elementary education and the bright pupil who could progress rapidly if permitted to do so, waste much of their time in school.

Despite under-enrollment and irregular attendance, the schools suffer from overcrowding and a shortage of good teachers. What is the remedy? Some have suggested resort to a double shift system, in which some children will attend mornings and others in the afternoon, under the same teachers in the same classrooms. The Education Department has, in fact, announced that it will experiment with such arrangements in one or two communities, and will endeavor to enlist parents' understanding and cooperation.

The double shift may help, but unless it is accompanied by greater regularity in attendance it can only shorten still further the number of hours which the average child—the interested child as well as the uninterested one—spends in school. Under present circumstances, which dictate rigorous economy in the use of resources, more drastic action appears to be required.

In frank recognition of present realities, it might be better to shorten the formal duration of schooling at the elementary level, and at the same time provide an intermediate school (or a modified senior school) for those who show an aptitude and a will to continue their studies. The educational authorities have expressed misgivings that children would be turned out of school at age 12 or 13 without prospects of employment for some years. This is indeed a problem which cannot be ignored, but it is one that already exists, since children now drop out of school early. Moreover, the need to find wholesome pursuits for young people should not be permitted to divert the schools from educational objectives. Admittedly as the schools are made a more valuable force in the life of the people, the problems of overcrowding will be automatically intensified; but this will be a transitional problem, since useful education will assuredly yield some of its dividends in higher productivity which in turn will support more adequate facilities. Parents and children are likely to accord a higher value to the privilege of school attendance when there is danger of losing it, and this would be a significant social gain.

Specifically, the Mission suggests that consideration be given to the following types of interrelated measures:

(1) A limitation of the standard primary school education to four years;

(2) A firm policy of cancelling the privilege of enrollment for any children who—for causes other than sickness or equally valid reasons—has had an attendance record of less than 60% during the preceding school year;

(3) The provision of postprimary, presecondary school classes for those children who have demonstrated ability beyond the primary level but are not old enough for secondary school;

(4) The provision of special continuation classes, meeting on two or three half-days a week, in which boys and girls who have finished primary school—and possibly even some who have dropped out—might acquire useful pre-vocational training;

(5) Gradual expansion of various auxiliary services and interests for young people, including museums, libraries, boys' and girls' clubs, scouting, junior 4-H clubs, and other similar activities;

(6) More extensive provision for young people in adult educa-

tion work and in other programs of the Jamaica Social Welfare Commission and in the work of various voluntary bodies.

Far from lowering the educational standards of the country, a program along these general lines should provide a basis and the incentives for a substantial improvement in standards. At the outset, more efficient use of teachers and buildings (under the first two measures) should release the staff and facilities necessary to enlarge post-primary opportunities for those ready to make good use of them.

The suggested changes will require some reorientation of the present educational staff and some additions to the supervisory staff assisting the Director of Education. An additional annual expenditure, estimated roughly at £ 20,000, might be necessary for strengthening the supervision and inspection of local schools, providing additional expert guidance to teachers facing new tasks and responsibilities, conducting intensive work with parents' groups as well as teachers to foster understanding and support of the program, and augmenting the central administrative staff of the Education Department. This would be a recurrent expenditure, beyond the normal rise of about £ 3,000 a year in the budgeting allowance for administration and inspectors.

Public Health

In accordance with our recommendations, expenditures on public health would rise to about £ 2.7 million by 1961-62 or by more than 50% over current levels. A considerable part of these larger outlays would be devoted to improving and expanding hospital facilities and raising gradually the standards of the curative services. The rest should make possible a significant enlargement of the preventive services.[1] Since the present shortage of physicians is likely to last a long time, it is particularly important not only to train sufficient medical auxiliaries, but, above all, to give more emphasis to those aspects of the public health program which will help to prevent disease.

Without undertaking to formulate a specific program, the Mission has identified several areas in which it recommends a strengthening of activities designed to prevent illness and improve health generally. In certain of these fields the government is already active, and the possibilities for fruitful extension will be readily evident; in others, the government will find it desirable to undertake a systematic valuation before deciding upon specific measures.

(1) NUTRITION

Medical officers commonly point to dietary imbalance as the root of much of the illness and debility which they observe. The Nutrition Committee of the Jamaican Branch of the British Medical Association made a general study in 1945, and in the following year the Medical Research Council published Dr. Waterlow's study of the nutritional condition of babies and young children. There have not

---

[1] The new mosquito control program launched with the help of the World Health Organization and the Internationl Children's Emergency Fund should permit in a few years an annual reduction of £ 30,000 below the amount made available for mosquito control in 1952-53. This saving will make possible a further expansion in other preventive activities.

been, however, more detailed and specific studies to determine precisely the dietary deficiencies or imbalances which now exist, their location and extent, and the specific implications for agricultural policy and practice. Studies showing what basic changes might appropriately be made in the island food supply and in the food-handling and eating habits of the people cannot be made by the medical profession alone, but they do require medical guidance.

Accordingly, the intention of the Medical Service to add a nutrition officer to its staff in 1953 is of great significance. He should be able to arrange for the needed studies and to provide leadership in the practical application of the findings. He can also guide and give new impetus to the efforts already being made to improve nutrition to the extent that this can be done without major changes in the food supply itself. These efforts have concentrated on teaching housewives what constitutes good diet and good cooking (as is done in the Social Welfare Commission's campaign for "Food for Family Fitness"), on providing lunches at schools, and on introducing a limited amount of food-yeast into the vitamin-deficient diet of the people.

Coordinated activity on the subject of nutrition might yield contributions of the highest order for preventive medicine.

(2) WATER SUPPLY

Water supply poses special health problems because impure supplies may spread disease directly; stagnant pools provide breeding places for disease-bearing mosquitoes and other insects; and shortages of water prevent healthful practices of personal hygiene and the safe dilution of sewage. These problems are acute in most rural areas and even in many urban places during some seasons. The importance of boiling water is widely taught, but the safeguard is widely ignored —even by the very schoolteachers who try to impress their pupils with its importance. It is, indeed, a generally impracticable substitute for the use of a safe source of water.

In its proposals for agricultural improvement, the Mission has included a ten-year program of water-supply improvement related to a rural housing program. The projected expenditures include £ 1.5 million of central government outlays on rural water supply— an amount that should as far as possible be supplemented by the parishes and by individual householders. The program is not, however, conceived on a scale to permit the piping of water into rural homes and, of itself, will not assure safe water supplies. As part of a general campaign of public health education people must be taught to handle water in such a way as to prevent pollution. Beyond this, they need guidance in locating and conserving safe supplies as a type of community enterprise.

(3) DENTAL CARE

With a ratio of only one dentist to each 17,000 of the population, dental care for adults at present is substantially limited to extraction of defective teeth. The school dental service in 10 parishes extends to prophylactic and other treatments and fillings, as well as extraction, for those children who are served, but it reaches only a fraction of the population. In this professional field, as in the practice of medicine, supplementary personnel and the most effective use of scarce skills are essential. The methods and importance of oral hygiene— and the effects of diet on the teeth—should be taught, not only in the schools, but also through the other resources of the health services.

(4) DIAGNOSIS AND INOCULATIONS

A substantial part of the credit for improving health conditions must be given to the preventive services performed by prenatal clinics, infant welfare clinics, various outpatient clinics, the organized corps of midwives, and the public health nurses. Much has been achieved through early diagnosis, inoculations, and treatment for a variety of ills in health centers, traveling health units, and dispensaries dealing with health problems generally, and through special clinics, special campaigns and selective surveys aimed particularly at tuberculosis, yaws, typhoid fever and venereal disease.

Some of these efforts might well be strengthened. The projected capital outlays for health services contemplate the expenditure, over the next decade, of £ 100,000 for five or possibly more district health centers; a contribution of £ 20,000 toward expansion of the British West Indies Institute for training public health personnel; and expansion of the outpatient clinics at Kingston Public Hospital, some of the country hospitals, and the Mental Hospital.

These improvements will require some expansion of staff. Beyond this, it appears that in some parts of the country the ratio of population to public health personnel is very high. For example, Clarendon, St. Elizabeth, and St. Thomas have comparatively few public health nurses. Enlargement of staff cannot, of course, be based on population ratios alone; it must be adjusted to the incident of preventable disease, the sparsity of population and ease of travel, and numerous other considerations. In general, however, the recent record suggests that modest additions to the present public health personnel would bring significant gains in many parts of the island.

(5) SANITATION

Problems of sanitary engineering will necessarily receive attention as an aspect of the general problem of water supply, since practices employed in disposing of wastes not only affect the purity of the water supply but also depend in some measure upon its adequacy. Efforts are already under way to assure that each household has a reasonably sanitary latrine and that the principles of sanitation are generally understood; these efforts could usefully be intensified.

Demonstrations and home visits of public health personnel should emphasize good methods of safeguarding and storing water and food, disposing of refuse, safeguarding latrines, and providing other sanitary facilities.

(6) PUBLIC HEALTH EDUCATION

Efforts in public health education should be coordinated with all the other important aspects of public health work, so as to win continuing popular cooperation in each type of activity. These educational activities, now conducted mainly through the special training of school teachers and through public lectures, exhibits, and cinema shows, might be extended to include special public health institutes for those leaders of community groups who, like the school teachers, are in strategic positions to disseminate information widely among the people.

Financing of the Program

The tables following show in greater detail how the projected expenditures given in Chapter IX were built up. The greater part of these expenditures was estimated after specific study of various fields of government activity by individual members of the Mission: the remainder was projected on the basis of certain assumptions. The totals for the entire period ending with the fiscal year 1961-62 represent the sum of expenditures allocated to each of the ten years. Only an annual allocation of expenditures could reveal whether or not the proposed acceleration of outlays was likely to prove feasible. In connection with these figures, however, we should like to make two points. First, all the estimates are unavoidably subject to varying degrees of error. The totals and their component parts indicate only the general magnitudes of the expenditures we recommend. Second, the phasing implied in the projected annual totals is purely illustrative. In no way does it reflect a desire or attempt to draw up annual budgets for a ten-year period—a task we consider impossible. In essence the primary object of the estimates was to determine whether the Mission's recommendations were likely to fall within the probable financial limitations.

Table 1 gives details of what we have called the "Development Program," and Table 2 gives a more detailed account of the expenditures for the agricultural program. While most of the items in Table 1 can be regarded in a broad sense as capital expenditure, this does not mean that they cannot be financed from general revenues. On the contrary, the estimates for the government budget (Table 4) show an accumulated surplus of £ 8.3 million over the period which will be available as a contribution to the expenditure. No particular significance should therefore be attached to the fact that a particular item of expenditure appears in the Development Program instead of in Table 3, "Development and Welfare Expenditure within the Budget."

TABLE 1

DEVELOPMENT PROGRAM

(£ thousands)

	1952-53	1953-54	1954-55	1955-56	1956-57	1957-58	1958-59	1959-60	1960-61	1961-62	Total
1. a) Agricultural Development	—	319	538	1,108	1,904	1,372	1,160	1,080	980	580	9,041
b) Production & Development Loans (Net of Repayment)	—	510	643	768	566	525	482	554	416	176	4,640
2. Railway (Capital Investment)	—	118	161	95	75	75	51	45	25	25	670
3. Harbors	—	30	50	—	—	—	—	—	—	—	80
4. Airports	350	300	350	200	—	—	—	—	—	—	1,200
5. Land Survey	—	170	180	75	75	75	75	—	—	—	650
6. Sugar Mill	—	—	—	—	—	1,000	1,000	—	—	—	2,000
7. IDC (Development Loans)	—	200	250	300	350	400	450	500	500	550	3,500
8. IDC Technical Service	—	10	12	14	16	18	18	18	18	18	142
9. Rural Housing & Water Supplies	—	80	330	430	330	670	470	430	510	250	3,500
10. Urban Housing	—	—	220	220	300	300	290	240	220	210	2,000
11. Education (Capital Outlay)	—	529	519	565	510	455	449	442	456	476	4,401
12. Health (Capital Outlay)	—	300	300	300	300	300	300	300	300	300	2,700
Total	350	2,566	3,553	4,075	4,426	5,190	4,745	3,609	3,425	2,585	34,524

TABLE 2

PHASING OF TEN-YEAR AGRICULTURAL PROGRAM
(£ thousands)

Expenditures	1952-53	1953-54	1954-55	1955-56	1956-57	1957-58	1958-59	1959-60	1960-61	1961-62	Total
1. Soil Conservation[1]		70	120	200	420	420	420	420	420	210	2,700
2. Pasture Rehabilitation[1]		30	60	100	180	180	180	180	180	110	1,200
3. Afforestation		40	50	100	130	130	130	130	130	130	970
4. Irrigation		125	210	470	900	300	120	70	—	—	2,195
5. Reclamation		4	8	8	24	112	120	100	80	20	476
6. Administration of Schemes		50	90	230	250	230	190	180	170	110	1,500
Total Non-recoverable		319	538	1,108	1,904	1,372	1,160	1,080	980	580	9,041
7. Loans[2]											
a) Crop Loans		400	900	1,500	1,800	2,100	2,400	2,800	3,100	3,300	18,300
b) Development		75	90	88	102	105	110	125	125	120	940
c) Soil Conservation[3]		25	40	65	140	140	140	140	140	70	900
d) Pasture Rehabilitation		10	20	33	60	60	60	60	60	37	400
Total Recoverable		510	1,050	1,686	2,102	2,405	2,710	3,125	3,425	3,527	20,540
8. Repayments on Loans											
a) Crop Loans		—	400	900	1,500	1,800	2,100	2,400	2,800	3,100	15,000
b) Developments		—	—	—	—	6	14	23	32	42	117
c) Soil Conservation		—	5	12	24	50	78	102	123	146	540
d) Pasture Rehabilitation		—	2	6	12	24	36	46	54	63	243
Total Repayments		—	407	918	1,536	1,880	2,228	2,571	3,009	3,351	15,900
9. Net Total of Loan Expenditure		510	643	768	566	525	482	554	416	176	4,640
Area under cultivation (arable and orchards 1,000 acres)		453	460	470	485	500	525	550	575	600	(Increase 33%)
Value of agricultural production (million £)		25.5	26.5	27	27.5	28.5	30	32	34	36	(Increase 44%)

[1] Grants only, loan part under 8c and 8d.

[2] Amounts to be disbursed in the indicated years.

[3] Repayable in five years.

269

Table 3 shows the effect of our recommendations on particular items of budget expenditure with which the Mission was concerned. In this table the expenditure figures for 1952-53 have been taken from the current estimates and include all expenditure on the items whether they appear as "Ordinary Estimates" or "Development Estimates" and whether financed from general revenue or from Colonial Development and Welfare Funds.[1] One point worth noting is the slight fall in expenditure on Education and Health from 1952-53 to 1953-54. This arises because for the years after 1952-53 all the capital expenditure in these fields for the latter year has been shown in Table 1, items 11 and 12, and only the costs of operation and maintenance are shown in Table 3, whereas capital expenditures for 1952-53 are included with operation and maintenance costs in Table 3.

In Table 4, total budget government expenditure and revenue are projected. The first line is taken from the totals shown in Table 3. The item for "Other Budget Expenditure," which covers all items other than those in line 1 (except debt service), had to be estimated arbitrarily. We have assumed it would increase by approximately 2% per year, or a rate equivalent to the population increase. The service charges on the public debt have been estimated by adding to the existing net debt charges the amounts required to service, at the rate of 5½% (assuming 4½% interest and 1% sinking fund), that proportion of the new borrowing which will have to be serviced from general revenue. From the total of these items is subtracted the reduction in the railway deficit and a small sum for the savings which will follow from the land survey. The resulting net budget expenditure can be compared with the revenue estimates which are assumed to increase by 5% per year in line with the national income. (In the first year the increase is slightly larger as there is some prospect that revenue was conservatively estimated in the 1952-53 budget.) The remainder of the Colonial Development and Welfare allocation has been prorated over the last three years of the Ten Year Plan.

---

[1] Except expenditure on "Hurricane Rehabilitation." All the special hurricane relief expenditure has been eliminated from all the tables.

TABLE 3

DEVELOPMENT AND WELFARE EXPENDITURE WITHIN THE BUDGET

(£ thousands)

	1952-53	1953-54	1954-55	1955-56	1956-57	1957-58	1958-59	1959-60	1960-61	1961-62
1. Roads¹	844	945	945	945	950	970	980	995	1,010	1,030
2. Public Works other than Roads, Schools and Hospitals	703	700	700	710	710	720	720	730	730	730
3. Education	1,700	1,614	1,798	1,953	2,096	2,238	2,342	2,441	2,541	2,626
4. Health	2,200	1,900	2,000	2,100	2,200	2,300	2,400	2,500	2,600	2,700
5. Social Welfare	500	600	600	650	650	700	700	750	750	800
6. Tourist Trade Publicity (Net of Passenger Duty)	80	80	94	118	132	136	130	124	118	112
7. Additional Expenditure for Department of Agriculture	—	50	75	100	124	124	124	124	124	124
	6,027	5,889	6,212	6,576	6,362	7,188	7,396	7,664	7,873	8,122

¹ This expenditure is composed of the following items:—

	1952-53	1953-54	1954-55	1955-56	1956-57	1957-58	1958-59	1959-60	1960-61	1961-62
Road Maintenance (including shops)	396	416	450	462	530	540	550	565	580	600
New Road Works	284	280	220	275	290	300	300	300	300	300
New Stores, Warehouse, etc.	—	20	20	—	—	—	—	—	—	—
New Road Machinery, etc.	134	84	78	78	—	—	—	—	—	—
12½% replacement on machinery	—	55	57	60	60	60	60	60	60	60
Flood Damage	30	70	70	70	70	70	70	70	70	70
New Workshops	—	20	50	—	—	—	—	—	—	—
	844	945	945	945	950	970	980	995	1,010	1,030

271

TABLE 4

ESTIMATE OF BUDGET REVENUE AND EXPENDITURE
(£ millions)

	1952-53	1953-54	1954-55	1955-56	1956-57	1957-58	1958-59	1959-60	1960-61	1961-62
Development & Welfare Expenditure (from Table 3)	6.03	5.89	6.21	6.58	6.86	7.19	7.40	7.66	7.87	8.12
Other Budget Expenditure	6.03	6.04	6.05	6.10	6.20	6.34	6.49	6.60	6.78	6.98
Service of Net Public Debt	.58	.80	.80	1.02	1.02	1.24	1.24	1.35	1.35	1.35
Total Expenditure	12.64	12.73	13.06	13.70	14.08	14.77	15.13	15.61	16.00	16.45
Less: a) Reduction in Railway Deficit	—	.16	.21	.24	.25	.27	.29	.30	.30	.30
b) Savings of Public Works Dept. on Surveys	—	—	—	—	—	.02	.04	.05	.05	.05
Net Budget Expenditure	12.64	12.57	12.85	13.46	13.83	14.48	14.81	15.26	15.65	16.10
Estimated Budget Revenue	11.42	12.30	12.90	13.55	14.21	14.90	15.65	16.45	17.26	18.22
Colonial Development and Welfare	.87	.62	.62	.62	—	—	—	—	—	—
Total Revenue	12.29	12.92	13.52	14.17	14.21	14.90	15.65	16.45	17.26	18.22
Budget Surplus	.35[1] (deficit)	.35	.67	.71	.38	.42	.85	1.19	1.61	2.12
										= 8.30

[1] The slight difference between this figure and that in the government's 1952-53 estimates is attributable to the omission of the hurricane rehabilitation program in our estimates. The receipts and expenditures envisaged under this program for the year are not exactly equal.

If these assumptions are realistic it appears that the budget will be able to contribute some £ 8.3 million to the expenditure on the Development Program given in Table 1.

For the reduced program given in Tables 5, 6 and 7 the general method used is the same. In the Development Program itself, it has been assumed that the agricultural program will be spread over fifteen instead of ten years. The amount allowed for loans by the Industrial Development Corporation has been lowered from £ 3.5 million to £ 3 million. The rural housing and water supply program has been reduced along with the agricultural program and the urban housing program has also been slightly reduced. The capital outlay on education has been reduced by £ 240,000 which represents half the cost of the program to increase the school accommodation. Thus the program provides for only 20,000 new places instead of 40,000. Corresponding reductions have been made in the estimates for operation and maintenance in Table 6. The amounts for the health and social welfare programs have been left unchanged. The road program has been reduced and we recommend that this cut should fall on new road construction as far as possible and that the road maintenance expenditures should be maintained.

In Table 7 the effect of these reductions upon the budget estimates is shown. But if even this scale of expenditure is to be met it will be necessary to hold down expenditure in the remainder of the budget below the amount allowed in the main program. If this can be done the whole program should be within the capacity of the revenues which, in this case, increase at only 4% per year in accordance with the smaller rise which is expected in the national income.

We have not, in general, discussed the question of which expenditure should be financed from the different sources of finance such as general reserve, external borrowing, internal borrowing and Colonial Development and Welfare funds. However, as will be seen in Table 2, we have allowed for a net increase in crop loans outstanding of £ 3.3 million by the end of the period and we would expect that a large proportion of this could be carried by the commercial banks, partly, if necessary, with a government guarantee.

273

TABLE 5

REDUCED PROGRAM
(£ thousands)

	1952-53	1953-54	1954-55	1955-56	1956-57	1957-58	1958-59	1959-60	1960-61	1961-62	Total
1. a) Agricultural Development		200	400	800	1,400	1,000	800	800	700	700	6,800
b) Production and Development Loans (Net of repayment)		270	300	500	400	400	300	400	200	—	2,770
2. Railway (Capital Investment)		118	161	95	75	75	51	45	25	25	670
3. Harbors		30	50	—							80
4. Airports	350	300	350	200	—						1,200
5. Land Survey		170	180	75	75	75	75				650
6. Sugar Mill		—			—	1,000	1,000				2,000
7. IDC Loans		100	200	250	300	350	400	450	450	500	3,000
8. IDC Technical Service		10	12	14	16	18	18	18	18	18	142
9. Rural Housing and Water		40	70	120	230	240	350	350	350	350	2,100
10. Urban		—	220	220	240	240	240	200	180	160	1,700
11. Education (Capital Outlay)		503	493	539	483	428	422	415	429	449	4,161
12. Health (Capital Outlay)		300	300	300	300	300	300	300	300	300	2,700
	350	2,041	2,736	3,113	3,519	4,126	3,956	2,978	2,652	2,502	27,973

TABLE 6

DEVELOPMENT AND WELFARE EXPENDITURE WITHIN THE BUDGET—REDUCED PROGRAM

(£ thousands)

	1952-53	1953-54	1954-55	1955-56	1956-57	1957-58	1958-59	1959-60	1960-61	1961-62
1. Roads	844	945	945	895	875	870	880	895	910	930
2. Public Works other than Roads, Schools and Hospitals	703	700	700	710	710	720	720	730	730	730
3. Education	1,700	1,614	1,788	1,933	2,066	2,198	2,292	2,381	2,471	2,546
4. Health	2,200	1,900	2,000	2,100	2,200	2,300	2,400	2,500	2,600	2,700
5. Social Welfare	500	600	600	650	650	700	700	750	750	800
6. Tourist Trade Publicity (net of Passenger Duty)	80	80	94	118	132	136	130	124	118	112
7. Additional Expenditure for Department of Agriculture	—	50	75	100	124	124	124	124	124	124
	6,027	5,889	6,202	6,506	6,757	7,048	7,246	7,504	7,703	7,942

275

TABLE 7

ESTIMATE OF BUDGET REVENUE AND EXPENDITURE (REDUCED PROGRAM)
(£ millions)

	1952-53	1953-54	1954-55	1955-56	1956-57	1957-58	1958-59	1959-60	1960-61	1961-62
Development and Welfare Expenditure (from Table 3(a))	6.03	5.89	6.20	6.51	6.76	7.05	7.25	7.50	7.70	7.94
Other Budget Expenditure	6.03	6.03	6.04	6.10	6.15	6.18	6.25	6.37	6.45	6.55
Service of Net Public Debt	.58	.80	.80	1.02	1.02	1.02	1.18	1.18	1.19	1.19
Total Expenditure	12.64	12.72	13.04	13.63	13.93	14.25	14.68	15.05	15.34	15.68
Less: a) Reduction in Railway Deficit	—	.16	.21	.24	.25	.27	.29	.30	.30	.30
b) Savings of Public Works Dept. on Surveys	—	—	—	—	—	.02	.04	.05	.05	.05
Net Budget Expenditure	12.64	12.56	12.83	13.39	13.68	13.96	14.35	14.70	14.99	15.33
Estimated Budget Revenue	11.42	12.30	12.80	13.31	13.86	14.40	15.00	15.60	16.20	16.87
Colonial Development and Welfare Funds	.87	.62	.62	.62	—	—	—	—	—	—
Total Revenue	12.29	12.92	13.42	13.93	13.86	14.40	15.00	15.60	16.20	16.87
Budget Surplus	.35	.36	.59	.54	.18	.44	.65	.90	1.21	1.54
										= 6.41

276

Inflation and the Currency System

In countries with a fully independent monetary system any attempt to increase the rate of investment is liable to create an adverse balance of payments and a consequent loss of foreign exchange reserves. It is therefore necessary, when judging proposals for development, to insure that they do not create a demand for foreign exchange larger than the probable supply. The danger is that an expansion of money incomes proceeds faster than the expansion of real output thus creating an upward pressure on the price level and an increase in imports—assuming that imports can be freely purchased. Government borrowing from a central bank and the consequent opportunity for an expansion of bank credit can increase money expenditure on investment much faster than the real available resources and thus bring about this kind of problem.

Ideally it is desirable that money incomes and output, including that part of output which can be exported, should increase at the same rate so that foreign exchange income and the demand for imports may be balanced.[1] If this can be done it matters little whether investment is financed from abroad or from domestic savings. What is important is that the rate of money expenditure on investment should not exceed the amount available from both domestic savings and external capital.

The existence in Jamaica of a rigid sterling exchange standard in the form of 100% sterling cover for the note issue means that the effect on the internal economy of changes in its international accounts must operate according to certain rules. For example, in the event of a sudden inflow of capital in a country with an independent monetary system the central bank can, if it wishes, sterilize the excess reserves and thus prevent any effect on the internal money supply. Conversely it may offset an outflow of capital or a fall in exports by

---

[1] If there is a change in the propensity to import, corresponding adjustments in exports and in production for domestic consumption will be necessary.

an expansion of bank credit. True, its freedom is limited by the condition of its foreign exchange reserves but insofar as these are above what is regarded as the necessary minimum, some freedom of action does exist. In contrast, Jamaica has no central bank; there is only a Currency Board which operates according to inflexible rules. This means that the money supply is determined by the net effect of payments into and out of the country except insofar as there may be changes in commercial bank credit. But commercial bank cash reserves consist of either sterling or Jamaican notes which are convertible into sterling so that, if the banks are sound, convertibility of the money supply into sterling is assured.

This system means that Jamaica cannot have a "balance of payments" problem as that term is now commonly understood. Its only problem is that of supplying the rest of the world with sufficient goods and services to enable it to purchase from the rest of the world those things which it desires. In this sense any arbitrarily defined "economy" such as a state of the United States, an English county, a town or even a family can have a "balance of payments problem." (It is sometimes pointed out that, in this sense, most Americans suffer from a "dollar shortage.") It is true that if there were to be a sudden decline in Jamaica's ability to supply goods and services to the rest of the world—a drop in export prices or a crop failure, for example—imports would have to be curtailed. But this necessity would manifest itself not in a "shortage of foreign exchange"[2] but in a simple lack of purchasing power in the hands of the public.

In strict logic it is therefore unnecessary to discuss, as a separate problem, whether Jamaica's future exports will be enough to purchase any "necessary" amount of imports. The real problem should be stated somewhat differently. Is there any guarantee that the supply of money, as determined by the total balance of payments, will always adjust itself to what is most desirable for the economy as

---

[2] All that is said here refers, of course, to the system as it operates within the "inner ring" of the sterling area. The amount of non-sterling currency available to Jamaica is a matter which depends on the central foreign exchange reserves of the whole sterling area.

a whole (assuming such an optimum can be agreed upon)? It is clearly possible to imagine a situation where exports equal imports (both visible and invisible) and there are no capital movements. In such circumstances, if the banks (and the public) had no excess cash reserves, the supply of money would be held constant. Any increase in the volume of purely domestic production and consumption would therefore necessitate a reduction in the cost-price structure of the domestic economy which would, of course, affect the relative prices of imports and exports and hence the trade balance.

A discussion of whether such a mechanism of adjustment is more or less desirable than the operation of an independent monetary system at the present stage of Jamaica's economic and political evolution is a complex question. Moreover, it is not solely a question of monetary theory. At the present time, however, we do not think that a change in the system can in any way be regarded as a necessity for economic development and since it did not fall specifically within our terms of reference, we have not pursued the matter.

Note on the Banking System

Banking services are provided primarily by four commercial banks, three Canadian and one British. The only other banks in the island are the Peoples Cooperative Banks which make loans for agricultural purposes to small farmers. These banks come under the general supervision of the Agricultural Loan Societies Board.

There is no central bank. The commercial banks' cash reserves are held partly in Jamaican pounds and partly in accounts in their London offices. As they are dependent upon London for any temporary emergency accommodations, they are thus subject to the general monetary policy of the Bank of England.

At the end of the war, the commercial banks were in a very liquid position. The table shows the movement of the banks' assets and liabilities since the end of the war. In December 1945 their cash reserves, including balances in London, amounted to almost 40% of their total deposit liabilities. Their loans and advances amounted to only £ 2,808,000 and they held investments amounting to £ 5,531,-000. From the end of 1945 to the end of 1951 total deposits rose by only 22% (from £ 13,654,000 to £ 16,705,000) but the banks' loans and advances rose by 279% (from £ 2,808,000 to £ 10,611,-000). As a consequence, their cash reserves fell to only 20.3% of deposit liabilities. Over this period, loans to industry increased from £ 582,000 to £ 3,233,000 and loans to agriculture rose from £ 613,000 to £ 1,604,000.

The banks' lending activities are generally confined to providing for the working capital requirements of industry, agriculture and commerce. They seldom undertake medium-term loans for the purchase of equipment, etc. The only organizations in Jamaica from which long-term capital can be obtained are the Colonial Development Corporation and Barclay's Overseas Development Corporation. The amount of development loans outstanding from these two corporations is very small. With the establishment of the Industrial Development corporation, a new source of long-term finance for industry has been provided and it is the first one whose interest is confined to Jamaica instead of embracing the whole of the British Colonial territories.

COMMERCIAL BANKS' STATISTICS[1]

Liabilities
(£ thousands)

Month ending	Total Liabilities	Notes	Deposits			Balance due to Banks		Other Liabilities
			De-mand	Time	Sav-ings	In Jamaica	Abroad	
1944								
December	13,959	174	6,398	915	4,780	89	139	1,464
1945								
December	15,382	140	7,105	1,053	5,496	159	164	1,265
1946								
December	15,477	140	6,838	893	5,491	30	374	1,711
1947								
December	15,112	75	7,528	922	5,139	87	307	1,054
1948								
December	15,151	82	7,703	844	4,930	54	475	1,083
1949								
December	15,046	56	7,748	714	4,944	59	572	953
1950								
December	16,816	70	9,057	725	5,320	148	512	984
1951								
December	18,761	81	10,288	660	5,757	87	282	1,606

[1] Four commercial banks.

ASSETS
(£ thousands)

Month ending	Total Assets	Cash	Balance due by Banks		Loans and Advances				Investments		Other Assets
			In Jamaica	Abroad	Indus-try	Com-merce	Agri-culture	Other	Local	Other	
December 1944	13,959	973	385	4,827	945	*	695	1,729	618	1,137	2,650
December 1945	15,382	965	301	4,468	582	*	613	1,613	1,329	4,202	1,309
December 1946	15,477	1,075	196	3,205	531	*	933	2,244	1,743	3,626	1,924
December 1947	15,112	1,051	450	1,935	1,488	*	1,475	4,768	2,740	223	982
December 1948	15,151	847	527	1,169	1,481	*	1,989	5,204	2,254	510	1,170
December 1949	15,046	1,084	344	877	1,676	3,700	2,194	2,208	1,661	456	846
December 1950	16,816	956	461	1,494	3,074	4,081	1,617	1,515	1,633	765	1,220
December 1951	18,761	1,320	448	2,079	3,233	3,923	1,604	1,851	1,682	708	1,913

* Not available.

282

INDEX